D1766306

Frontline Intelligence 2
New Plays for the Nineties

Blasted by Sarah Kane, **Foreign Lands** by Karen Hope, **Hurricane Roses** by David Spencer, **The Life of the World to Come** by Rod Williams

Books are to be returned on or before

Frontl.... *bserver* as 'a selection of the ....

Blasted receives its première on the main stage of the Royal Court Theatre, London, in spring 1995. It is the first full length play written by Sarah Kane, whose monologues have been performed by fringe companies throughout Britain.

Foreign Lands opened the Women's Work season at the Finborough Arms, London in 1993 to critical acclaim: 'A chilling and extremely accomplished play' *Independent*. 'It is tense with ideas, feeling and power' *Sunday Times*. 'She combines mystery, suspense, atmosphere and moral purpose in a way that has you grasping for superlatives . . . one of the best plays in London' *Guardian*.

Hurricane Roses was produced by the Royal National Theatre Studio in London in 1994, and is the most recent play by two times Verity Bargate Award winner David Spencer.

The Life of the World to Come was premièred at the Almeida Theatre, London, in July 1994 and greeted as 'a funny, futuristic version of David Mamet's *Glengarry Glen Ross*' *The Times*. 'Audaciously original . . . a highly polished and recommended piece of new writing' *Daily Mail*. 'Williams shows himself a brilliant master of state-of-the-art jargon' *Sunday Telegraph*.

Each play has an afterword written by its author or director of its original production and the volume opens with an introduction by Pamela Edwardes, Editorial Director of Methuen Drama.

Frontline Intelligence 2

New Plays for the Nineties

Blasted
Sarah Kane

Foreign Lands
Karen Hope

Hurricane Roses
David Spencer

The Life of the World to Come
Rod Williams

Introduced by Pamela Edwardes

Methuen Drama

Methuen New Theatrescripts

First published in Great Britain 1994
by Methuen Drama
an imprint of Reed Consumer Books Ltd
Michelin House, 81 Fulham Road, London SW3 6RB
and Auckland, Melbourne, Singapore and Toronto
and distributed in the United States of America
by Heinemann
a division of Reed Elsevier Inc,
361 Hanover Street, Portsmouth, New Hampshire 03801 3959

ISBN 0 413 68980 8

A CIP catalogue record for this book is available from the British Library

Front cover photograph shows 'The irrepressible British Tommy' by Sgt Len Chetwyn,
26 October 1942
Reproduced courtesy of the Imperial War Museum, London

Typset by Wilmaset, Birkenhead, Wirral
Printed by Clays Ltd, St Ives, plc

Contents

Introduction

Frontline Intelligence 2 is the second in Methuen's series of volumes of plays from the most original and exciting new voices for the nineties. It features four playwrights whose work demonstrates a preoccupation with crime. The images are strong and topical: Sarah Kane's *Blasted* focuses on war crimes as an hotel in Leeds comes under mortar attack; in Karen Hope's *Foreign Lands* a mass murderer is on parole; *Hurricane Roses* by David Spencer is a painful attack on the greatest 'crime' against humanity, the world's failure to find a way to share its wealth; and, in more light-hearted style, Rod Williams's *The Life of the World to Come* takes a comic look at the deceit of overenthusiastic businessmen who measure their honesty against their share price.

All four plays were staged, or are due to be staged, in London at venues honoured for their commitment to new writing and the imagination and daring of their productions: the Royal Court, the Finborough Arms, the Royal National Theatre Studio and the Almeida Theatre.

Frontline Intelligence 2 represents but a small proportion of the new plays published recently by Methuen Drama. To gain a fuller picture, you might care to read *Night After Night* by Neil Bartlett, *Tuesday* by Edward Bond, *The Lodger* by Simon Burke, Ken Campbell's *Pigspurt*, Michael Frayn's *Here*, Jonathan Harvey's *Babies* and *Beautiful Thing*, Declan Hughes's *Digging for Fire & New Morning*, Terry Johnson's *Dead Funny* and *Hysteria*, Philip Ridley's *Ghost from a Perfect Place*, Michael Palin's *The Weekend* and Sue Townsend's *The Queen and I*, not to mention the plays in our other new writing anthologies: *Black Plays 3*, *Gay Plays 5*, *Plays By Women 10* and *Made in Scotland*, our first collection of new Scottish plays, edited by Ian Brown and Mark Fisher.

Much recent work in the theatre has not been text-based and must be reflected in print by other means than a published script. *Live 1 – food for the soul – a new generation of British theatremakers* is the first of Methuen's regular series of books focusing on specific issues in contemporary theatre. *Food for the soul* launches an investigation into the new spirit of innovation within British theatre by profiling a number of remarkable theatremakers. The volume features individual artists such as Bobby Baker, Stephen Daldry, Katie Mitchell and Jeremy Weller and the work of companies including Théâtre de Complicité, DV8, Gloria and Adventures in Motion Pictures. *Live* is edited by David Tushingham, with photographs by Simon Annand.

Pamela Edwardes
Editorial Director
Methuen Drama
October 1994

Blasted

Sarah Kane

Characters

Ian
Cate
Soldier

Blasted is due to première at the Royal Court Theatre Upstairs, London, in January 1995, in a production directed by James Macdonald and designed by Franziska Wielcken.

For Vincent O'Connell, with thanks.

Scene One

A very expensive hotel room in Leeds – the kind that is so expensive it could be anywhere in the world.

There is a large double bed.
A mini-bar and champagne on ice.
A telephone.
A large bouquet of flowers.
Two doors – one is the entrance from the corridor, the other leads off to the bathroom.

*Two people enter – **Ian** and **Cate**.*

Ian *is 45, Welsh born but lived in Leeds much of his life and picked up the accent.*

Cate *is 21, a lower middle class Southerner with a South London accent and a stutter when under stress.*

They enter.

Cate *stops at the door amazed at the classiness of the room.*
Ian *comes in, throws a small pile of newspapers on the bed, goes straight to the mini-bar and pours himself a large gin.*
He looks briefly out of the window at the street, then turns back to the room.

Ian   I've shat in better places than this.

He gulps down the gin.

      I stink.
      You want a bath?

Cate   *(shakes her head)*

Ian *goes into the bathroom and we hear him run the water. He comes back in with only a towel around his waist and a revolver in his hand. He checks it is loaded and puts it under his pillow.*

Ian   Tip that wog when he brings up the sandwiches.

He leaves fifty pence and goes into the bathroom.
Cate *comes into the room. She puts her bag down and bounces on the bed. She goes around the room, looking in every drawer, touching everything. She smells the flowers and smiles.*

Cate   Lovely.

Ian *comes back in, hair wet, towel around his waist, drying himself off. He stops and looks at **Cate** a moment, who is sucking her thumb.*
He goes back in the bathroom where he dresses.

We hear him coughing terribly in the bathroom.
He spits in the sink and re-enters.

Cate   You all right?

Ian   It's nothing.

He pours himself another gin, this time with tonic, ice and lemon, and sips it at a more normal pace.
He collects his gun and puts it in his under arm holster.
He smiles at **Cate**.

Ian   I'm glad you've come. Didn't think you would.

He offers her champagne.

Cate   (*shakes her head*) I was worried.

Ian   This? (*He indicates his chest.*) Don't matter.

Cate   I didn't mean that. You sounded unhappy.

Ian   (*Pops the champagne. He pours them both a glass*)

Cate   What we celebrating?

Ian   (*Doesn't answer. He goes to the window and looks out*)

Hate this city. Stinks. Wogs and Pakis taking over.

Cate   You shouldn't call them that.

Ian   Why not?

Cate   It's not very nice.

Ian   You a nigger-lover?

Cate   Ian, don't.

Ian   You like our coloured brethren?

Cate   Don't mind them.

Ian   Grow up.

Cate   There's Indians at the day centre where my brother goes.
They're really polite.

Ian   So they should be.

Cate   He's friends with some of them.

Ian   Retard, isn't he?

Cate   No, he's got learning difficulties.

Ian   Aye. Spaz.

Cate   No he's not.

Ian   Glad my son's not a Joey.

Cate Don't c- call him that.

Ian Your mother I feel sorry for. Two of you like it.

Cate Like wh- what?

Ian *looks at her, deciding whether or not to continue. He decides against it.*

Ian You know I love you.

Cate (*smiles a big smile, friendly and non-sexual*)

Ian Don't want you ever to leave.

Cate I'm here for the night.

Ian *drinks. She's made her point.*

Ian Sweating again. Stink.
You ever thought of getting married?

Cate Who'd marry me?

Ian I would.

Cate I couldn't.

Ian You don't love me. I don't blame you, I wouldn't.

Cate I couldn't leave mum.

Ian Have to one day.

Cate Why?

Ian (*opens his mouth to answer but can't think of one*)

There is a knock at the door.
Ian *starts, and* **Cate** *goes to answer it.*

Ian Don't.

Cate Why not?

Ian I said.

He takes his gun from the holster and goes to the door.
He listens.
Nothing.

Cate (*giggles*)

Ian Shh.

He listens.
Still nothing.

Ian Probably the wog with the sarnies. Open it.

Cate *opens the door.*
There's no-one there, just a tray of sandwiches on the floor.
She brings them in and examines them.

Cate Ham. Don't believe it.

Ian (*takes a sandwich and eats it*) Champagne?

Cate (*shakes her head*)

Ian Got something against ham?

Cate Dead meat. Blood. Can't eat an animal.

Ian No-one would know.

Cate No, I can't, I actually can't, I'd puke all over the place.

Ian It's only a pig.

Cate I'm hungry.

Ian Have one of these.

Cate I CAN'T.

Ian I'll take you out for an Indian.
Jesus, what's this? Cheese.

Cate *beams.*
She separates the cheese sandwiches from the ham ones, and eats.
Ian *watches her.*

Ian Don't like your clothes.

Cate (*looks down at her clothes*)

Ian You look like a lesbos.

Cate What's that?

Ian Don't look very sexy, that's all.

Cate Oh. (*She continues to eat.*) Don't like your clothes either.

Ian (*looks down at his clothes. Then gets up, takes them all off, and stands in front of her, naked*)

Put your mouth on me.

Cate (*stares. Then bursts out laughing*)

Ian No? Fine.
Because I stink?

Cate (*laughs even more*)

Ian *attempts to dress, but fumbles with embarrassment. He gathers his clothes and goes into the bathroom where he dresses.*
Cate *eats, and giggles over the sandwiches.*
Ian *returns, fully dressed.*
He picks up his gun, unloads and reloads it.

Ian You got a job yet?

Cate No.

Ian Still screwing the taxpayer.

Cate Mum gives me money.

Ian When are you going to stand on your own feet?

Cate I've applied for a job at an advertising agency.

Ian (*laughs genuinely*) No chance.

Cate Why not?

Ian (*stops laughing and looks at her*)
Cate. You're stupid. You're never going to get a job.

Cate I am. I am not.

Ian See.

Cate St- stop it. You're doing it d- deliberately.

Ian Doing what?

Cate C- confusing me.

Ian No, I'm talking, you're just too thick to understand.

Cate I am not, I am not.

Cate *begins to tremble.* **Ian** *is laughing.*
Cate *faints.*
Ian *stops laughing and stares at her motionless body.*

Ian Cate?

He turns her over and lifts up her eyelids.
He doesn't know what to do.
He gets a glass of gin and dabs some on her face.
Cate *sits bolt upright, eyes open but still unconscious.*

Ian Fucking Jesus.

Cate *bursts out laughing, unnaturally, hysterically, uncontrollably.*

Ian Stop fucking about.

Cate *collapses again and lies still.*
Ian *stands by helplessly.*
After a few moments, **Cate** *comes round as if waking up in the morning.*

Ian   What the Christ was that?

Cate   Have to tell her.

Ian   Cate?

Cate   She's in danger.

She closes her eyes and slowly comes back to normal.
She looks at **Ian** *and smiles.*

Ian   What now?

Cate   Did I faint?

Ian   That was real?

Cate   Happens all the time.

Ian   What, fits?

Cate   Since dad came back.

Ian   Does it hurt?

Cate   I'll grow out of it the doctor says.

Ian   How do you feel?

Cate   (*smiles*)

Ian   Thought you were dead.

Cate   Suppose that's what it's like.

Ian   Don't do it again, fucking scared me.

Cate   Don't know much about it, I just go. Can be away for minutes or months sometimes, then I come back just where I was.

Ian   It's terrible.

Cate   I didn't go far.

Ian   What if you didn't come round?

Cate   Wouldn't know. I'd stay there.

Ian   Can't stand it.

Cate   What?

Ian   Death. Not being.

He goes to the mini-bar and pours himself another large gin and lights a cigarette.

Cate   You fall alseep and then you wake up.

Ian   How do you know?

Cate   Why don't you give up smoking?

Ian   (*laughs*)

Cate   You should. They'll make you ill.

Ian   Too late for that.

Cate   Whenever I think of you it's with a cigarette and a gin.

Ian   Good.

Cate   They make your clothes smell.

Ian   Don't forget my breath.

Cate   Imagine what your lungs must look like.

Ian   Don't need to imagine. I've seen.

Cate   When?

Ian   Last year. When I came round, surgeon brought in this lump of rotting pork, stank. My lung.

Cate   He took it out?

Ian   Other one's the same now.

Cate   But you'll die.

Ian   Aye.

Cate   Please stop smoking.

Ian   Won't make any difference.

Cate   Can't they do something?

Ian   No. It's not like your brother, look after him and he'll be all right.

Cate   They die young.

Ian   I'm fucked.

Cate   Can't you get a transplant?

Ian   Don't be stupid. They give them to people with a life. Kids.

Cate   People die in accidents all the time. They must have some spare.

Ian   Why? What for? Keep me alive to die of cirrhosis in three months time.

Cate   You're making it worse, speeding it up.

Ian   Enjoy myself while I'm here.

He inhales deeply on his cigarette and swallows the last of the gin neat.

Ian   [I'll] Call that coon, get some more sent up.

Cate   (*shakes*)

Ian   Wonder if the conker understands English.

He notices **Cate**'s *distress and cuddles her. He kisses her.*
She pulls away and wipes her mouth.

Cate   Don't put your tongue in, I don't like it.

Ian   Sorry.

The telephone rings loudly. **Ian** *starts, then answers it.*

Ian   Hello?

Cate   Who is it?

Ian   (*covers the mouthpiece*) Shh.

(*Into the mouthpiece.*) Got it here.

(*He takes a notebook from the pile of newspapers and reads down the phone.*)

A serial killer slaughtered British tourist Samantha Scrace in a sick murder ritual comma, police revealed yesterday point new par. The bubbly 19 year old from Leeds was among seven victims found buried in identical triangular tombs in an isolated New Zealand forest point new par. Each had been stabbed more than twenty times and placed face down comma, hands bound behind their backs point new par. Caps up, ashes at the site showed the maniac had stayed to cook a meal, caps down point new par. Samantha comma, a beautiful redhead with dreams of becoming a model comma, was on the trip of a lifetime after finishing her A levels last year point. Samantha's heartbroken mum said yesterday colon quoting, we pray the police will come up with something, dash, anything comma, soon point still quoting. The sooner this lunatic is brought to justice the better point end quote new par. The Foreign Office warned tourists down under to take extra care point. A spokesman said colon quoting, common sense is the best rule point end quote, copy ends.

(*He listens. Then he laughs.*)

Exactly.

(*He listens.*)

That one again, I went to see her. Some scouse tart, spread her legs. No. Forget it. Tears and lies, not worth the space. No.

He presses a button on the phone to connect him to room service.

Ian   Tosser.

Cate   How do they know you're here?

Ian   Told them.

Cate   Why?

Ian   In case they needed me.

Cate   Silly. We came here to be away from them.

Ian Thought you'd like this. Nice hotel. (*Into the mouthpiece.*) Bring a bottle of gin up, son.

He puts the phone down.

Cate We always used to go to yours.

Ian That was years ago. You've grown up.

Cate (*smiles*)

Ian I'm not well any more.

Cate (*stops smiling*)

Ian *kisses her.*
She responds.
He puts his hand inside her shirt and moves it towards her breast.
With the other hand he undoes his trousers and starts masturbating.
He begins to undo her shirt.
She pushes him away.

Cate Ian, d- don't.

Ian What?

Cate I don't w- want to do this.

Ian Yes you do.

Cate I don't.

Ian Why not? You're nervous, that's all.

He starts to kiss her again.

Cate I t- t- t- t- t- t- t- told you. I really like you but I c- c- c- c- can't do this.

Ian (*kissing her*) Shhh. (*He starts to undo her trousers.*)

Cate *panics.*
She starts to tremble and make inarticulate crying sounds.
Ian *stops, frightened of bringing another 'fit' on.*

Ian All right, Cate, it's all right. We don't have to do anything.

He strokes her face until she has calmed down.
She sucks her thumb. Then.

Ian That wasn't very fair.

Cate What?

Ian Letting me lie there like that, making a prick of myself.

Cate I f- f- felt –

Ian   Don't pity me, Cate. You don't have to fuck me 'cause I'm dying, but don't push your cunt in my face then take it away 'cause I stick my tongue out.

Cate   I- I- Ian.

Ian   What's the m- m- matter?

Cate   I k- k- kissed you, that's all. I l- l- like you.

Ian   Don't give me a hard-on if you're not going to finish me off.
It hurts.

Cate   I'm sorry.

Ian   Can't switch it on and off like that. If I don't come my cock aches.

Cate   I didn't mean it.

Ian   Shit. (*He appears to be in considerable pain.*)

Cate   I'm sorry. I am. I won't do it again.

Ian, *apparently still in pain, takes her hand and grasps it around his penis, keeping his own hand over the top.*
Like this, he masturbates until he comes with some genuine pain.
He releases **Cate**'*s hand and she withdraws it.*

Cate   Is it better?

Ian   (*nods*)

Cate   I'm sorry.

Ian   Don't worry.
Can we make love tonight?

Cate   No.

Ian   Why not?

Cate   I'm not your girlfriend anymore.

Ian   Will you be my girlfriend again?

Cate   I can't.

Ian   Why not?

Cate   I told Shaun I'd be his.

Ian   Have you slept with him?

Cate   No.

Ian   Slept with me before. You're more mine than his.

Cate   I'm not.

Ian   What was that about then, wanking me off?

Cate   I d- d- d- d-

Ian   Sorry. Pressure, pressure. I love you, that's all.

Cate   You were horrible to me.

Ian   I wasn't.

Cate   Stopped phoning me, never said why.

Ian   It was difficult, Cate.

Cate   Because I haven't got a job?

Ian   No, pet, not that.

Cate   Because of my brother?

Ian   No, no, Cate. Leave it now.

Cate   That's not fair.

Ian   I said leave it.

He reaches for his gun.
There is a knock at the door.
Ian *starts, then goes to answer it.*

Ian   I'm not going to hurt you, just leave it. And keep quiet. It'll only be Sooty after something.

Cate   Andrew.

Ian   What do you want to know a conker's name for?

Cate   I thought he was nice.

Ian   After a bit of black meat, eh? Won't do it with me but you'll go with a whodat.

Cate   You're horrible.

Ian   Cate, love. I'm trying to look after you. Stop you getting hurt.

Cate   You hurt me.

Ian   No, I love you.

Cate   Stopped loving me.

Ian   I've told you to leave that.
Now.

He kisses her passionately, then goes to the door.
When his back is turned, **Cate** *wipes her mouth.*

Ian *opens the door. There is a bottle of gin outside on a tray.*
Ian *brings it in and stands, unable to decide between gin and champagne.*

Cate   Have champagne, better for you.

Ian   Don't want it better for me.

Cate   You'll die quicker.

Ian   Thanks. Don't it scare you?

Cate   What?

Ian   Death.

Cate   Whose?

Ian   Yours.

Cate   Only for mum. She'd be unhappy if I died. And my brother.

Ian   You're young.
When I was your age –
Now.

Cate   Will you have to go to hospital?

Ian   Nothing they can do.

Cate   Does Stella know?

Ian   What would I want to tell her for?

Cate   You were married.

Ian   So?

Cate   She'd want to know.

Ian   So she can throw a party at the coven.

Cate   She wouldn't do that. What about Matthew?

Ian   What about Matthew?

Cate   Have you told him?

Ian   I'll send him an invite for the funeral.

Cate   He'll be upset.

Ian   He hates me.

Cate   He doesn't.

Ian   He fucking does.

Cate   Are you upset?

Ian   Yes. His mother's a lesbos. Am I not preferable to that?

Cate   Perhaps she's a nice person.

Ian   She don't carry a gun.

Cate I expect that's it.

Ian I loved Stella till she became a witch and fucked off with a dyke, and I love you, though you've got the potential.

Cate For what?

Ian Sucking gash.

Cate (*utters an inarticulate sound*)

Ian You ever had a fuck with a woman?

Cate No.

Ian Do you want to?

Cate Don't think so. Have you? With a man.

Ian You think I'm a cocksucker? You've seen me. (*He vaguely indicates his groin.*) How can you think that?

Cate I don't. I asked. You asked me.

Ian You dress like a lesbos. I don't dress like a cocksucker.

Cate What do they dress like?

Ian Hitler was wrong about the Jews who have they hurt the queers he should have gone for scum them and the wogs and fucking football fans send a bomber over Elland Road finish them off.

He pours champagne and toasts the idea.

Cate I like football.

Ian Why?

Cate It's good.

Ian And when was the last time you went to a football match?

Cate Saturday. United beat Liverpool 2–0.

Ian Didn't you get stabbed?

Cate Why should I?

Ian That's what football's about. It's not fancy footwork and scoring goals. It's tribalism.

Cate I like it.

Ian You would. About your level.

Cate I go to Elland Road sometimes. Would you bomb me?

Ian What do you want to ask a question like that for?

Cate Would you though?

Ian Don't be thick.

Cate   But would you?

Ian   Haven't got a bomber.

Cate   Shoot me, then. Could you do that?

Ian   Cate.

Cate   Do you think it's hard to shoot someone?

Ian   Easy as shitting blood.

Cate   Could you shoot me?

Ian   Could you shoot me stop asking that could you shoot me you could shoot me.

Cate   I don't think so.

Ian   If I hurt you.

Cate   Don't think you would.

Ian   But if.

Cate   No, you're soft.

Ian   With people I love.

He stares at her, considering making a pass.
She smiles back, friendly.

Ian   What's this job, then?

Cate   Personal Assistant.

Ian   Who to?

Cate   Don't know.

Ian   Who did you write the letter to?

Cate   Sir or madam.

Ian   You have to know who you're writing to.

Cate   It didn't say.

Ian   How much?

Cate   What?

Ian   Money. How much do you get paid.

Cate   Mum said it was a lot. I don't mind about that as long as I can go out sometimes.

Ian   Don't despise money. You got it easy.

Cate   I haven't got any money.

Ian   No and you haven't got kids to bring up neither.

Cate   Not yet.

Ian   Don't even think about it. Who would have children.
You have kids, they grow up, they hate you and you die.

Cate   I don't hate mum.

Ian   You still need her.

Cate   You think I'm stupid. I'm not stupid.

Ian   I worry, that's all.

Cate   Can look after myself.

Ian   Like me.

Cate   No.

Ian   You hate me, don't you.

Cate   You shouldn't have that gun.

Ian   May need it.

Cate   What for?

Ian   (*drinks*)

Cate   Can't imagine it.

Ian   What?

Cate   You. Shooting someone. You wouldn't kill anything.

Ian   (*drinks*)

Cate   Have you ever shot anyone?

Ian   Your mind.

Cate   Have you though?

Ian   Leave it now, Cate.

She takes the warning.
Ian *kisses her and lights a cigarette.*

Ian   When I'm with you I can't think about anything else.
You take me to another place.

Cate   It's like that when I have a fit.

Ian   Just you.

Cate   Like the world don't exist, not like this. Looks the same
but –
Time slows down.
Like a dream I get stuck in, can't do nothing about it.
One time –

Ian   Make love to me.

Cate   Blocks out everything else.
Once –

Ian   [I'll] Make love to you.

Cate   It's like that when I touch myself.

Ian *is embarrassed.*

Cate   Just before I'm wondering what it'll be like, and just after
I'm thinking about the next one, but just as it happens
it's lovely, I don't think of nothing else.

Ian   Like the first cigarette of the day.

Cate   That's bad for you though.

Ian   Stop talking now, you don't know anything about it.

Cate   Don't need to.

Ian   Don't know nothing. That's why I love you, want to make love to you.

Cate   But you can't.

Ian   Why not?

Cate   I don't want to.

Ian   Why did you come here?

Cate   You sounded unhappy.

Ian   Make me happy.

Cate   I can't.

Ian   Please.

Cate   No.

Ian   Why not?

Cate   Can't.

Ian   Can.

Cate   How.

Ian   You know.

Cate   Don't.

Ian   Please.

Cate   No.

Ian   I love you.

Cate   I don't love you.

Ian *turns away.*
He sees the bouquet of flowers and picks them up.

Ian   These are for you.

Blackout.

Scene Two

The same.

Very early the following morning.
Bright and sunny – it's going to be a very hot day.
The bouquet of flowers is now ripped apart and scattered around the room.

Cate *is still asleep.*
Ian *is awake, glancing through the newspapers.*

Ian *goes to the mini-bar. It is empty.*
He finds the bottle of gin under the bed and pours half of what is left into a glass.
He stands looking out of the window at the street.
He takes the first sip and is overcome with pain.
He waits for it to pass, but it doesn't. It gets worse.
Ian *clutches his side – it becomes extreme.*
He begins to cough, and experiences intense pain in his chest, each cough tearing at his lungs.

Cate *wakes and watches* **Ian**.

Ian *drops to his knees, puts the glass down carefully, and gives in to the pain.*
It looks very much as if he is dying.
His heart, lungs, liver and kidneys are all under attack, and he is making involuntary crying sounds.

Just at the moment when it seems he cannot survive this, it begins to ease. Very slowly, the pain decreases until it has all gone.

Ian *is a crumpled heap on the floor.*

He looks up and sees **Cate** *watching him.*

Cate   Cunt.

Ian *gets up slowly, picks up the glass and drinks.*
He lights his first cigarette of the day.

Ian   I'm having a shower.

Cate   It's only six o'clock.

Ian   Want one?

Cate   Not with you.

Ian   Suit yourself. Cigarette?

Cate *makes a noise of disgust.*
They are silent.

Ian stands, smoking and drinking neat gin. When he's sufficiently numbed, he comes and goes between the bedroom and the bathroom, undressing and collecting discarded towels. He stops, towel around his waist, gun in hand, and looks at **Cate**. *She is staring at him with hate.*

Ian Don't worry, I'll be dead soon.

(*He tosses the gun onto the bed.*)

Have a pop.

Cate *doesn't move.*
Ian *waits, then chuckles and goes into the bathroom.*
We hear the shower running.

Cate *stares at the gun.*
She gets up very slowly and dresses.
She packs her bag.
She picks up **Ian**'s *jacket and smells it.*
She rips the arms off at the seams.
She picks up his gun and examines it.
We hear **Ian** *coughing up in the bathroom.*
Cate *puts the gun down and he comes in.*
He dresses. He looks at the gun.

Ian No?

(*He chuckles, unloads and reloads the gun and tucks it in his holster.*)

We're one, yes?

Cate (*sneers*)

Ian We're one.
Coming down for breakfast? It's paid for.

Cate Choke on it.

Ian Sarky little tart this morning aren't we?

He picks up his jacket and begins to put it on.
He stares at the damage, then looks at **Cate**.
A beat, and then she goes for him, slapping him around the head hard and fast.
He wrestles her onto the bed, her still kicking, punching and biting.
She takes the gun from his holster and points it at his groin.
He backs off rapidly.

Ian Easy, easy, that's a loaded gun.

Cate I d- d- d- d- d- d- d- d- d-

Ian Catie, come on.

Cate d- d- d- d- d- d- d- d- d- d-

Ian   You don't want an accident. Think about your mum.
       And your brother. What would they think?

Cate   I d- d- d- d- d- d- d- d- d- d- d- d-

Cate *trembles and starts gasping for air. She faints.*
Ian *goes to her, takes the gun and puts it back in the holster.*
He lies her on the bed, on her back.
He puts the gun to her head, lies between her legs, and simulates sex.
As he comes, **Cate** *sits bolt upright with a shout.*
Ian *moves away, unsure what to do, pointing the gun at her from behind.*
She laughs hysterically, as before, but doesn't stop.
*She laughs and laughs and laughs until she isn't laughing anymore, she's crying her heart
out.*
She collapses again and lies still.

Ian   Cate? Catie?

Ian *puts the gun away.*
He kisses her and she comes round.
She stares at him.

Ian   You back?

Cate   Liar.

Ian *doesn't know if this means yes or no, so he just waits.*
Cate *closes her eyes for a few seconds, then opens them.*

Ian   Cate?

Cate   Want to go home now.

Ian   It's not even seven. There won't be a train.

Cate   I'll wait at the station.

Ian   It's raining.

Cate   It's not.

Ian   Want you to stay here. Till after breakfast at least.

Cate   No.

Ian   Cate. After breakfast.

Cate   No.

Ian *locks the door and pockets the key.*

Ian   I love you.

Cate   I don't want to stay.

Ian   Please.

Cate   Don't want to.

Ian   You make me feel safe.

Cate   Nothing to be scared of.

Ian   I'll order breakfast.

Cate   Not hungry.

Ian   (*lights a cigarette*)

Cate   How can you smoke on an empty stomach?

Ian   It's not empty. There's gin in it.

Cate   Why can't I go home?

Ian   (*thinks*)
It's too dangerous.

Outside, a car backfires – there is an enormous bang.
Ian *throws himself flat on the floor.*

Cate   (*laughs*) It's only a car.

Ian   You. You're fucking thick.

Cate   I'm not. You're scared of things when there's nothing to be scared of.
What's thick about not being scared of cars?

Ian   I'm not scared of cars. I'm scared of dying.

Cate   A car won't kill you. Not from out there. Not unless you ran out in
front of it.

She kisses him.

What's scaring you?

Ian   Thought it was a gun.

Cate   (*kissing his neck*) Who'd have a gun?

Ian   Me.

Cate   (*undoing his shirt*) You're in here.

Ian   Someone like me.

Cate   (*kissing his chest*) Why would they shoot at you?

Ian   Revenge.

Cate   (*runs her hands down his back*)

Ian   For things I've done.

Cate   (*massaging his neck*) Tell me.

Ian   Tapped my phone.

Cate   (*kisses the back of his neck*)

Ian   Talk to someone and I know I'm being listened to. I'm sorry I stopped calling you but –

Cate   (*strokes his stomach and kisses between his shoulder blades*)

Ian   Got angry when you said you loved me, talking soft on the phone, people listening to that.

Cate   (*kissing his back*) Tell me.

Ian   In before you know it.

Cate   (*licks his back*)

Ian   Signed the Official Secrets Act, shouldn't be telling you this.

Cate   (*claws and scratches his back*)

Ian   Don't want to get you into trouble.

Cate   (*bites his back*)

Ian   Think they're trying to kill me. Served my purpose.

Cate   (*pushes him onto his back*)

Ian   Done the jobs they asked. Because I love this land.

Cate   (*sucks his nipples*)

Ian   Stood at stations, listened to conversations and given the nod.

Cate   (*undoes his trousers*)

Ian   Driving jobs. Picking people up, disposing of bodies, the lot.

Cate   (*begins to perform oral sex on* **Ian**)

Ian   Said you were dangerous.

So I stopped.

Didn't want you in any danger.

But

Had to call you again

Missed

This

Now

I do

The real job

I

Am

A

Killer

On the word 'killer' he comes.
As soon as **Cate** *hears the word she bites his penis as hard as she can.*
Ian*'s cry of pleasure turns into a scream of pain.*
He tries to pull away but **Cate** *holds on with her teeth.*
He hits her and she lets go.
Ian *lies in pain, unable to speak.*
Cate *spits frantically, trying to get every trace of him out of her mouth.*
She goes to the bathroom and we hear her cleaning her teeth.
Ian *examines himself. He is still in one piece.*
Cate *returns.*

Cate   You should resign.

Ian   Don't work like that.

Cate   Will they come here?

Ian   I don't know.

Cate   (*begins to panic*)

Ian   Don't start that again.

Cate   I c- c- c- c- c-

Ian   Cate, I'll shoot you myself you don't stop.
I told you because I love you, not to scare you.

Cate   You don't.

Ian   Don't argue I do. And you love me.

Cate   No more.

Ian   Loved me last night.

Cate   I didn't want to do it.

Ian   You enjoyed it.

Cate   Did not.

Ian   Made enough noise. .

Cate   It was hurting.

Ian   Went down on Stella all the time, didn't hurt her.

Cate   You bit me. It's still bleeding.

Ian   Is that what this is all about?

Cate   You're cruel.

Ian   Don't be stupid.

Cate   Stop calling me that.

Ian   You sleep with someone holding hands and kissing you wank me off then say we can't fuck get into bed but don't want me to touch you what's wrong with you Joey.

Cate   I'm not. You're cruel. I wouldn't shoot someone.

Ian   Pointed it at me.

Cate   Wouldn't shoot.

Ian   It's my job. I love this country. I won't see it destroyed by slag.

Cate   It's wrong to kill.

Ian   Planting bombs and killing little kiddies, that's wrong.
That's what they do. Kids like your brother.

Cate   It's wrong.

Ian   Yes, it is.

Cate   No. You. Doing that.

Ian   When are you going to grow up?

Cate   I don't believe in killing.

Ian   You'll learn.

Cate   No I won't.

Ian   Can't always be taking it backing down letting them think they've got a right turn the other cheek SHIT some things are worth more than that have to be protected from shite.

Cate   I used to love you.

Ian   What's changed?

Cate   You.

Ian   No. Now you see me. That's all.

Cate   You're a nightmare.

She shakes.
Ian *watches a while, then hugs her.*
She is still shaking so he hugs tightly to stop her.

Cate   That hurts.

Ian   Sorry.

He hugs her less tightly.
He has a coughing fit.

He spits into his handkerchief and waits for the pain to subside.
Then he lights a cigarette.

Ian How you feeling?

Cate I ache.

Ian (*nods*)

Cate Everywhere.
I stink of you.

Ian You want a bath?

Cate *begins to cough and retch.*
She puts her fingers down her throat and produces a hair.
She holds it up and looks at **Ian** *in disgust. She spits.*
Ian *goes into the bathroom and turns on one of the bath taps.*
Cate *stares out of the window.*
Ian *returns.*

Cate Looks like there's a war on.

Ian Turning into wogland.
You coming to Leeds again?

Cate 26th.

Ian Will you come and see me?

Cate I'm going to the football.

She goes to the bathroom.
Ian *picks up the phone.*

Ian Two English breakfasts, son.

He finishes the remainder of the gin.
Cate *returns.*

Cate I can't piss. It's just blood.

Ian Drink lots of water.

Cate Or shit. It hurts.

Ian It'll heal.

There is a knock at the door. They both jump.

Cate DON'T ANSWER IT DON'T ANSWER IT DON'T ANSWER IT

She dives on the bed and puts her head under the pillow.

Ian Cate, shut up.

He pulls the pillow off and puts the gun to her head.

Cate   Do it. Go on, shoot me. Can't be no worse than what you've done already. Shoot me if you want, then turn it on yourself and do the world a favour.

Ian   (*stares at her*)

Cate   I'm not scared of you, Ian. Go on.

Ian   (*gets off her*)

Cate   (*laughs*)

Ian   Answer the door and suck the cunt's cock.

Cate *tries to open the door. It is locked.*
Ian *throws the key at her. She opens the door.*
The breakfasts are outside on a tray. She brings them in.
Ian *locks the door.*
Cate *stares at the food.*

Cate   Sausages. Bacon.

Ian   Sorry. Forgot. Swap your meat for my tomatoes and mushrooms. And toast.

Cate   (*begins to retch*) The smell.

Ian *takes a sausage off the plate and stuffs it in his mouth, and keeps a rasher of bacon in his hand.*
He puts the tray of food under the bed with a towel over it.

Ian   Will you stay another day?

Cate   I'm having a bath and going home.

She picks up her bag and goes into the bathroom, closing the door.
We hear the other bath tap being turned on.
There are two loud knocks at the outer door.
Ian *draws his gun, goes to the door and listens.*
The door is tried from outside. It is locked.
There are two more loud knocks.

Ian   Who's there?

Silence.
Then two more loud knocks.

Ian   Who's there?

Silence.
Then two more knocks.

Ian *looks at the door.*
Then he knocks twice.

Silence.
Then two more knocks from outside.

Ian *thinks.*
Then he knocks three times.

Silence.
Three knocks from outside.

Ian *knocks once.*
One knock from outside.

Ian *knocks twice.*
Two knocks.

Ian *puts his gun back in the holster and unlocks the door.*

Ian   (*under his breath*) Speak the Queen's English fucking nigger.

He opens the door.
Outside is a **Soldier** *with a sniper's rifle.*
Ian *tries to push the door shut and draw his revolver.*
The **Soldier** *pushes the door open and takes* **Ian**'s *gun easily.*
The two stand, both surprised, staring at each other.
Eventually.

Soldier   What's that?

Ian *looks down and realises he is still holding a rasher of bacon.*

Ian   Pig.

The **Soldier** *holds out his hand.*
Ian *gives him the bacon and he eats it quickly, rind and all.*
The **Soldier** *wipes his mouth.*

Soldier   Got any more?

Ian   No.

Soldier   Got any more?

Ian   I –
No.

Soldier   Got any more?

Ian   (*points to the tray under the bed*)

The **Soldier** *bends down carefully, never taking his eyes or rifle off* **Ian**, *and takes the tray from under the bed.*
He straightens up and glances down at the food.

Soldier   Two.

Ian   I was hungry.

Soldier   I bet.

He sits on the edge of the bed and very quickly devours both breakfasts. He sighs with relief and burps.
He nods towards the bathroom.

Soldier   She in there?

Ian   Who?

Soldier   I can smell the sex.

(*He begins to search the room.*)

You a journalist?

Ian   I –

Soldier   Passport.

Ian   What for?

Soldier   (*looks at him*)

Ian   In the jacket.

The **Soldier** *is searching a chest of drawers.*
He finds a pair of **Cate**'s *knickers and holds them up with a smile.*

Soldier   Hers?

Ian   (*doesn't answer*)

Soldier   Or yours.

He closes his eyes and rubs them gently over his face, smelling with pleasure.

Soldier   What's she like?

Ian   (*doesn't answer*)

Soldier   Is she soft?
Is she – ?

Ian   (*doesn't answer*)

The **Soldier** *puts* **Cate**'s *knickers in his pocket and goes to the bathroom.*
He knocks on the door. No answer.
He tries the door. It is locked. He forces it and goes in.
Ian *waits, in a panic.*
We hear the bath taps being turned off.
Ian *looks out of the window.*

Ian   Jesus Lord.

The **Soldier** *returns.*

Soldier   Gone. Taking a risk. Lot of bastard soldiers out there.

Ian looks in the bathroom. **Cate** *isn't there.*
The **Soldier** *looks in* **Ian**'s *jacket pockets and takes his keys, money and passport.*

Soldier   (*reading the passport*) Ian Jones, occupation journalist.

Ian   Oi.

Soldier   Oi.

They stare at each other.

Ian   If you've come to shoot me –

The **Soldier** *reaches out to touch* **Ian**'s *face.*

Ian   You taking the piss?

Soldier   Me?

(*He smiles.*)

Our town now.

(*He stands on the bed and urinates over the pillows.*)

Ian *is disgusted.*

There is a huge explosion.

Blackout.

Scene Three

The hotel has been blasted by a mortar bomb.

There is a large hole in one of the walls, and everything is covered in dust which is still falling.

The **Soldier** *is unconscious, rifle still in hand.*
He has dropped **Ian***'s gun which lies between them.*

Ian *lies very still, eyes open.*

Ian   Mum?

Silence.
The **Soldier** *wakes and turns his eyes and rifle on* **Ian** *with the minimum possible movement. He instinctively runs his free hand over his limbs and body to check that he is still in one piece. He is.*

Soldier   The drink.

Ian *looks around.*
There is a bottle of gin lying next to him with the lid off.
He holds it up to the light.

Ian   Empty.

The **Soldier** *takes the bottle and drinks the last mouthful.*

Ian   (*chuckles*) Worse than me.

Soldier   (*holds the bottle up and shakes it over his mouth, catching any remaining drops*)

Ian   (*finds his cigarettes in his shirt pocket and lights up*)

Soldier   Give us a cig.

Ian   Why?

Soldier   'Cause I've got a gun and you haven't.

Ian   (*considers the logic. Then takes a single cigarette out of the packet and tosses it at the* **Soldier**)

Soldier   (*picks up the cigarette and puts it in his mouth.*
        Looks at **Ian***, waiting for a light*)

Ian   (*looks back, considering*)

Soldier   (*waits*)

Ian   (*holds out his cigarette*)

Soldier   (*leans forward, touching the tip of his cigarette against the lit one, eyes always on* **Ian**)

        He smokes.

Never met an Englishman with a gun before, most of them
don't know what a gun is. You a soldier?

Ian Of sorts.

Soldier Which side, if you can remember.

Ian Don't know what the sides are here. Don't know where . . .

(*He trails off, confused, and looks at the* **Soldier**.)

Think I might be drunk.

Soldier No. It's real.

(*Picks up the revolver and examines it.*)

Come to fight for us?

Ian No, I –

Soldier No, course not. English.

Ian I'm Welsh.

Soldier Sound English, fucking accent.

Ian I live there.

Soldier Foreigner?

Ian English and Welsh is the same. British. I'm not an import.

Soldier What's fucking Welsh, never heard of it.

Ian Come over from God knows where have their kids and call them
English they're not English born in England don't make you English.

Soldier Welsh as in Wales?

Ian It's attitude.

(*He turns away.*)

Look at the state of my fucking jacket. The bitch.

Soldier Your girlfriend did that, angry was she?

Ian She's not my girlfriend.

Soldier What, then?

Ian Mind your fucking own.

Soldier Haven't been here long have you.

Ian So?

Soldier Learn some manners, Ian.

Ian Don't call me that.

Soldier What shall I call you?

Ian Nothing.

Silence.
The **Soldier** *looks at* **Ian** *for a very long time, saying nothing.*
Ian *is uncomfortable.*
Eventually.

Ian   What?

Soldier   Nothing.

Silence.
Ian *is uneasy again.*

Ian   My name's Ian.

Soldier   I
Am
Dying to make love, Ian.

Ian   (*looks at him*)

Soldier   You got a girlfriend?

Ian   (*doesn't answer*)

Soldier   I have. Col. Fucking beautiful.

Ian   Cate –

Soldier   Close my eyes and think about her.
She's –
She's –
She's –
She's –
She's –
She's –
She's –
When was the last time you – ?

Ian   (*looks at him*)

Soldier   When? I know it was recent, smell it, remember.

Ian   Last night. I think.

Soldier   Good?

Ian   Don't know. I was pissed. Probably not.

Soldier   Three of us.

Ian   Don't tell me.

Soldier   Went to a house just outside town. All gone. Apart from a small boy hiding in the corner. One of the others took him outside. Lay him on the

ground and shot him through the legs. Heard crying in the basement. Went down. Three men and four women. Called the others. They held the men while I fucked the women. Youngest was twelve. Didn't cry, just lay there. Turned her over and –
Then she cried. Made her lick me clean. Closed my eyes and thought of –
Shot her father in the mouth. Brothers shouted. Hung them from the ceiling by their testicles.

Ian   Charming.

Soldier   Never done that?

Ian   No.

Soldier   Sure?

Ian   I wouldn't forget.

Soldier   You would.

Ian   Couldn't sleep with myself.

Soldier   What about your wife?

Ian   I'm divorced.

Soldier   Didn't you ever –

Ian   No.

Soldier   What about that girl, locked herself in the bathroom.

Ian   (*doesn't answer*)

Soldier   Ah.

Ian   You did four in one go, I've only ever done one.

Soldier   You killed her?

Ian   (*makes a move for his gun*)

Soldier   Don't I'll have to shoot you. Then I'd be lonely.

Ian   Course I haven't.

Soldier   Why not, don't seem to like her very much.

Ian   I do.
She's . . . a woman.

Soldier   So.

Ian   I've never –
       It's not –

Soldier   What?

Ian   (*doesn't answer*)

Soldier   Thought you were a soldier.

Ian   Not like that.

Soldier   Not like that, they're all like that.

Ian   My job –

Soldier   Even me. Have to be.
         My girl –
         Not going back to her. When I go back.
         She's dead, see. Fucking bastard soldier, he –

He stops.
Silence.

Ian   I'm sorry.

Soldier   Why?

Ian   It's terrible.

Soldier   What is?

Ian   Losing someone, a woman, like that.

Soldier   You know, do you?

Ian   I –

Soldier   Like what?

Ian   Like –
       You said –
       A soldier –

Soldier   You're a soldier.

Ian   I haven't –

Soldier   What if you were ordered to?

Ian   Can't imagine it.

Soldier   Imagine it.

Ian   (*imagines it*)

Soldier   In the line of duty. For your country. Wales.

Ian   (*imagines harder*)

Soldier   Foreign slag.

Ian   (*imagines harder. Looks sick*)

Soldier   Would you?

Ian   (*nods*)

Soldier   How.

Ian   Quickly. Back of the head. Bam.

Soldier   That's all.

Ian   It's enough.

Soldier   You think?

Ian   Yes.

Soldier   You never killed anyone.

Ian   Fucking have.

Soldier   No.

Ian   Don't you fucking –

Soldier   Couldn't talk like this. You'd know.

Ian   Know what?

Soldier   Exactly. You don't know.

Ian   Know fucking what?

Soldier   Stay in the dark.

Ian   What? Fucking what? What don't I know?

Soldier   You think –

>   (*He stops and smiles*)

>   I broke a woman's neck. Stabbed up between her legs, on the fifth stab snapped her spine.

Ian   (*looks sick*)

Soldier   You couldn't do that.

Ian   No.

Soldier   You never killed.

Ian   Not like that.

Soldier   Not
Like
That

Ian   I'm not a torturer.

Soldier   You're close to them, gun to head. Tie them up, tell them what you're going to do to them, make them wait for it, then . . . what?

Ian   Shoot them.

Soldier   You haven't got a clue.

Ian   What, then?

Soldier   You never fucked a man before you killed him?

Ian   No.

Soldier   Or after?

Ian   Course not.

Soldier   Why not?

Ian   What for, I'm not queer.

Soldier   Col, they buggered her. Cut her throat. Hacked her ears and nose off, nailed them to the front door.

Ian   Enough.

Soldier   Ever seen anything like that?

Ian   Stop.

Soldier   Not in photos?

Ian   Never.

Soldier   Some journalist, that's your job.

Ian   What?

Soldier   Proving it happened. I'm here, got no choice. But you. You should be telling people.

Ian   No-one's interested.

Soldier   You can do something, for me –

Ian   No.

Soldier   Course you can.

Ian   I can't do anything.

Soldier   Try.

Ian   I write . . . stories. That's all. Stories. This isn't a story anyone wants to hear.

Soldier   Why not?

Ian   (*takes one of the newspapers from the bed and reads*)

'Kinky car dealer Richard Morris drove two teenage prostitutes into the country, tied them naked to fences and whipped them with a belt before having sex. Morris, from Sheffield, was jailed for three years for unlawful sexual intercourse with one of the girls, aged 13.'

(*He tosses the paper away*)

Stories.

Soldier Doing to them what they done to us, what good is that? At home I'm clean. Like it never happened. Tell them you saw me. Tell them . . . you saw me. Make it concrete.

Ian It's not my job.

Soldier Whose is it?

Ian I'm a home journalist, for Yorkshire. I don't cover foreign affairs.

Soldier Foreign affairs, what you doing here?

Ian I do other stuff. Shootings and rapes and kids getting fiddled by queer priests and schoolteachers. Not soldiers screwing each other for a patch of land. It has to be . . . personal. Your girlfriend, she's a story. Soft and clean. Not you. Filthy, like the wogs. No joy in a story about blacks who gives a shit? Why bring you to light?

Soldier You don't know fuck all about me.

Ian What makes you special?

Soldier Nothing.
I went to school.
I made love with Col.
Bastards killed her, now I'm here.
Now I'm here.

(*He pushes the rifle in* **Ian**'s *face*.)

Turn over, Ian.

Ian Why?

Soldier Going to fuck you.

Ian No.

Soldier Kill you, then.

Ian Fine.

Soldier See. Rather be shot than fucked and shot.

Ian Yes.

Soldier And now you agree with anything I say.

(*He kisses* **Ian** *very tenderly on the lips.*
They stare at each other)

You smell like her. Same cigarettes.

He gets up and turns **Ian** *over with one hand.*
He holds the revolver to **Ian**'s *head with the other.*
He pulls down **Ian**'s *trousers, undoes his own and rapes him – eyes closed and smelling*
Ian's *hair.*
The **Soldier** *is crying his heart out.*

Ian's *face registers pain but he is silent.*

When the **Soldier** *has finished he pulls up his trousers and pushes the revolver up* **Ian**'s
anus.

Soldier   Bastard pulled the trigger on Col.
What's it like?

Ian   (*tries to answer. He can't*)

Soldier   (*withdraws the gun and sits next to* **Ian**)

You never fucked by a man before?

Ian   (*doesn't answer*)

Soldier   Didn't think so. It's nothing. Saw thousands of people packing into
trucks like pigs trying to leave town. Women threw their babies on board
hoping someone would look after them. Crushing each other to death. Insides
of people heads came out of their eyes. Saw a child most of his face blown off,
young girl I fucked hand up inside her trying to claw my liquid out, starving
man eating his dead wife's leg. Gun was born here and won't die. Can't get
tragic about your arse. Don't think your Welsh arse is different to any other
arse I fucked. Sure you haven't got any more food, I'm fucking starving.

Ian   Are you going to kill me?

Soldier   Always looking after your own arse.

The **Soldier** *grips* **Ian**'s *head in his hands.*

He puts his mouth over one of **Ian**'s *eyes, sucks it out, bites it off and eats it.*

He does the same to the other eye.

Soldier   He ate her eyes.
Poor bastard.
Poor love.
Poor fucking bastard.

Blackout.

Scene Four

The Same.

The **Soldier** *lies close to* **Ian**, *the revolver in his hand. He has blown his own brain out.*

Cate enters through the bathroom door, soaking wet and carrying a baby. She steps over the **Soldier** *with a glance.*
Then she sees **Ian**.

Cate   You're a nightmare.

Ian   Cate?

Cate   It won't stop.

Ian   Catie? You here?

Cate   Everyone in town is crying.

Ian   Touch me.

Cate   Soldiers have taken it over.

Ian   They've won?

Cate   Most people gave up. They didn't cry at all, now they can't stop.

Ian   You seen Matthew?

Cate   No.

Ian   Will you tell him for me?

Cate   He isn't here.

Ian   Tell him –
Tell him –

Cate   No.

Ian   Tell him –

Cate   No.

Ian   Don't know what to tell him.
I'm cold.
Tell him –
You here?

Cate   A woman gave me her baby.

Ian   You come for me, Catie? Punish me or rescue me makes no difference I love you Cate tell him for me do it for me touch me Cate.

Cate   Don't know what to do with it.

Ian   I'm cold.

Cate   Keeps crying.

Ian   Tell him –

Cate   I can't.

Ian   Will you stay with me, Cate?

Cate   No.

Ian   Why not?

Cate   I have to go back soon.

Ian   Shaun know what we did?

Cate   Nothing.

Ian   Better tell him.

Cate   No.

Ian   He'll know. Even if you don't.

Cate   How?

Ian   Smell it. Soiled goods. Don't want it, not when you can have someone clean.

Cate   What's happened to your eyes?

Ian   I need you to stay, Cate. Won't be for long.

Cate   Do you know about babies?

Ian   No.

Cate   What about Matthew?

Ian   He's twenty four.

Cate   When he was born.

Ian   They shit and cry. Hopeless.

Cate   Bleeding.

Ian   Will you touch me?

Cate   No.

Ian   So I know you're here.

Cate   You can hear me.

Ian   Won't hurt you, I promise.

Cate   (*goes to him slowly and touches the top of his head*)

Ian   Help me.

Cate   (*strokes his hair*)

Ian   Be dead soon, anyway, Cate. And it hurts. Help me to –
Help me –
Finish
It

Cate   (*withdraws her hand*)

Ian   Catie?

Cate   Got to get something for baby to eat.

Ian   Won't find anything.

Cate   May as well look.

Ian   Fucking bastards ate it all.

Cate   It'll die.

Ian   Needs its mother's milk.

Cate   Ian.

Ian   Stay. Nowhere to go, where are you going to go?
Bloody dangerous on your own, look at me. Safer here with me.

Cate   (*considers. Then sits down with the baby some distance from* **Ian**)

Ian   (*relaxes when he hears her sit*)

Cate   (*rocks the baby*)

Ian   Not as bad as all that, am I?

Cate   (*looks at him*)

Ian   Will you help me, Catie?

Cate   Don't know how.

Ian   My gun.

Cate   (*thinks. Then gets up and searches around, baby in arms. She sees the revolver in the* **Soldier**'*s hand and stares at it for some time*)

Ian   Found it?

Cate   No.

(*She takes the revolver from the* **Soldier** *and fiddles with it. It springs open and she stares in at the bullets.*
She removes them and closes the gun)

Ian   That it?

Cate   Yes.

Ian   Can I have it?

Cate   I don't think so.

Ian   Catie.

Cate   What?

Ian   Come on.

Cate   Don't tell me what to do.

Ian   I'm not, love. Can you keep that baby quiet.

Cate   It's not doing anything. It's hungry.

Ian   We're all bloody hungry, don't shoot myself I'll starve to death.

Cate   It's wrong to kill yourself.

Ian   No it's not.

Cate   God wouldn't like it.

Ian   There isn't one.

Cate   How do you know?

Ian   No God. No Father Christmas. No fairies. No Narnia. No fucking nothing.

Cate   Got to be something.

Ian   Why?

Cate   Doesn't make sense otherwise.

Ian   Don't be fucking stupid, doesn't make sense anyway. No reason for there to be a God just because it would be better if there was.

Cate   Thought you didn't want to die.

Ian   I can't see.

Cate   My brother's got blind friends. You can't give up.

Ian   Why not?

Cate   It's weak.

Ian   I know you want to punish me, trying to make me live.

Cate   I don't.

Ian   Course you fucking do, I would. There's people I'd love to suffer but they don't, they die and that's it.

Cate   What if you're wrong?

Ian   I'm not.

Cate   But if.

Ian   I've seen dead people. They're dead. They're not somewhere else, they're dead.

Cate   What about people who've seen ghosts?

Ian   What about them? Imagining it. Or making it up or wishing the person was still alive.

Cate   People who've died and come back say they've seen tunnels and lights –

Ian   Can't die and come back. That's not dying, it's fainting.
When you die it's the end.

Cate   I believe in God.

Ian   Everything's got a scientific explanation.

Cate   No.

Ian   Give me my gun.

Cate   What are you going to do?

Ian   I won't hurt you.

Cate   I know.

Ian   End it. Got to, Cate, I'm ill. Just speeding it up a bit.

Cate   (*thinks hard*)

Ian   Please.

Cate   (*gives him the gun*)

Ian   (*takes the gun and puts it in his mouth.
He takes it out again*)

Don't stand behind me.

Ian   (*Puts the gun back in his mouth.
He pulls the trigger. The gun clicks, empty.*

He shoots again. And again and again and again.
He takes the gun out of his mouth)

Fuck.

Cate   Fate, see. You're not meant to do it. God –

Ian   The cunt.

He throws the gun away in despair.

Cate   (*Rocks the baby and looks down at it*)

Oh no.

Ian   What.

Cate   It's dead.

Ian   Lucky bastard.

Cate *bursts out laughing, unnaturally, hysterically, uncontrollably. She laughs and laughs and laughs and laughs and laughs.*

Blackout.

Scene Five

The Same.

Cate *is burying the baby under the floorboards.*

She looks around and finds two pieces of wood. She rips the lining out of **Ian***'s jacket and binds the wood together in a cross which she jams between the boards.*
She collects a few of the scattered flowers and places them under the cross.

Cate   I don't know her name.

Ian   Don't matter. No-one's going to visit.

Cate   I was supposed to look after her.

Ian   Can bury me next to her soon. Dance on my grave.

Cate   Don't feel no pain or know nothing you shouldn't know –

Ian   Cate?

Cate   Shh.

Ian   What you doing?

Cate   Praying. Just in case.

Ian   Will you pray for me?

Cate   No.

Ian   When I'm dead, not now.

Cate   No point when you're dead.

Ian   You're praying for her.

Cate   She's baby.

Ian   So?

Cate   Innocent.

Ian   Can't you forgive me?

Cate   Don't see bad things or go bad places –

Ian   She's dead, Cate.

Cate   Or meet anyone who'll do bad things.

Ian   She won't, Cate, she's dead.

Cate   Amen.

She starts to leave

Ian   Where you going?

Cate   I'm hungry.

Ian Cate, it's dangerous. There's no food.

Cate Can get some off a soldier.

Ian How?

Cate (*doesn't answer*)

Ian Don't do that.

Cate Why not?

Ian That's not you.

Cate I'm hungry.

Ian I know so am I. But.
I'd rather –
It's not –
Please, Cate.
I'm blind.

Cate I'm hungry.

She goes

Ian Cate? Catie?
If you get some food –
Fuck.

Darkness.
Light.

Ian *masturbating.*

Ian cunt cunt cunt cunt cunt cunt cunt cunt cunt cunt cunt

Darkness.
Light.

Ian *strangling himself.*

Darkness.
Light.

Ian *shitting.*
And then trying to clean it up.

Darkness.
Light.

Ian *laughing hysterically.*

Darkness.
Light.

Ian *having a nightmare.*

Darkness.
Light.

Ian *crying, huge bloody tears.*
He is hugging the **Soldier**'s *body for comfort.*

Darkness.
Light.

Ian *lying very still, weak with hunger.*

Darkness.
Light.

Ian *tears the cross out of the ground, rips up the boards and lifts the baby's body out.*

He eats the baby.

He puts the sheet the baby was wrapped in back in the hole. A beat, then he climbs in after it and lies down, head poking out of the floor.

He dies with relief.

It starts to rain on him, coming through the roof.

Eventually.

Ian   Shit.

Cate *enters carrying some bread, a large sausage and a bottle of gin. There is blood seeping from between her legs.*

Cate   You're sitting under a hole.

Ian   I know.

Cate   Get wet.

Ian   Aye.

Cate   Stupid bastard.

She pulls a sheet off the bed and wraps it around her.
She sits next to **Ian**'s *head.*

She eats her fill of the sausage and bread, then washes it down with gin.

Ian *listens.*

She feeds **Ian** *with the remaining food.*

Cate   Did it in the back of a van.
He smelt of cigarettes and sweat.
What he did –
What he did with his wife he said.

Did it quickly. Made me bleed.
Gave me a sausage, some bread and this.

(*She pours gin in* **Ian***'s mouth*)

Want to go home now.

She finishes feeding **Ian** *and sits apart from him, huddled for warmth.*

She drinks the gin.
She sucks her thumb.

Silence.

It rains.

Ian   Thankyou.

Blackout.

Blasted

Blasted now exists independently of me – as it should do – and to attempt to sum up its genesis and meaning in a few paragraphs would be futile and of only passing interest. If a play is good, it breathes its own air and has a life and voice of its own. What you take that voice to be saying is no concern of mine. It is what it is. Take it or leave it.

Sarah Kane
July 1994

Sarah Kane was born in 1971. Her monologues *Comic Monologue*, *Starved* and *What She Said* have been performed by fringe companies throughout Britain. *Blasted* is her first full length play and she is currently working on a commission for the Royal Court.

Foreign Lands

Karen Hope

Foreign Lands was first performed at the Finborough Theatre, London on 5 January 1993, with the following cast:

Rosie	Steph Bramwell
Ellen	Tracy Gillman
Barbara	Marlene Sidaway
Madeleine	Julia Tarnoky

Directed by Jessica Dromgoole
Designed by Joanne Nellis
Lighting by Isla Stewart
Sound by Alan Gwinnett

Characters

Ellen *late twenties*
Rosie *late thirties*
Barbara *early sixties*
Madeleine *late twenties*

The play is set in the North East of England.

Scene One: Evening. March 14th 1986. Bedroom.
Scene Two: Same room. Evening. One week later.
Scene Three: Same room. Morning. Two weeks later.

Scene One

Upstairs bedroom in terraced house in the North East of England. Medium sized, a bit cluttered: against rear wall is a large old fashioned wardrobe with a full-length mirror, a small kitchen table with a table lamp on it, and a chair. There is a large window rear left. Beneath, along left side wall is a bed. The bedroom door is set into right side wall. An armchair is front right of stage, with its back to audience. A few framed pictures on walls – faded black and white family photographs, a reproduction of a painting of flowers. The room is virtually in darkness. It is an early winter evening. Light from a street lamp outside the window provides some illumination. The bedroom door is slightly ajar, also letting in light. Because the window is open, sounds from the street can be heard; the vague hum of distant cars, but predominantly the voices of girls playing in the street below. They are skipping, singing an accompanying song. The words are not really distinguishable, but the rhyme goes:

> Peggy Bow, Peggy Bow,
> Watching the boys from her window,
> Catch her eye, watch her smile,
> She'll take you out for a little while,
> Past the pit, down to the Tyne,
> Peggy doesn't need much time
> Tell her you'll go home instead,
> Cos if you don't, this time you're DEAD.

The sound of footsteps coming upstairs heralds the arrival of **Ellen**. *She is carrying a cassette player. She makes no attempt to switch on the light, stands stiffly in the doorway, looking around her, swaying slightly backwards and forwards on the balls of her feet.*

Ellen (*she has slight speech impediment*) Six o clock. Friday. March the fourteenth. Nineteen eighty six.

Closes door behind her, chuckling to herself.

Ellen Supper. Seven o clock. Beans on toast. (*Makes happy, throaty, appreciative sounds.*) Nine o clock. Windows. Clean Ellen's windows. (*Excited sounds.*)

Goes across to window. Caresses window frame. Strokes cheek against window panes. Her attention is suddenly taken by girls skipping ouside. Watching them, begins to jump up and down herself. Recites rhyme along with them.

Ellen

> Peggy Bow, Peggy Bow,
> Watching the boys from her window,
> Catch her eye, watch her smile,
> She'll take you out for a little while,
> Past the pit, down to the Tyne,
> Peggy doesn't need much time
> Tell her you'll go home instead,
> Cos if you don't, this time you're DEAD.

She begins to sway from side to side, her arms hugging herself, but still holding the cassette player. Goes across to wardrobe. Peers very closely at herself. Pulls a lipstick out of her trouser pocket, applies it to face, although audience can't make out what she is doing, since her back is to them. Admires handiwork. Moves back to window. Stands in profile, switches on cassette. It is instrumental – a hymn. She begins to sing in Latin. She has a beautiful voice; a soprano of extraordinary purity. She doesn't move at all while she sings, in fact stands quite stiffly to attention. Half-way through the song she abruptly switches off the cassette and stops singing. She has heard someone coming upstairs. She looks around anxiously for somewhere to hide, clambers onto window sill and pulls curtains closed around her, leaving her radio cassette on the bed.

Voice coming upstairs (Rosie)   Your daughter has a beautiful voice, Mrs Goodison.

Second voice (Barbara)   I told her not to go upstairs. I'm never quite sure what she'll get up to. (*Shouting.*) Ellen.

They open bedroom door.

Barbara   (*calling*) Ellen.

She switches light switch by door, but nothing happens.

Barbara   (*flustered*) Oh dear. The bulb must've gone. What a time for it to happen.

Rosie   (*pleasantly*) That's no problem, Mrs Goodison.

Barbara   Please call me Barbara. (*Thinks for a while.*) I should have some bulbs in the kitchen cupboard. Would you mind just waiting for a moment?

Rosie   Not at all. If I pull open the curtains, it'll give us a bit more light, don't you think, Barbara?

Barbara   Oh don't go bothering yourself, Miss McDonald. You might trip over in the dark.

Rosie   (*laughs*) Someone once told me I could see like a cat in the dark.

Barbara   Oh, well . . . I'd better get the bulb, then. Sorry about this.

Exit **Barbara**, *calling for* **Ellen**.

Rosie *moves, feeling her way, across room. She discovers table lamp, switches it on, and trains it on window. She pulls back curtains. There is a moment of horror.* **Ellen** *is standing, as if crucified, with her back against the window. The palms of her hands, her mouth and her forehead appear to be smeared and running with blood. Her eyes are closed and her head is drooping.* **Rosie** *gives a short scream.* **Ellen** *looks up, her eyes meet* **Rosie***'s, and there is a moment of recognition.*

Rosie   Ellen.

Barbara *comes running in, heavily out of breath.*

Barbara   What's wrong? What's wrong?

Ellen *begins to scramble down, but not before* **Barbara** *has realized what she has done.*

Barbara Ellen! If I've told you once . . . Miss McDonald, I'm really sorry . . . Ellen, how could you? . . . Are you alright Miss McDonald? . . . That's my best lipstick, I'll bet, Ellen, I could . . . honestly, I could . . . Oh dear . . . I just . . .

Rosie (*interrupting, laughing a little*) It's alright, Barbara. There's no harm done. I was just taken by surprise, that's all.

Ellen *is standing in middle of room, ramrod straight. She looks at neither of them.*

Barbara Oh dear, I'm so sorry, I really am. First the light bulb, then this. It's no way to go about renting a room. (*With resignation.*) Ellen! Go and wash your face.

Exit **Ellen**. **Barbara** *wedges open the bedroom door to let in a little more light. She puts chair beneath light fitting.*

Rosie Could I put it in for you?

Barbara No, I couldn't . . . I've already . . . Maybe you could be so kind as to hold up the lamp so I can see what I'm doing. If you don't mind.

Rosie Not at all, Barbara.

Barbara *gets up onto chair.* **Rosie** *shines lamp up for her. She shines it a little too directly onto* **Barbara**'*s face.*

Barbara (*holding one hand up to her eyes*) Oh . . . em . . . that's a bit too . . .

Rosie Oh. Sorry, Barbara.

Rosie *slowly moves the position of the lamp.* **Barbara** *fits the new bulb, gets off chair and switches on light. The room looks a little in need of decoration, but otherwise quite homely.*

Rosie Very nice.

Barbara (*pleased*) Do you think so?

Rosie *moves around room, touching things.*

Rosie (*pointing to photograph on wall*) Is that you?

Barbara No. That's my mother. Everyone said we were very alike.

Rosie Yes, you are. Is she . . . ?

Barbara No – she's dead now. (*Quickly.*) That one's me.

Rosie Oh yes. That's a very nice photograph. Very pretty. How old were you?

Barbara (*remembering and smiling*) Seventeen. (*Laughs girlishly.*) That boy with the smart jacket . . . Colin Davies. He went to New Zealand about forty years ago. We were sweethearts. (*Laughs again.*) That's my best friend Pam stood next to him. And behind her are Veronica and Beth and Lily Lewis with the kiss curls. Oh, I had lots of friends in those days.

Rosie   Your best friend. Does she still live in the neighbourhood.

Barbara   (*too smoothly*) Went to New Zealand. With Colin. (*Quickly.*) I could take them down if you want . . . if you decide to take the room . . . only . . . they've been up so long the wallpaper underneath is a different colour . . . I need to decorate really.

Rosie   No, no, leave them. I like them. (*Points to another.*) This one . . . aha . . . is that Ellen?

Barbara   Yes. Now how long ago was that taken. I think it was, let's see . . . well, I think she was about six at the time. That would make it . . . 1965. But she could tell you if you asked her. Right down to the date – day, month, year, the lot. Probably even what time. Yes, she was living at her auntie's, and I'd taken her out. Yes, that's right. I had a weekend off work, and I took her out. The only place she wanted to visit was this church. St. Mary's. She didn't want to go to the pictures, or the coast. Just this church.

Rosie   What a beautiful window.

Barbara   Yes. It's supposed to be one of the best stained glass windows in Gateshead. Very old. Beautiful colours. It would have looked a lovely photograph in colour.

Rosie   Yes – all that light flooding in. I can imagine what the colours must have looked like all over her face and dress – and the way she's lifted up her face. . . . Look at the delight in her eyes. (*Pause.*) Didn't she live with you as a child?

Barbara   (*cautious*) Not all of the time. I had a live-in job for a while you see . . . (*Quickly, moving across to the window.*) As I said over the phone, there's quite a nice view. That's the River Tyne just down the valley there. You can get across the fields and down to the river bank quite quickly now. It's quite a nice walk of a summer Sunday, but you have to be careful. There was . . . well, you know, all these stories in the papers.

Rosie   I'll take it.

Barbara   Are you sure? It's not too expensive for you?

Rosie   No. It's fine.

Barbara   (*seems at a loss for words*) Em . . . I could always give you your dinner as well if you're in the house. It's no extra work. I've got to make something for me and Ellen anyway.

Rosie   (*laughs*) Breakfast and evening meal will be just fine. I never eat lunch anyway.

Barbara (*wistfully*) That's how you keep your figure, is it? I've got too used to four square meals a day. Well, right then . . . (*Smiles.*) Hope you'll enjoy it here.

Enter **Ellen**, *clean and scrubbed.*

Barbara Let's have a look at that face. (*She examines* **Ellen**'*s face as though she were a child, turning it from side to side, and examining beneath the chin, and the neck.*) That's much better, Ellen. Did you put my lipstick back as well?

Ellen Lipstick back.

Barbara Thank you, Ellen. Now, we've got some good news. Miss McDonald is coming to live with us.

Rosie Please call me Rosie.

Barbara She'll be moving in right away.

Ellen *looks from mother to* **Rosie** *and back. Goes to leave room.*

Barbara (*slightly hurt*) Manners, Ellen. (*Smiles apologetically at* **Rosie**.) Ellen, what birthday? Ask Rosie, what birthday?

Ellen Know.

Barbara (*puzzled*) What do you mean, no?

Ellen (*explaining*) Not 'no'. (*Shakes head.*) Know. (*Nods head.*)

Barbara Don't be silly. You can't know. (*To* **Rosie**.) When were you born? If you give the date, the month and the year, Ellen can tell you what day you were born on.

Rosie (*to* **Ellen**) Eighth of April 1948.

Ellen Thursday.

Rosie No.

Barbara Oh! (*Pause.*) Wasn't it? (*Pause.*) Are you sure? I've never known her to get it wrong.

Rosie Positive. Thursday's child has far to go. No. I was born on a Monday.

Ellen *looks agitated, without saying a word.*

Barbara Monday's child is fair of face. Yes, I can see that. (*Puzzled, changing the subject.*) Would you like a cup of tea?

Rosie Yes please.

Barbara I'll give you a shout when it's ready.

Rosie Oh – Barbara – why don't we drink it up here – if you don't mind.

Barbara Right you are, then. How do you like it?

Rosie Milk. One sugar.

Barbara   You take sugar, then? I thought maybe you'd be watching your figure . . . Oh, sorry . . . you probably don't need to. I didn't mean . . .

Rosie   What's the point of life if not to indulge yourself every once in a while. Don't you think, Barbara?

Barbara   (*chuckling*) I do, oh I do indeed. (*To* **Ellen**.) Come on, pet, you can carry Miss Mc . . . (*Smiles.*) Rosie's things upstairs for her.

Exit **Barbara** *and* **Ellen**. **Ellen** *stops briefly and turns in doorway, gives strange look to* **Rosie**. **Rosie** *looks at her impassively. When the two women have gone* **Rosie** *turns away, a slight smile on her face as though amused. She walks slowly around room, her arms stretched out sideways, her head thrown back, touching the walls with her fingertips. It is a voluptuous gesture, her fingers caressing the surfaces she encounters. She inhales deeply, eyes closed, a smile on her face, then turns abruptly to the window, stands in profile, face turned slightly towards window, one hand absent-mindedly caressing the window pane. Enter* **Ellen**, *carrying a large travelling bag. She puts it down in centre of room, stares at* **Rosie**, *rocking backwards and forwards on balls of feet.*

Ellen   (*her tongue lingering over first syllable of word*) Thursday!

Rosie   (*turns face slowly towards her, whispers, confirming the date*) Thursday.

Ellen *looks satisfied now, makes contented chuckling sounds.*

Ellen   Ellen window.

Rosie   What can you see from the window, Ellen?

Ellen   (*ignoring question*) Mr Pothequeue. Mr Pothequeue, blue . . . Mr Pothequeue blue gate.

Rosie   Mr Pothequeue.

Ellen   Mr Pothequeue blue gate run run. (*Chuckles.*)

Sound of **Barbara** *coming upstairs. Enter* **Barbara** *bearing tea tray.*

Barbara   Do you like ginger snaps?

Rosie   I do. Yes.

Barbara   Oh good. (*To Ellen.*) What's the joke?

Ellen *chuckles, rocks her upper body back and forth.*

Ellen   Mr Pothequeue.

Barbara   Ah. It's Mr Pothecary, is it?

Ellen   Mr Pothequeue.

Barbara   Mr Pothequeue, blue gate.

Ellen   (*gleefully*) Mr Pothequeue blue gate. (*Chuckles.*)

Barbara (*to* **Rosie**) Mr Pothecary had a blue gate. Mr Pothecary lived across the road from Ellen when she was a child. She used to stand by the window and watch him.

Ellen Mr Pothequeue, blue gate, run run.

Barbara (*to* **Ellen**) Mr Pothequeue blue gate run run. (*To* **Rosie**.) He was gassed in the first world war. On bad days he still thought he was fighting the Germans – used to dash down his front path, fumble with the gate – he couldn't hardly drink a cup of tea for his hands shaking – and he'd be bawling and shouting down the street, waving his stick so much he sometimes fell over. (*To* **Ellen**.) What made you think of that? It's years since you mentioned him? (*To* **Rosie**.) What made her start talking about Mr Pothecary?

Rosie I don't know. (*Pause.*) I asked her what she could see from the window.

Barbara Oh. (*Pause.*) She's talking about the wrong window. Whatever made her talk about Mr Pothecary?

Ellen *has started to pour the tea. There are four cups.*

Rosie Four cups?

Barbara Two for Ellen.

Rosie I see.

Barbara She always has two. One's half full, one's three quarters full. She has two sugars in the three quarters full cup, and one sugar in the half full cup.

Rosie Always? What happens if she doesn't?

Barbara What happens? (*Laughs.*) She always does. There's no question of it. She has a way of doing everything, and that's the way she does it.

Rosie (*smiling*) A woman of determination.

Barbara You would definitely be right there.

Ellen *is putting milk and sugar in tea. She puts two sugars in* **Rosie**'*s tea.*

Barbara (*noticing*) Ellen! That's too many sugars. Why didn't you ask?

Ellen (*looking confidently at* **Rosie**) Two sugars. Two sugars.

Rosie (*to* **Barbara**) That's okay. (*To* **Ellen**.) Thank you.

Ellen *hands out tea.*

Barbara Next time ask, Ellen.

Rosie Very nice.

Ellen *takes her tea and leaves room.*

Barbara   She always drinks her tea separately. She'll come back when she's finished.

Rosie   (*politely*) Has she always . . . ?

Barbara   She's autistic. They're like that, some of them. Little rituals, you know. Keeps her happy.

Rosie   Autistic?

Barbara   Aye. No-one seems to know what it is, what causes it. The doctors call it 'abnormal self-absorption'. (*Laughs.*) I have a little laugh at that, you know. When I think of me father . . . took his tea into the kitchen away from all us kids and me mam, and sat poring over his racing paper. Only things he ever really talked about were the horses and his motor bike and side-car. Then after he died and I lived with me mother . . . she was another one . . . obsessed with coloured people moving into the area . . . 'specially when she got older, lost her faculties; had a terrible time of it trying to strike up a proper conversation with her – had to give up in the end – always on about coloured people this, coloured people that. I don't know about abnormal. Next to horses, motor bikes and coloured people, windows and dates don't seem so bad. We've all got our obsessions.

Rosie   (*sipping tea*) Mmm. Although I should think that you're not a lady to be obsessed with anything. Not in any negative sense of the word.

Barbara   (*flattered but unsure*) Oh. What do you mean?

Rosie   Well, Barbara, you strike me as being, what's the word I'm looking for? . . . wise, I suppose.

Barbara   Wise? (*Laughs, flattered but embarrassed.*) Can't say I'd call meself that.

Rosie   Yes, wise. (*Pause.*) Any obsessions you had would be, I don't know . . . healthy ones, I suppose.

Barbara is silent for a while, drinking tea to gain herself time.

Barbara   (*serious*) For a while I . . . (*Changes tack, tone of voice becomes more hearty*) Some people might say that the bingo is my biggest obsession. Couple of nights a week. But, you know, it gets you out of the house, lets you meet people. And there's set nights when Ellen has favourite programmes on television, so if I go out those nights, she's alright in on her own. (*Pause*) Are you a one for going out in the evenings?

Rosie   Not really.

Pause.

Rosie   I should think I'll be working in my room most of the time.

Barbara   It's funny. I always thought that my first lady would be a teacher.

Rosie   Did you really?

Barbara I would have liked to become a teacher. It was difficult though, in those days, for someone like me. Anyway, there was me mother, and after that, well, there was only really domestic work or shop work that I was qualified for. (*Pause.*) Is it difficult, teaching by correspondence course?

Rosie Not difficult. Just different.

Barbara What is it you teach them?

Rosie I have a degree in social sciences.

Barbara Oh. (*Impressed.*) A degree. (*Pause, embarrassed.*) What's social sciences?

Rosie Psychology. Sociology. Anthropology.

Barbara Oh. (*Still doesn't understand.*) You must spend a lot of time writing.

Rosie Yes, a lot.

Barbara I'll have to introduce you to Mrs Allen. She's a one for writing. You wouldn't think it to look at her, but she writes all these romantic stories. But you know, (*Begins to laugh.*) I can't get over it – she calls all the men Ronald. I said to her, Mrs Allen, what d'you call them all Ronald for? She says to me, it's a lovely name, very masculine.

Rosie That would be nice, but I shall probably be very busy.

Barbara Oh yes, of course.

Enter **Ellen**. *She returns mugs to tray.*

Ellen Cheese on toast.

Barbara (*laughs*) But you had cheese on toast at tea time.

Ellen Cheese on toast, geddaway window.

Barbara Oh yes, I forgot. We were sitting in the living room, just before you came, Ellen with her cheese on toast, me with my ginger cake, when we saw this man looking at us through the window.

Ellen Geddaway window, geddaway.

Barbara I opened the front door and asked him what he was doing. He asked if this was the house with the room to let, but I wasn't going to tell him. (*Carefully.*) I'm not quite sure how it affects me allowances, that's why, you known . . .

Rosie Yes, you said.

Barbara He said he was looking for someone.

Rosie (*very interested, trying to appear disinterested*) Looking for someone?

Barbara A well-spoken man, too, creeping around – didn't even seem to know who he was looking for. I told him I would call the police.

Rosie The police?

Barbara But just in case he was from, you know . . . I didn't. (*Brusquely.*) Could have been a man out to track down his girlfriend, I suppose. You know, if they'd had a tiff and she said she was going to look for somewhere else to live. Probably a married man. That's why he was snooping. They don't like to get caught out, these married men.

Rosie Don't they?

Barbara No. (*Pause.*) Well not from what you gather reading the papers. There was that politician. Got his girlfriend in trouble and then just didn't want to know. Did his career no harm, though, not like hers. (*Pause.*) Yes.

Rosie But he went away?

Barbara Who?

Rosie The man.

Barbara Oh. (*Pause.*) Him. (*Disinterested.*) Yes.

Rosie *moves upstage, to window, looks out.*

Rosie (*quietly*) Nice view . . . familiar . . .

Barbara Do you know this area then?

Rosie No . . . well . . . I've seen old photographs . . . I used to live somewhere very similar once, but . . . I've moved around a bit since then, lived abroad . . .

Barbara (*interrupting*) I knew it. Something about you . . . When I saw you get out of the cab, pay the man his money, it was a bit like when Pam and Colin came over from New Zealand, didn't know the money properly, still a bit, em, you know – looking around, up, at everything. (*Excited at her own detective work.*) I'll bet you haven't been in this country for long, right? (*Hesitates.*) Oh, I'm sorry. (*Sheepish.*) I was getting a bit carried away.

Ellen *has moved across to window. Can still hear vague sounds of children playing outside. As it has got darker, street lamp seems brighter and familiar urban night sounds have entered the room; dogs barking, a train in the distance.* **Ellen** *begins to hum rhythm of children's skipping song without actually saying the words. She is in a world of her own, begins to skip, softly, almost imperceptibly.* **Rosie** *watches her as she speaks, as if she is not really concentrating on what she is saying.*

Rosie Yes. You're right. It's . . . (*Voice trails away as watches* **Ellen***, then seems to force herself out of her reverie.*) Are you musical, Barbara?

Barbara Me? (*Laughs.*) Musical? I couldn't carry a tune in a paper bag. Not me.

Rosie Then it must be Mr Goodison?

Barbara Her granda? A sing-song in the club, maybe. . . .

Rosie (*slightly confused*) Your husband.

Pause.

Barbara I don't know where she gets it from.

Rosie Then it's a gift from God.

Barbara From God!

Rosie Don't you believe in God, Barbara?

Barbara Yes. I do believe. But not like I once did. Once. . . . It's hard to believe sometimes, with what happens in this world. If there is . . . well, I find it hard to see, sometimes, the purpose . . .

Rosie No. There is purpose. In everything.

Barbara (*a little worried*) Are you . . . a Jehovah's Witness, or something?

Rosie (*laughs*) No – You won't find me hosting bible meetings up here – don't you worry about that. It's just . . . well . . . I believe it's up to every individual to find their peace with God. I have. It wasn't easy. But I feel at peace now.

Barbara Our Ellen – now she's a different kettle of fish. Cannot keep her out of the churches. Seven, she goes to, on and off. She's in the choir of each of them. Sometimes, on a Sunday, she's just backwards and forwards on the buses, catching a bit of each of the services. It's the windows, and the music – maybe something else . . . I don't know . . . St Edmund Campion – that's the Catholic church at the bottom of the rise; St Alban's – that's C of E; the Methodist chapel over Windy Nook – I've never thought their windows very interesting, but just goes to show – maybe wire netting has a beauty all of it's own; The Church of the Lord High . . . oh, what's it called? – One of these born again places – very stern and grey; how many's that? . . . one, two, three, four . . . oh yes, another C of E, St George's – now that's a nice church for you, only just sandblasted clean, flower arrangements like you've never seen before; and, what are the others? . . . You'd have to ask Ellen. Ellen!

Ellen *doesn't reply. She is still too wrapped up in the children's game outside.*

Rosie She's too busy to answer.

Barbara She's always too busy. Aren't you, pet? (*Pause.*) Sometimes they get a bit funny, you know, these vicars and that. If she misses them out for a while. They're convinced the other side has won her over. No-one's ever been courted so well as this one, by the churches. They all give her the solo's. She listens once to a piece of music, and the second time she can remember it, music, words, and all. Even the Latin. I can't get over it. She'll be in demand in a fortnight's time, you'll see, with Easter, and all that.

Rosie   Yes. Easter. (*Pause.*) Brings back memories.

Barbara   This reminds you of your old home, I can tell. Bringing back the memories.

Rosie   (*as if to herself*) When you're away, you think you remember, but you don't really. It takes coming back to make you realise that.

Silence.

Barbara   I'd better leave you to your unpacking, then. (*Calling.*) Ellen! Come downstairs with me, while Rosie sorts out her things. (*To* **Rosie**.) Is there anything you'll be needing?

Rosie   No thank you. I think I have everything I need.

Barbara   Howway then, Ellen.

Rosie   She's alright here if she wants to stay.

Barbara   If you're sure? If she's any trouble . . . I expect she'll be down soon anyway to sort out her beans on toast. I'll see you later.

Exit **Barbara**.

Rosie   (*to* **Ellen**) Mr Potheque . . . (*Voice trails away.*) Lynne West, three yellow windows . . .

Ellen   (*suddenly interested*) Lynne West, three yellow windows . . .

Rosie and **Ellen**   (*together*) No curtains.

Rosie   (*laughs*) Lived with . . . ?

Ellen   Mr Doorstop.

Rosie   (*laughs*) Mr Dawlston.

Rosie *puts her arm around* **Ellen***'s shoulders, gently but firmly moves her to more central position in front of window. Points into distance.*

Rosie   That was then. And over there?

Ellen *shakes head.*

Rosie   Yes. You do know.

Ellen *moves free of* **Rosie***'s arm.*

Ellen   Seven o'clock. Supper. Beans on toast.

Ellen *moves firmly to door.* **Rosie** *moves with her, stands in front of door, looks at* **Ellen**. *She seems about to say something, but changes her mind and moves aside. She* *laughs. Exit* **Ellen**. **Rosie** *moves to centre of room. She looks around, a little unsure now she is completely on her own, seems to feel the cold, shivers a little, hugs herself. Visibly pulls herself together, smiles triumphantly, smugly. Moves across to window and looks out.*

Rosie Can't see properly.

She switches off light. Only illumination is from street light and table lamp. Returns to window.

Rosie Kids and their games. (*Pause.*) There it is, how I remember it, the Tyne snaking into the distance, cold glitter of the water. (*Pause.*) But not those lights, all those lights. And roads, where there never were roads before. (*Pause.*) Still the old pit, though. Grass and weeds as high as your head, rippling like waves when the wind howls across the hills. I just knew it would be the same. People change but . . . (*laughs.*) Ellen. Ellen.

Sound of footsteps coming upstairs. There is a knock on her bedroom door.

Barbara (*from corridor*) Rosie. I'm leaving you the electric fire outside the door in case you're feeling the chill.

Rosie Thanks very much, Barbara.

Barbara Don't mention it.

Footsteps recede downstairs. **Rosie** *closes curtains, switches on light again, brings in electric fire and plugs it in. She opens suitcase. There are very few clothes inside. Instead there is a portable electronic typewriter, several card index boxes, a bible, and a number of paperback books. She puts the typewriter on the desk, arranges the paperbacks next to it. The clothes and the index boxes she locks inside the wardrobe, and carefully puts the key inside the pocket of her jacket. She moves table till she is satisfied with its new position, sits down in front of typewriter, facing audience.*

Rosie This is it.

Lights go down.

Scene Two

Same room, one week later. Evening drawing in.

Rosie *is typing. From downstairs can hear doorbell ring, sound of front door being opened, muffled sound of womens' voices. Someone rushes upstairs. Tap on* **Rosie***'s door.* **Rosie** *quickly takes paper out of typewriter.*

Rosie   Yes?

Ellen's voice   Friday. March twenty first. Nineteen eighty six. Door lady. Vis-it.

Rosie   Oh. A visitor.

Sound of two people coming upstairs. Knock on **Rosie***'s door.*

Barbara's voice   Rosie. You have a visitor. A young lady. Is it alright to show her in?

Rosie   (*to herself*) Maddy.

Rosie *gets up and opens door.*

Rosie   Yes, of course. Come in.

Enter **Barbara** *and* **Madeleine**. **Ellen** *hangs around in the doorway.*

Rosie   Hello Maddy. Barbara. This is Madeleine. One of my students.

Madeleine   How do you do.

Barbara   Pleased to meet you.

Rosie   Madeleine. This is Barbara, who has been so kind in letting out this room to me. I feel so much at home here, I might have lived here for years. And Ellen. We mustn't forget Ellen. A very important young lady.

Madeleine   Important?

Rosie   Maddy. This is Ellen.

Barbara   (*flattered*) Oh well. It's nice to have a bit of company. Not that Ellen's not company . . . but, you know . . . (*To* **Madeleine**.) I've been telling Rosie. She should get out a bit. It's not good to be cooped up all day between four walls. (*To* **Rosie**.) I don't think I've seen you go out once since you came here.

Madeleine   Not once?

Rosie I have so much work to do at the moment. Unfortunately. But the view from the window makes up for it. Have you seen the view, Maddy?

Rosie *walks* **Madeleine** *to the window.* **Ellen** *follows.*

Ellen (*to* **Madeleine**) Fave-rite. Win-dow.

Madeleine *doesn't respond.*

Rosie Your favourite window?

Madeleine I beg your pardon?

Rosie Ellen wants to know your favourite window.

Ellen Fave-rite.

Madeleine I really don't know.

Rosie Think.

Madeleine (*laughs, confused*) Um . . . oh . . .

Ellen Colour.

Rosie Come on, Maddy. Think of all the houses you've lived in – all the places you've visited.

Madeleine Well. (*Pause.*) The window frame is brown. The window itself is five hundred years old, like the house. The pane is mullioned.

Ellen Mul-yund.

Madeleine That means it is divided up into lots of little panes.

Barbara Ooh. That sounds lovely.

Ellen See. Mul-yund.

Madeleine I . . . (*She doesn't understand* **Ellen**.)

Rosie What can you see from the window.

Madeleine What can I see? (*Pause.*) Meadows. Water meadows. And cows grazing in the distance. And not too far away a tiny chapel, whose bell chimes softly on Sundays.

Barbara I can just imagine it. So peaceful. That sounds like a nice window, Ellen.

Ellen (*to* **Rosie**) Favourite. (*Chuckles.*) Mr Potheque, blue gate, run run.

Barbara Don't be silly, Ellen. How can that be Rosie's favourite window? She doesn't know it at all. That's your auntie Bellas' window from when you were a little girl. (*To* **Rosie**.) Unless she's given that window to you.

Sometimes she does. (*To* **Ellen**.) But Rosie doesn't know your auntie Bella. (*To* **Rosie**.) I can't follow the connection, though.

Pause.

Come on, then, Ellen. Time we got on with some tidying up downstairs.

Ellen (*to* **Madeleine**) Date.

Madeleine *looks helplessly at* **Rosie**.

Barbara Oh Ellen . . . maybe later.

Ellen Date.

Rosie Tell Ellen when you were born.

Madeleine Um . . .

Rosie Look. Just give her the date, the month and the year, and she'll tell you which day of the week it was.

Madeleine Sixteenth of July 1958.

Ellen Wednesday.

Barbara Did she get it right?

Madeleine Yes. That's amazing. How did she do it?

Barbara No-one can work out. (*Pause.*) She got it wrong with Rosie, though. I'm not sure why. (*Pause.*) It wasn't a leap year, was it? . . . Though that doesn't normally make any difference. (*Pause.*) Alright then, my girl, no more games, we've got work to do. (*To* **Madeleine**.) Very pleased to meet you. Feel free to call by any time.

Exit **Barbara** *and* **Ellen**.

Silence.

Rosie *and* **Madeleine** *begin to speak at the same time.*

Rosie Wednesday's child is full of woe.

Madeleine Very cosy indeed.

Pause.

Rosie As I was saying – Wednesday's child is full of woe.

Madeleine It's not bloody surprising, is it? You've got to be out of your head.

Rosie Is that so?

Madeleine You were supposed to meet me at the airport.

Rosie So I caught a train to Newcastle instead.

Madeleine Are you crazy?

Rosie Not at all. I just had a change of mind since our last conversation.

Madeleine Do you know what I've been through in the last week? Worrying. Worrying about what might have happened.

Rosie You should have known that I would have everything under control.

Madeleine What about me? I went through hell.

Rosie I'm sorry. (*Pause.*) But obviously if I'd told you first that I wasn't coming with you, then it would have made things more difficult.

Madeleine Who for? For you?

Rosie Don't be selfish, Maddy. It's just that I knew if I presented it as a fait accompli, then it would be less of a problem overall. You see. I'm okay. Nothing untoward has happened to me.

Madeleine But you haven't been out.

Silence.

Rosie By the way, I appreciated the description of the window.

Madeleine It's just the way I described it to you. Many times. Peaceful. Safe.

Rosie And the tiny chapel on Sunday.

Silence.

Madeleine I spent a lot of time staring out of that window wondering what had happened to you.

Rosie You should have reported me missing to the police.

Madeleine Ha, ha.

Pause.

Rosie Well, anyway. Here I am.

Madeleine Why?

Rosie Why? (*Pause.*) Because this is where it all happened.

Madeleine Exactly.

Rosie So. It brings it all back. Fresh. I couldn't write about it anywhere else.

Madeleine That's not what you told me.

Rosie I didn't know till they let me out. Then it all became much clearer.

Madeleine We were getting really worried.

Rosie We?

Madeleine Were getting worried.

Rosie You mean your father was getting worried about his investment.

Madeleine That's not fair. To give him his due . . .

Rosie   (*laughs*) That'll be a first for you.

Madeleine   . . . He has put himself on the line. For both of us.

Rosie   And for his bank balance, of course.

Madeleine   What have I done wrong? Why all the digs?

Rosie   I knew you wouldn't understand. I showed you this view from my window here and your eyes just slipped over it without registering anything.

Madeleine   I was too busy looking at you.

Rosie   You know what I look like. But this, this is important. This is what kept me going.

Silence

Madeleine   I'm sorry. But not hearing from you . . . One fears the worst . . .

Rosie   Maddy!

Madeleine   Okay, okay. How is it coming on?

Rosie   Slowly. I keep remembering . . . and then, (*Starts to laugh.*) a chance in a million . . .

Madeleine   What? Why are you laughing?

Rosie   I'll tell you, *show* you later.

Pause.

Rosie   I want to visit her grave.

Madeleine   Oh.

Rosie   But you'll have to locate it for me first. I don't want to have to wander around the cemetery. I want just to be able to go straight there, put some flowers beside her headstone. I've had to wait twenty years to do this. I want to be able to find her straightaway.

Madeleine   I don't know . . .

Rosie   You've got to. (*Pause.*) Unless you want me to make myself conspicuous, scanning the tombstones for her name . . . asking people . . . they might wonder why . . .

Madeleine   No of course I don't want you to . . . (*In a rush.*) But I also don't want you to end up like her.

Rosie   Mrs Craddock's dead now.

Madeleine   Mrs Craddock is, yes. But what about the other parents?

Rosie   (*grudgingly*) Yes . . .

Madeleine   So they could do the same to you.

Rosie   I'm not an easy target like Lesley was. That crack . . . sounded like a car backfiring . . . I remember . . . her . . . sinking . . . almost gracefully . . . in the dock . . . as if . . . as if she needed suddenly to sit down . . . (*Pause.*) And that woman. Standing tall in the public gallery . . . staring . . . the gun still smoking in her hands . . . (*Pause.*) The second day of the trial . . . they didn't want to hear our side of it . . .

Madeleine   Yes, I know.

Pause.

Rosie   And now? I'm a new woman. A good two stone lighter – *despite* that awful stodgy food – or maybe because of it. Hair greying. Quite distinguished looking, don't you think? And the accent. Ironed out. Not completely, but enough, more than enough.

Madeleine   You're so confident, Peggy . . .

Rosie   Don't! Not even in private. It's Rosie now.

Madeleine   I'm sorry. Rosie. But you are. You're so absolutely confident in yourself. Too confident.

Rosie   You've got to be. But not your kind of confident.

Madeleine   What do you mean? My kind of confident?

Rosie   It's not something that has been bought . . .

Madeleine   Bought!

Rosie   Come on, Maddy. You know what I mean.

Madeleine   How can you say that? Bought? Did I choose to have money flung at me?

Rosie   No you didn't.

Madeleine   Did I ask for nannies . . . private schools . . . ponies . . .

Rosie   I don't suppose you did.

Madeleine   All the stupid coinage of privilege . . .

Rosie   You're getting upset, Maddy. Here. Come here.

Madeleine   No. It's alright for you. You haven't had to live with everyone's assumptions that only daddy's cheque book stands between you and utter uselessness. . . .

Rosie   I've never made that assumption.

Madeleine   No. You haven't. Because you took the time to get to know me.

Rosie   That's right. I did. And I respect the way you've used your situation to *your* advantage . . . used your contacts . . . funds . . . made things a little more difficult for your father and people like him to live the way they do . . .

Madeleine   Yes, well – it's a pity a few more people can't see things the way you do.

Rosie   Oh, Maddy – you're too sensitive about all this. All I meant was that our confidence was born of nothing except . . . ignorance, and yet not ignorance . . . I'm not putting this very well. (*Pause.*) What Lesley and I had was something which we felt would get us out of here, out of the paint factory to something else . . . that's what we always wanted . . . something else.

Madeleine   Lesley, Lesley, Lesley . . .

Rosie   She was my one and only. You know that.

Madeleine   Doesn't this count for anything?

Madeleine *kisses* **Rosie** *passionately.*
There is a knock at the door.

Madeleine   (*whispering*) Tell them to go away.

Ellen's voice   Teeea. Ellen's teeea.

Rosie *rearranges her clothing, moves over to window.*

Rosie   Thank you very much, Ellen. Come in.

Madeleine   Cheers, Rosie.

Enter **Ellen**, *carrying tray with tea and biscuits.*

Rosie   Just put it on the table, Ellen. Thank you. (*To* **Madeleine**.) Would you like a ginger snap.

Madeleine   Yes. Why not? Just what I want.

Ellen *seems a bit uneasy at the atmosphere. She takes a biscuit.*

Rosie   (*to* **Madeleine**) Tea?

Madeleine   (*sarcastic*) Mmmm. Yes please.

Rosie   The answer to your question is, yes, it counts. But not in the same way. What we had was closer to . . . innocence.

Madeleine   Innocence.

Silence.

Rosie   Yes. Me and Lesley.

Ellen *drops biscuit, looks uncomfortable. She wraps her arms around her body, rocks herself gently.*

Ellen Mr. Po . . . th . . .

Rosie (*to* **Ellen**) She's alright. She's okay.

Ellen Special window. Col . . . col . . . special colours. Sing Ellen, sing. (*Unsure.*) Never back. Promised. Ellen promised.

Rosie *puts her arms around* **Ellen**, *who seems to recoil, there is a mixture of fear and fascination in her eyes.*

Rosie Shush. Don't worry, pet. I'll make it up to you, pet. You know that, don't you?

Ellen *moves away.*

Ellen Tea time. Blue Peter. Dogs, nice dogs. Favourite programme. Play-y-y-school. Through the round window.

Exit **Ellen**.

Madeleine What the hell was all that about?

Rosie Nothing.

Madeleine How do you understand her? I can't comprehend anything she says. It's like another language.

Rosie You speak French?

Madeleine You know I do. Otherwise we'd have problems when we start travelling.

Rosie A little Spanish, also?

Madeleine Yes . . .

Rosie Reasonable German from your former, how shall I put it, political connections?

Madeleine (*flattered*) Don't tell me you're jealous over what I told you about Dieter. That was a long time ago.

Rosie Not at all. What I'm getting at, is that Ellen does speak another language. And you wouldn't think twice about learning it if it was, say, Italian or, whatever.

Madeleine Mmm.

Rosie And this is a unique language. It's all her own. That's something to impress your friends with; 'I speak fluent Ellen.'

Madeleine   This is all quite immaterial. I don't *care* . . . Look – this isn't how I thought it would be . . .

Rosie   How did you think it would be?

Madeleine   I thought it would be simply a question of getting you away, without anyone noticing, and having you write in peace and tranquility and safety, and me being able to help you.

Rosie   So did I.

Madeleine   The car's just outside.

Rosie   Uh huh.

Madeleine   I'll help you pack your things.

She gets up, as if to begin packing.

Rosie   No.

Madeleine   You've got to. It's dangerous here.

Rosie   I've got things to do.

Madeleine   Okay. I'll find the grave now. I'll even buy the flowers. Then that's everything done.

Rosie   Oh, that's only the beginning.

Madeleine   What?

Rosie   Calm down. Sit down.

Rosie *pulls* **Madeleine** *down to sit on the bed.*

Rosie   Wait a moment.

Rosie *gets up and switches the light off, so the only light in the room is that of the anglepoise lamp on the table, and the street lamp shining through the open window.* **Rosie** *stands in profile to the window.*

Rosie   Close your eyes. You don't have the excuse of looking at me, so you can see what I want to show you.

Madeleine   I don't want to . . .

Rosie   Just close your eyes.

Silence.

Rosie   A tiny window, with a cobweb in the corner. I never cleaned the cobweb away because I loved watching that spider. Spinning. Spinning a little world of its own. Outside, through the bars, brown brick walls, and other tiny windows. Tiny faces, sometimes faraway voices, not always tiny, shouting, sometimes crying.

Madeleine I know those windows . . .

Rosie Yes. You did. But not for twenty years. How long was it? Six months? Less remission.

Madeleine I wasn't trying to compare . . .

Rosie No. I know you weren't. (*Pause.*) So it's working. You can see. (*Pause.*) Okay. Another. (*Pause.*) Nice white net curtains. I can see down the hill. On the horizon I can see three flashing orange lights. They each flash at different frequencies. They're the lighthouses on the coast. Seven or eight miles away. At night the lights of the chemical works on the riverside reflect off the water. When the mists draw in, you can hear the sound of the ships' foghorns. Terrifying, like prehistoric monsters coming ashore. Right across the road there's an old man who wrestles with his rickety old blue painted gate to fight imaginary Germans in the front street. And on the other side of the houses are fields, seems like miles of them, pitted and scarred with old mine workings, where you have to be careful you don't fall in, or you'll never be heard of again.

Madeleine Is that this window?

Rosie No. It doesn't exist any more. I drove past where it used to be in the taxi. The driver had never even heard of the street. It's a block of flats now. (*Pause.*) But it's almost the same view. I was lucky.

Pause.

Rosie You keep a picture in your head . . . The other women inside worried about the old man – would he have a new woman? Would she be younger? Prettier? Would he still be there, even? Not me. People . . . It's the lights across the river I saw when I closed my eyes at night. The touch of dying autumn grass, rippled by the wind, against my bare legs, as I lay naked on my bunk in the dark. The cries of children playing in the old colliery and down by the river's edge, entering my dreams. That's what I had fallen in love with. Not the people. Not the people.

Madeleine Mmmm. (*Pause.*) Are you going to put that in the book?

Rosie Oh yes. It will all be different when it's published. I should think that a lot of people will be shamed by it. I've never had the opportunity to put our side of it. People only know what they've read in the papers. Only bad things.

Madeleine Rosie.

Rosie Yes.

Madeleine I love you.

Rosie I know you do.

Silence.

Rosie *leaves window, and goes over to* **Madeleine**. *She pulls her to the floor.*
Madeleine *responds sexually, but* **Rosie** *doesn't have sex in mind.*

Rosie   Imagine. Imagine you work in a factory with the smell of paint so
strong that you can smell it in your dreams. Now you're sitting here. It's
Sunday afternoon. The sun is high above you. You lean back. Feel the sun on
your face. And you can smell the grass, and the damp earth, because it's been
raining overnight. It's another world. For a while it seems like it's all for you,
just for you.

Madeleine   Mmmm.

Rosie *puts her arms around* **Madeleine**, *kisses her.*

Rosie   Perfect, isn't it?

Madeleine   Yes.

Rosie   But you've got to go back. To all that. Haven't you?

Madeleine   I suppose so.

Rosie   No *I suppose so*. You have to go back.

Pause.

Rosie   And you look around you at the children playing.

Madeleine   (*uneasy*) Yes.

Rosie   You look around, and there's a little girl, it's you, and another little
girl, it's you, and another, and another . . . All you. What's the answer for
them?

Madeleine   And you'd be playing games with your friends and the boys
would come along. They always have to spoil things, don't they?

Rosie   Do they?

Madeleine   Yes. It's alright when you're at the age when you're stronger
than them, but that doesn't last long. That's the golden age in any womans'
life. Don't you think? They start off young, interrupting games, chasing you
round the grounds . . .

Rosie   (*laughs*) The *grounds*?

Madeleine   (*misses a beat*) The *play*grounds. Then as they get older . . .

Rosie   Yes?

Madeleine   You know – I told you about the squat, didn't I? And the
revolutionary newspaper. It was all my money, and we were supposed to be
working collectively, but it was the men like Dieter who took over . . .

Rosie   Sssh. (*She isn't listening.*)

The door is opening gently. **Ellen** *slides in.*

Rosie   (*whispering*) Ellen. I knew you would come. Sit down next to me and Lesley.

Madeleine   Lesley?

Rosie   (*to* **Madeleine**) Ssh. (*To* **Ellen**.) Grassy green.

Ellen   Grassy green, river . . . boat window?

Rosie   Yes. Boat window. Over there. (*Points to imaginary ship*.)

Ellen   Newcastle Big Ear.

Rosie   Yes. The Newcastle Brigadier. They were building it, remember. And the windows. They had special names.

Ellen   Parcels.

Rosie   Portholes.

Ellen   Peggy. Ellen . . .

Rosie   Yes.

Ellen   What date?

Rosie   Second of June 1966.

Ellen   Johnny. Johnny Crad-d-d . . .

Madeleine *leaps up.*

Madeleine   What . . . ?

Knock on the door.

Barbara's voice   It's only me. Ellen isn't bothering you, is she?

Rosie   (*getting up and switching on light*) Not at all, Barbara. Come in and join us.

Enter **Barbara**.
Ellen *scrambles to her feet, looks with confusion at* **Madeleine**, *takes up defensive position near window.*

Barbara   Can I clear away these tea things for you, then?

Madeleine *is also unsure. She observes* **Ellen**. *She seems indecisive about whether to go or to stay.*

Madeleine   I'll be on my way now. I'll look up that old friend of yours for you. Maybe when you've seen how she is, you'll change your mind.

Barbara   Oh. Bye, pet.

Madeleine *hurries out.*

Rosie   She's in a hurry.

Barbara   Do you know someone from round here, then?

Rosie   Some way away. I'm not even sure where she lives.

Barbara *picks up the cups.*

Barbara   She's a very well spoken young lady.

Rosie   Yes. She is, isn't she?

Barbara   Lovely. Like the television.

Rosie   You have a lovely voice, Barbara.

Barbara   No-o-o. Don't be daft.

Rosie   No. You have. Hasn't anyone ever told you before. Soft. Gentle. Ellen gets the music in her voice from you.

Barbara   (*flattered*) Well I don't know about that . . . (*Pause.*) Well. Better get on with me dolls, then.

Ellen   Dolls. Bizzy bee dolls.

Ellen *smirks and claps her hands.*

Barbara   Oh Ellen. You know they're not called busy bees. (*To* **Rosie**.) I'm doing sentries at the moment. You know – like the one's who stand guard outside Buckingham Palace, with their big busbies on their heads.

Ellen   Bizzy bees. (*She sniggers.*)

Barbara   The man's coming to collect them tomorrow night, and I've still got a fair few to do. It's piecework, you see. Not much in the way of pay, but it all helps with me pension.

Rosie   Bring them up here. I'll give you a hand if you like.

Barbara   (*doubtful*) Are you sure? It's a bit boring, just sticking belts and buckles and whatnot onto dolls with bits of glue. And a bit messy.

Rosie   Of course not. We'll hardly notice once we're having a bit of a chat.

Barbara   Oh. Well. If you don't mind. (*Pause.*) I've got a Battenberg cake in the cupboard. It's only shop bought, mind you, but it'll go down nice with some fresh tea. I won't be a minute.

Exit **Barbara**. **Rosie** *looks at* **Ellen**, *who turns her head away. Suddenly* **Ellen** *leaves the room.* **Rosie** *looks after her, thoughtfully. She takes all of the papers from her desk and locks them in the wardrobe.* **Ellen** *returns. She is carrying a large box full of plastic dolls.* **Rosie** *takes one out. She moves across to the window and examines it minutely.*

Rosie   (*whispering*) Hey. Ellen. They haven't got any you-know-whats.

Ellen *pretends not to hear, but she obviously finds this very funny. She is not very good at concealing her feelings.*

Rosie   (*still whispering*) Ellen. Are they all like that?

Ellen *sniggers to herself. She glances, without fear, at* **Rosie**. *Enter* **Barbara**, *carrying tray.*

Barbara Thanks Ellen.

Ellen *takes dolls out of box. She arranges them in three equal piles. Between them she puts glue, dolls clothing, etc.*

Rosie You'll have to show me what to do, Barbara.

Barbara It's very simple. They've all got a little red jacket and pair of trousers. The trousers come in two bits – one for each leg. You glue them on, then you have to glue on their little belts and swords and then their busbies.

Ellen Bizzy bees.

Barbara Oh shut up, Ellen. They've already got their boots and gloves painted on them, so that's one good thing.

Rosie It must be difficult, getting the glue in just the right places.

Barbara Oh don't worry about that. A bit of glue showing round the edges doesn't really matter. Mr Philips – that's the man that picks them up – he says, it's only for southerners and foreigners. That's who buys them. (*Pause.*) D'you know what? I'd love to go down to London and just look in some of them shop windows, and be able to say, I made them. Well – I *dressed* them, would be more like. Just think how many countries my little dolls could be in by now. I've been doing them years. They could be all over the world. Couldn't they?

Rosie Amazing.

Barbara Yes. That's what it is. Amazing.

The three of them sit on the floor and start working on the dolls.
Barbara *hands round tea and cake.* **Ellen** *gives her tea back.*

Barbara Oh! She's staying! Do you have many students come to see you?

Rosie No. Not many.

Barbara It's quite nice to have visitors. Don't you think?

Rosie Sometimes. But not always.

Barbara I like having visitors. I don't think I'm ever too out of sorts that having someone call round doesn't give me a lift. Don't you find that? Just talking to someone. It can have that good an effect.

Rosie Sometimes. But I like to think that I'm the most capable person there is at helping myself. After all, I know myself better than anyone else.

Barbara   I don't know – sometimes you can be the last person to understand yourself properly. Set yourself up good and proper, when everyone else can see what you've got coming to you a long, long time before you can.

Rosie   Is that what you've found?

Barbara   Oh yes. I've found that in the past.

Pause.

Rosie   I suppose that depends on the individual concerned.

Barbara   You haven't found that yourself?

Rosie   No. There's a calm centre inside of me all the time, looking around and ahead, seeing all possible outcomes, evaluating, never taken by surprise. (*Pause*) Do you think that's strange?

Barbara   I just suppose it's different to me. Things just seem to *happen* . . .

Rosie   (*holding out doll*) Is that right, Barbara?

Barbara   Let's have a closer look. I should really be wearing me reading glasses for close-up work like this.

Ellen   Glasses.

Barbara   Yes. That's dandy. Are you sure you don't mind?

Rosie   Of course not. It's quite relaxing, isn't it?

Ellen   Glasses. Downstairs. Blu-u-u-e, br-r-r-ring.

Barbara   So that's where I left them.

Rosie   I suppose you put them down on the telephone table when the doorbell rang.

Barbara   Oh . . . You've really begun to understand Ellen. People have known her for years and still not been able to . . .

Ellen   Glasses.

Ellen *stands up.*

Barbara   Okay. If you don't mind, pet.

Exit **Ellen**.

I don't really want them. It's for her really. She just wants to try them on while I'm not there. She likes to look at windows through them. Makes them different. It's not always a good idea, though. Sometimes she gets frightened.

She's got such a routine, you see, everything fits into such a pattern. Sometimes it disturbs her.

Rosie The answer is to prepare for every eventuality.

Barbara Pardon?

Rosie The answer is to prepare for every eventuality. Then the challenge and the excitement is in responding to what actually does happen. Controlling it.

Barbara Mmm. (*She is out of her depth.*) How long have you been a teacher, then?

Rosie Years. Coming on for twenty years.

Barbara Always abroad?

Rosie Yes.

Barbara Which countries have you lived in?

Rosie Oh . . . France, Germany, Switzerland . . . America.

Barbara Ooh. Isn't that just lovely. I've never been abroad. Not once. I've been up to Scotland a couple of times. You know – the Edinburgh tattoo. And Great Yarmouth once. I had an auntie lived down there, just after the war. Were you in . . . Paris?

Rosie Yes. Very beautiful.

Barbara Did you ever visit the Eiffel Tower? They say it's just like Blackpool Tower except without the ballroom. I've been there for the illuminations. Ellen loved it. I don't know how many times I had to walk that Golden Mile. Me feet felt like puddings afterwards. And still she wanted to carry on.

Rosie Oh yes. And the Champs Elysées. Very beautiful.

Barbara Oh – you speak the language?

Rosie Are you a linguist yourself?

Barbara A linguist? Oh . . . I see . . . No. There's some would say that I have difficulty gettin' by in English, let alone French.

Rosie Now, now, Barbara. You're a very articulate woman. Many of my students don't express themselves as well as you.

Barbara Eeeh. Don't be daft. (*Pause.*) It must be grand to have a degree. If I had a degree I think I would have it framed and on me wall, just to show that I'm not stupid, that I've got a few brains in me head.

Rosie You don't need to do that, Barbara. Anyone can see how intelligent you are.

Barbara (*pause*) You don't need to say these things to me, you know. I know I'm not clever, I know I haven't got the knack of saying things just right . . .

Rosie (*interrupting*) Of course I don't tell you what I think of you just for the sake of it. You should have every confidence in your own abilities. Surely other people – your husband, for example – have told you exactly the same things . . .

Barbara (*quickly*) I've worked and worked all my life, and have so little to show for it . . . If I'd been clever . . . now there you have it . . . if I'd been clever . . .

She is distracted by entrance of **Ellen.**

Ellen   Geddaway. Geddaway window.

Barbara   What?

Ellen   (*agitated*) Geddaway window.

Barbara   It must be that man again. Where was he, Ellen?

Ellen   Back gar-din.

Barbara   What was he doing?

Ellen   Eyes man. Ooking.

Barbara   What was he looking at?

Ellen   Ellen Goodison.

Barbara   Is he still there?

Ellen   Gone. Geddawayed. (**Ellen** *mimes how she gestured him away.*) Geddaway Ellen Goodison's window.

Barbara   I think I should call the police.

Ellen *talks to herself in background, as* **Rosie** *and* **Barbara** *speak.*

Ellen   Polis. (*She mimics sound of police siren.*) Ello, ello, ello. (*Sniggers.*) Dikon of Dox Green. (*She hums theme tune.*)

Rosie   No. Don't. (*Hesitates.*) If I told you . . . that somehow this might be connected with me . . .

Barbara   Oh. What . . . ?

Rosie   I think that someone may be looking for me.

Barbara   But who . . . ?

Rosie   It's . . . personal . . . connected with . . . my time . . . abroad.

Barbara   (*confused*) I see . . .

Rosie   Nothing to worry about. Simply someone trying to verify where I am.

Barbara   Don't you want them to know.

Rosie   No. Not really. Not at the moment anyway.

Barbara   Personal . . . Is it . . . a man? If I'm being too forward . . . ?

Rosie Of course not. I may be renting this room from you, but above all I see you as a friend.

Barbara (*extremely flattered*) That's very nice of you.

Rosie It is a man, yes. But not as simple as . . .

Barbara I knew it. (*Pause.*) I . . . (*She hesitates.*) . . . When it comes to men, I . . . You can't trust them, that's my opinion . . . I lost my faith . . .

Silence.

(*Abruptly.*) Go and put on the kettle please, Ellen.

Ellen Bizzy Bees.

Ellen *continues to clothe dolls.*

Barbara (*sternly*) Tea, Ellen. You can do that when you come back.

Ellen *hesitates, then exits with dirty tea cups.*

Barbara They don't know what causes it, you know.

Rosie (*confused*) Sorry?

Barbara Oh sorry, pet. I'm jumping ahead of meself. Autism. They don't know what causes it.

Rosie Yes. I remember you telling me.

Pause.

Barbara For years I thought it was my fault.

Rosie That's silly. Why blame yourself?

Barbara Because . . .

Silence.

There's never been a Mr Goodison, you see. Just a man I thought I . . . (*Pause.*) You see, because of me dad being dead, and no man about the house, we had to get a man in to do little repairs and what not. And with me mam being so poorly all the time, and confined to the house, and noticing when things didn't work properly, like the tap dripping all the time and getting on her nerves . . . Well, we had to get someone in. We got his name out the newspaper, a Mr Stephens. It wasn't even as if he was very handsome. I noticed the veins on his arms stood out when he was busy fixing underneath the sink, and I was that fascinated, I got all embarrassed when I realized he'd noticed me looking. I hadn't had much time for men, since Colin took up with Pam and emigrated. Me mam took a lot of looking after. He came a few times. He never said that much. I suppose he was about forty. He mentioned his wife and the kids once or twice, in passing. I suppose he thought that would square us up, me knowing, understanding the score. But I was a thirty one year old girl. One day he said, 'Call me David', in a voice so soft, like an angel's breath, that I knew it was inevitable what would happen. It just took the once. Next time he came, I told him I was expectin', and, I can tell you, he was no angel about it. Said it was up to me what happened, nothing to do with him. *Nothing to do with him.* Can you imagine it? I wanted to die when it started showin'. I was the talk of the neighbourhood. But I never told anyone who the father was. I might have been stupid, I might have been naive, but I never lost me pride. You're the only one now, apart from me, and him – if he's still alive – that knows.

Rosie   Thank you for telling me, Barbara. I'm honoured.

Barbara   That's why, when you first came, last week, and you asked me if I believed in God, I couldn't . . . you see. I felt God must have punished me for something I did, and I don't know what – doubly punished me.

Rosie   That's the wrong way to look at it. There is always a purpose. It's all part of a plan. Sometimes you can't see the pattern, but it's there. And God has planned it that way.

Enter **Ellen**.

Ellen   Kettle on.

Barbara   Thank you, Ellen. (*To* **Rosie**.) You won't . . .

Rosie   Thank you for telling me.

Rosie *holds her finger against her lips. They all continue with dolls.*

Barbara   What does . . . What do you get when you pass a degree? Is it a . . . certificate? Or like a . . . medallion or . . . something?

Rosie   It's a certificate. With your name and your subject and your pass mark.

Barbara   Have you . . . got yours here?

Rosie   (*hesitates*) Yes.

Barbara   Could I . . . You see I've never . . . won anything like that . . . well, I've called house at the bingo a couple of times, but I've never actually . . . *passed* anything . . .

Rosie   You'd like to look at it?

Barbara   Em, yes. If you didn't mind.

Rosie   We-e-ll. Yes. But. You see I'll need to search it out. I'll look for it. Maybe tonight. (*Pause.*) I'd like to show it to you. I was thinking of having it (*Laughs.*) framed. (*Quickly.*) Not to prove anything to anyone else, you know.

Just for myself. It wasn't easy. I had to fight for . . . (*Smiles.*) It's nothing, really. Just a piece of paper. With my name on it.

Barbara   It's what it means, isn't it?

Rosie   Yes. You're right. It is.

Silence. They continue with dolls.
Night sounds drift in through window.
Ellen *grows listless. She checks her wristwatch.*

Ellen   Nine o'clock. Clean Ellen's windows.

She takes out a cloth from her pocket and goes across to window.

Ellen   Clean. Hmm. Hmm.

She cleans panes by breathing on window first. Sound of girls skipping from outside.

Barbara   I wonder sometimes, you know. Nine o'clock and there's bairns still playing outside. I know they're just playing round the houses, but . . . you read about it in the papers. (*Pause.*) Have they got their skippy rope round the lamp post, Ellen?

Ellen *says nothing. She is resting her head against the window, engrossed in the game.*
Rosie *moves to window.*

Rosie   Isn't it strange? Just watching them from the window over the past week . . . They all seem so more grown-up than we were at that age. (*Pause.*) And yet . . . they're still playing the same games I played, thirty years ago. (*Pause.*) Different song, though. (*Pause.*) What is it, Ellen? What are they singing?

Ellen *looks uncomfortable, turns her back on* **Rosie***, begins cleaning again.*

Barbara   Ellen! Manners! I'm sorry, Rosie, there's something . . .

Skipping sounds from outside.

Rosie   Don't you know it, then, Ellen?

Barbara   Yes she does. She does. But we . . .

Rosie   Oh. I'm sorry. I don't want to . . . If there's some problem . . . It was just curiosity.

She returns to **Barbara***.* **Ellen** *jumps on spot, as if skipping. She recites rhyme, replacing all reference to Peggy Bow, with a humming sound.*

Ellen   Hmmm, hmmm, hmmm. Hmmm, hmmm, hmmm,
Watch the boys from her window,

Catch her eye, watch her smile,
She'll take you out for a little while.

Barbara *looks very uncomfortable.*

Barbara   That's alright now, Ellen.

Ellen   Past the pit, down to the Tyne . . .

Barbara   Come and finish the dolls, pet.

Ellen   Hmmm, hmmm, doesn't need much time . . .

Barbara   That's enough, Ellen.

Barbara *goes across to close window. It slams on the last word of the rhyme.*

Ellen   Tell her you'll go home instead,
'Cos if you don't this time you're DEAD.

Silence. **Ellen** *uncertain. Looks from* **Rosie** *to mother.*

Barbara   Ellen . . .

Ellen *becomes withdrawn.*

Barbara   (*helpless*) Ellen . . . I . . .

Barbara *tries to touch* **Ellen**, *who cringes.* **Barbara** *withdraws her hand. Silence.*

Rosie   Barbara. Is everything alright? I seem to have unintentionally . . .

Barbara   (*distant*) No. No. Not your . . . (*Pause.*) It's something else. (*Pause.*) You would think that with all the lamp posts in the street, they could choose another one for their games. Why ours? Why outside *my* house? (*Pause.*) But then, I hear that song . . . *have heard* that song so many times over the years. Sometimes just the rhythm of it, even, so far away the words are lost or garbled, but I *know* what they're singing. It's just a nursery rhyme to them, like ring a ring o' rosies. Even Ellen . . . *she* sings along, sits on the kerb and watches the rope twitch and turn as they jump in and then jump out again. (*Pause.*) No-one wants to be left still skipping when the song ends . . .

Silence.

Barbara   (*in normal manner*) I'm not the only one round here that feels that way.

Rosie   I don't understand.

Barbara   (*lowers voice so* **Ellen** *can't hear*) Did you never hear of Peggy Bow and Lesley Underhill?

Rosie   No. (*Pause.*) Should I?

Barbara   1968?

Ellen   1968? What date?

Barbara   (*worried*) No date, Ellen.

Silence as they work on dolls. **Ellen** *remains frozen in her withdrawn position.*

Barbara Howway Ellen. Finish them off.

Ellen Ellen's other window.

Exit **Ellen** *abruptly.*

Rosie 1968?

Barbara It was in all the papers.

Rosie I was abroad in 1968.

Barbara Yes. Of course . . .

Silence.

Barbara I'm surprised you never heard. Even after all these years, they're still famous. Have you never seen that picture of them . . . everyone knows it . . . the police taking them into the van outside the Old Bailey. Both of them. Smiling. And Peggy with her hand raised, as if she's waving. (*Pause.*) They were, what, eighteen, nineteen years old, and they murdered five little boys.

Rosie Oh. (*Pause.*) All at once?

Barbara No. One by one. Over a couple of years.

Rosie And they came from round here?

Barbara Yes. They've pulled the street down now. It needed pulling down anyway, but I reckon the council sorted it ten years sooner than they would've normally. There was never any peace for anyone. There was even sightseeing tours, people in trip buses. It wasn't right.

Rosie What happened to them?

Barbara Peggy was put away for life. So would Lesley have been, if it wasn't for one of the mothers. Shot her dead in the courtroom. Killed herself later, poor soul.

Rosie I sce. (*Pause.*) How did they find out . . . they were the murderers?

Barbara (*hesitates*) A boy got away. He couldn't describe them, but (*hesitates*) he remembered someone they were with.

Rosie Someone they were with?

Barbara *is saved from answering by sound of* **Ellen** *singing downstairs, the same hymn she sang at beginning of play. The two women listen in rapt silence. Doorbell rings.* **Ellen** *continues to sing.* **Rosie** *goes across to window.*

Rosie   That's Madeleine's car. (*Pause.*) Would you mind if she stayed overnight? Otherwise she has a very long drive home.

Barbara   Oh. (*Pause.*) I can make up the settee for her.

Rosie   Don't worry about that, Barbara. We can share my bed.

Barbara   Are you sure?

Rosie   Yes – it'll save on sheets.

Doorbell rings again. **Ellen** *continues to sing.*

Barbara   I'd better get the door.

Exit **Barbara**. **Rosie** *lies back on bed. Touches sheets in caressing gesture. Her door opens.* **Madeleine** *stands in doorway.*

Rosie   Hello Madeleine.

Enter **Madeleine** *and* **Barbara**. **Ellen** *watches them from doorway.*

Barbara   Tea. Can I get you some tea, Madeleine? The kettle's just boiled.

Madeleine   (*to* **Rosie**) Tea?

Rosie   I don't think I could manage any more tea.

Madeleine   (*to* **Rosie**) I'm not thirsty. (*To* **Barbara**.) Thank you very much, um . . .

Barbara   Barbara.

Madeleine   Sorry. Barbara. It's very kind of you to offer.

Silence.

Barbara   If you're sure you don't mind sharing.

Rosie   Well, we're all girls together, aren't we?

Madeleine   Sharing?

Rosie   The bed. It'll be much handier for you than driving all the way home.

Madeleine   Thank you. (*Pause.*) Barbara.

Pause.

Barbara   Alright then. (*Pause.*) Come on, Ellen. You can give me a hand.

She picks up remaining dolls, puts them in box.

Barbara   There's only a few left. I'll finish them downstairs. Thank you for your help. And the chat. I appreciate it.

Rosie   It's a pleasure.

Barbara   Night night, then.

Exit **Barbara** *and* **Ellen**, *though* **Ellen** *seems loath to go, and exits with long glance at* **Rosie**.

Silence.

Rosie   Did you find her?

Madeleine   No. I'll try again tomorrow.

Rosie *sits abruptly on bed, staring ahead, withdrawn. She holds out her hand to* **Madeleine**, *without looking at her. They embrace, without* **Rosie**'s *expression changing.* **Rosie** *kisses* **Madeleine** *forcefully.* **Madeleine** *pulls back.*

Madeleine   I can taste blood.

Madeleine *returns to* **Rosie**'s *embrace.*

Lights go down.

Sounds of skipping song, voices repeating 'you're dead' and childish laughter.

Scene Three

Rosie's bedroom. Early morning, one week later.
Curtains drawn shut, room in darkness. **Rosie** *and* **Madeleine** *are in bed. The alarm*
sounds. **Rosie** *switches it off.*

Rosie   Nine am. Friday. March 28th. 1986. Good Friday.

She gets briskly out of bed.

Madeleine   Ugh. (*Sleepily.*) Jesus Christ. Do you have to say the time, date
. . . bloody temperature in fahrenheit, centigrade and whatever bloody else?
. . . You're beginning to sound like *her*.

Rosie   Like who?

Madeleine   Like her . . . the walking calendar . . . *Ellen*.

Rosie   What's your problem?

Madeleine   No problem. None whatsoever.

Rosie   Good. (*Pause.*) I learned inside that time is an anchor. I wouldn't
expect you to understand. Time, for you, is expendable, a commodity. You
want more, buy more. How could you appreciate the value of it? You've let it
trickle through your fingers like water.

Madeleine   I know, I *know* . . . I've never had to count off the years like you
. . . eighteen . . . seventeen . . . sixteen . . .

Rosie   No. Worse than that. I could have been counting down a *lifetime* of
years. Can you imagine it? A lifetime in prison.

Pause.

Rosie *opens the curtains. Light floods in, through an almost completed 'stained glass'*
window, which **Rosie** *has made using tissue paper. It shows Jesus on the cross. The room*
is filled with different colours.

Rosie   She's sitting there.

Madeleine   Who?

Rosie   Ellen. (*She waves.*) Every morning. She knows I open the curtains at
nine o'clock. Sitting on the kerb opposite. To see our masterpiece unveiled.
She's got someone with her this morning. The old dear down the street with
the blue rinse. And yesterday a man out walking his dog stopped, to look.

People are beginning to notice. That's important. Good Friday and it only needs a few finishing touches . . . He was crucified and He rose again . . .

Madeleine   (*interrupting*) I don't like it.

Rosie   Don't like it?

Madeleine   Any of it. Particularly religion in the bedroom. Bad enough in the churches . . .

Rosie   And what would you prefer in the bedroom?

Madeleine   You.

Rosie   I see.

Madeleine   In *my* bedroom. *Our* bedroom.

Rosie   This *is* my bedroom.

Madeleine   No it isn't. It's a rented room in a poky terraced house. And whatever your soft spot may be for Barbara, it can't be because of her stimulating company. And as for Ellen . . .

Rosie   What about Ellen?

Madeleine   Well. Nothing. It's just that I haven't seen you for a week and yet you spend the whole evening doing the 'Blue Peter' number with *her* . . .

Rosie grabs **Madeleine** *by the shoulders.*

Madeleine   (*raising voice*) You're hurting me.

Rosie   Keep your voice down. (*The rest of the conversation is carried out virtually in a whisper. Menacing.*) Listen. This *poky terraced house* . . . compared to where I grew up . . . this is a palace . . . You don't know how privileged you are. Even when you were inside you had it easy . . .

Madeleine   I could have paid the fine. I didn't have to go inside. I *chose* to . . .

Rosie   Exactly. You had the choice. And once you'd made that choice, what happened? Word in the governor's ear from daddy . . .

Madeleine   That's not true. He wanted to, but I wouldn't let him . . .

Rosie   (*laughs*) When has he ever listened to anything you've ever said? Unless it suited him.

Madeleine   He didn't . . .

Rosie   Grow up, Maddy. How else do you think you managed to get such a cushy cell, cushy cell-mate. Lovely woman, wasn't she?

Madeleine   I despised her . . .

Rosie   Now, now. *Edwina. Craig-Donald.* Well known for her charitable works. Until the charities found out they were working for *her*, that is.

Madeleine   You're hurting my arm.

Rosie   *And* you got yourself a nice cushy job in the library. Can't remember you having to lie, cheat or sleep your way into that one. Like most other people have to.

Madeleine   You're hurting me.

Rosie *jolts* **Madeleine** *as if to emphasise what she is saying.*

Rosie   You come here. This is the second time you've stayed here. You take her hospitality.

Madeleine   I come here for *you.*

Rosie   This is Barbara's house. She tries to make you feel welcome by making you cups of tea.

Madeleine   Why do you defend her? You spend more time with her than you do with me. She's an old woman. You have nothing in common with her.

Rosie   What do I have in common with you?

Madeleine   Anything and everything. We're kindred spirits . . .

Rosie   (*laughs*) Kindred spirits. (*Laughs, then suddenly serious.*) Are you sure you know who you're kindred spirits with?

Madeleine   Get off me.

Rosie   Why? You like it. (*She wrenches* **Madeleine***'s head back onto the bed.*) You love it. (*She kisses her, roughly.*) You love it. (*Kisses her.*) That's why you come back for more.

Madeleine   No.

Silence.

Madeleine *slowly gets into sitting position.*

Madeleine   You were different inside.

Rosie   I was exactly the same.

Madeleine   You said we had a future together.

Rosie   *You* said we had a future together.

Madeleine   There is so much I wanted to show you.

Rosie   There's so much you wanted to *teach* me.

Madeleine   That's not so. There's a lot I wanted to share with you. Things you would appreciate . . . architecture, art, theatre – you've never been inside a theatre, have you?

Rosie   No.

Madeleine I wanted to take you to galleries, buy you books – lots more books – poetry . . . And foreign lands. I wanted most of all to travel with you, to see things afresh, through *your* eyes.

Rosie This is a foreign land. To me. I'm on a voyage of discovery. I have no maps, except up here. (*She taps her head.*) I'm adrift amid insubstantial memories. Everything has changed. The places. The people. I feel like an explorer. A lone explorer.

Madeleine Is that what you want? To be alone?

Rosie I went out yesterday. By myself. To buy more tissue paper for the window. The very first time in two weeks. I *dared* to go out. I watched for the reactions of other people. Nothing. (*Pause. Laughs.*) No. Not exactly. A man whistled at me.

Madeleine You think you're safe, don't you?

Rosie (*laughs*) Safe? What would be the point of being here, if I were safe?

Madeleine This is frightening. Your attitude is dangerous.

Pause.

Rosie Why are you with me?

Madeleine Why?

Rosie Why do you want to be with me?

Madeleine Why do I . . . ? I love you.

Rosie You love me . . . ? You love me. (*Pause.*) Do you love what I am?

Madeleine I love you for yourself.

Rosie Then part of it is the danger.

Madeleine No.

Rosie Come on . . . First of all, I'm a dangerous woman. For nearly twenty years had a label hung around my neck by the world, saying 'psychopath'. Secondly, every day I stay here, I run the danger of being discovered, revealed. There are still people out there who would kill me. Literally *kill* me. And you continue to visit. Every time that you visit, the danger increases. Your face is known to the press. *Sordid Sexploits of Rebel Publishing Magnate's Daughter and Murderess.* You can just see the headlines. And still you come. And still you *come.* Aah. *Feel* that moment. That delicious sensation. (*Pause.*) Imagine living your life around that. The expectancy. A rippling tide. Too much sometimes. Exquisite. To walk down a street, not knowing who or what might lie in wait for you. The *waiting.* A teasing not-knowing.

Madeleine You like to tease me.

Rosie And you enjoy it.

Madeleine I . . . (*Pause. She thinks.*)

Rosie   You like to be teased because you've never had to wait for anything before.

Madeleine   Tease me some more.

Rosie   No. (*She gets up.*)

Madeleine   Why not? I'm asking you to.

Rosie *laughs, looks out of window.*

Madeleine   I satisfy you, don't I?

Rosie   Yes.

Madeleine   So what's wrong?

Rosie   Wrong?

Madeleine   Am I better than the others?

Rosie   Which others?

Madeleine   Do you want me to name them? I don't know all their names.

Silence.

Madeleine   Alright then. That screw – how very apt – Ruby? Am I better than her?

Rosie   (*laughs*) Why do you want to know?

Madeleine   Am I? (*Her voice is getting louder.*) Am I? Look – tell me, tell me – am I?

Rosie *puts hand over* **Madeleine**'s *mouth.*

Rosie   Ssh. (*Pause.*) Yes. (*Pause.*) In some ways. But not in others.

Madeleine   (*struggles free of* **Rosie**'s *hand*) In what ways was she better than me? Tell me. In what ways?

Rosie   What does it matter?

Madeleine   I need to know. In what ways?

Rosie   It doesn't matter.

Madeleine   It does matter. It matters . . . I want you to want me. I want you to need me.

Rosie   I don't need anyone.

Madeleine   You do. You must do. Otherwise I wouldn't be here with you.

Silence.

Madeleine   You care for me. Say you care for me.

Rosie I first saw you across the dining hall. Your hair shone almost reddish under the fluorescent light. Like Lesley's. You kept apart, with your head held high, and your eyes seemed to flame whenever anyone tried to talk to you. I liked that. I wanted to cut through that proud intensity. I wanted to make you cry for pleasure, sob for more in a child's broken voice. (*Pause.*) You could open the curtains a little wider for me to the outside world. Studying had already drawn them aside a little. I felt assured and secure in prison. I had respect. I have a degree. My intelligence is beyond question. But I still thought I would need a guide outside. (*Laughs.*) I was allowed into sane society with a clean bill of psychological health, because I had studied the topic and knew the correct answers to give. It was like any examination. Cheating is not permitted, but . . . if you aren't caught out . . . And I wasn't. (*Pause.*) Do you know anything about psychopathy? (**Madeleine** *shakes her head.*) Maddy. Maddy. Kindred spirits. Remember. You ought to find out. (*Pause.*) It fascinates me. I learned that there is no such thing as a psychopath. Just someone with a concentration of traits common to everyone. Imagine it as . . . like . . . a queue of people. A long unbroken queue. Interesting, isn't it? The psychopath and the psychologist in the same queue. (*Pause.*) You, my sweetheart, dawdle with all the other relatively well-adjusted souls, at the bottom, whereas I head the queue. (*Pause.*) You wanted me to tell you I care for you. I told you before. I burn ice-cold.

Silence.

Madeleine I don't believe it.

Rosie *shrugs.*

Madeleine You're just protecting yourself. You've had a rough time. You just need to . . . trust me.

Rosie Do you trust me?

Madeleine Yes.

Rosie *laughs.*

Madeleine Is that so funny?

Rosie To trust in people? (*She shrugs.*) I trust in God alone.

Madeleine In God! In God!

Rosie Yes. In God.

Madeleine You're an intelligent women . . .

Rosie Yes. I am an intelligent woman who believes that God moves through her . . .

Madeleine This is ridiculous . . .

Rosie   Don't you think I am touched by God? I live, while Lesley dies. Against all the odds they release me from prison. And they don't just release me in the normal fashion. They make an exception. Strings are pulled. They're keeping it under wraps until I've had a chance to make a new life for myself. (*Pause.*) And there is the book. God wants me to put my side of the story, so that people will accept me again.

Madeleine   It's nothing . . . nothing to do with God. Lesley died because . . . it was Lesley. You would have got off lightly if she'd lived. Instead, you were the sacrificial lamb. You should be familiar with that concept . . . And all the rest was . . . Jesus fucking Christ – that was *me*. *I* worked tirelessly to make them re-examine your case. *I* got daddy to push and pull every which way to keep things quiet – and believe me – that took something stronger than God to move him. And *I*, *I* got you that publishing contract.

Rosie   Your father knows a business opportunity when he sees one. I'm sure he saw the situation as heaven sent.

Madeleine   It's not my father you owe it to, it's not God you owe it to, it's . . .

Rosie   You.

Silence.

Rosie   And like God, you think you can re-create me. In your image.

Silence.

Madeleine   Are you going to come back with me? Ever?

Rosie   I have a job to do here first.

Madeleine   And then . . . ?

Rosie   Then . . . ? (*She shrugs.*)

Madeleine   Are you trying to tell me something?

Rosie   I'm not trying to tell you anything. Except that at the moment my place is here.

Madeleine   I don't understand. You *were* different inside. Softer. You didn't seem so driven. I felt as if I could . . . protect you.

Rosie   Protect me? From whom?

Madeleine   From all the people who didn't understand you.

Rosie   And you understand me?

Madeleine   Yes. Yes I do.

Rosie   But it's beginning to seem from our conversation that you never really did. I told you inside about . . .

Madeleine I know. I know. About God. I know. I suppose I saw . . . I thought . . . it seemed like one way of surviving all the crap . . . I didn't think you would need it when you came out.

Rosie You've failed to see the purpose. You seem to see my life as a series of accidental events. God gave me salvation through our actions. It was ordained.

Madeleine This is absurd. You've just spent eighteen years in prison because you got involved with the wrong person.

Rosie I've just spent eighteen years in prison because I murdered five children. Five little boys.

She goes across to window and beckons to **Ellen**.

Madeleine It's all front. You're scared of getting involved. Don't be afraid. You're just trying to hold me away. You're not hard like this. You held me when I cried after we made love. The other women, inside, they all worshipped you – for your warmth, your compassion. They all wanted to make love to you, and you chose me.

Footsteps on stairs. Knock on bedroom door.

Rosie Come in, Ellen.

Enter **Ellen**. *She goes across to window and caresses tissue paper.*

Ellen Sing Morey chap-peal.

Rosie Saint Mary's chapel. (*Pause.*) Remember the window. (*She takes down from wall photo of* **Ellen** *as child, in church.*) Remember.

Ellen (*giggles*) Ellen . . . ba-airn.

Rosie Favourite.

Ellen (*nodding*) Mmm. Best window. Best window. Ellen fave-rite.

Rosie And I'm making it for you. For *you*. Specially. Because . . . Why am I making it for you, Ellen?

Ellen (*looks at* **Madeleine**) Can't.

Rosie She's alright. She won't tell anyone.

Ellen Can't . . . go . . . sing morey . . .

Rosie Why can't you, Ellen? Tell Madeleine.

Ellen Can't . . . tell . . . nobody . . .

Rosie Nobody? Are you sure?

Ellen
Rosie }Sure. Certain. Absolutely. Positively.

Madeleine   Rosie! What can't she tell me?

Rosie   So no-one must know?

Ellen   Nobody.

Rosie *suddenly grabs* **Ellen** *and shakes her violently.*

Rosie   Tell her. *Tell* her.

Ellen   (*dignified, pulling away*) No. *You* told me. Never, never. Nobody.

Rosie *presses her against wall.*

Ellen   (*adamant*) Peggy. Not tell nobody . . . sing morey . . .

Rosie *suddenly releases her.*

Rosie   Good girl, Ellen. Even after all these years, you remembered.

Ellen *moves across to window, touches tissue paper.*

Madeleine   Listen – last time I came here, you gave her a date. She started to say, 'Johnny Craddock'.

Rosie   It's all here.

Rosie *takes card index boxes from wardrobe and hands them to* **Madeleine**.

Rosie   Indexed. Cross-referenced. Cutting after cutting. (*Suddenly, to* **Ellen**.) Ellen. Here. Come here. Madeleine's going now. So I thought we could play a game.

Rosie *covers* **Ellen**'s *eyes with her hands.*

Rosie   Remember. Like the games we used to play. When you open your eyes she'll be gone. And we can play.

Rosie *indicates for* **Madeleine** *to hide behind armchair.* **Madeleine** *seems about to refuse, but is silenced by glance from* **Rosie**. *She hides.* **Rosie** *spins* **Ellen** *around.*

Rosie   Keep your eyes tightly closed, Ellen. Okay. Now. Open them. See. She's gone.

Ellen   Baddy gone.

Rosie   Yes. Maddy's gone.

Ellen   Remembered.

Rosie   I know you did. You knew I'd have to test you, didn't you?

Ellen   Test, Mmmm. What date?

Rosie   Second of June 1966.

Ellen Johnny Craddock. Town moor. Blue trousers. Brown jump-pa. Socks. One red. One green. Shoes. Brown. Lace-u-u-u-p. Blue jacket. Four blue buttons.

Rosie Good job you remembered about the four, isn't it?

Ellen (*nods smugly*) Next time . . . *Three* . . . oh dear.

Rosie So we had to look for it, didn't we?

Ellen Mmmm hmmmm.

Rosie Where did we find it?

Ellen Lesley's car. Under passalger seat.

Rosie Yes. That's right. And what else?

Ellen Pen-knife.

Rosie Which had fallen . . . (*She waits for* **Ellen** *to finish sentence.*)

Ellen Out of pocket . . . (*She smirks at own cleverness.*)

Rosie But everything else was still in his pocket, wasn't it?

Ellen Bus ticket. Lastic bands. Football pict-cha. Chewing gum. Ugh. *Old* chewing gum. Yuk yuk.

Rosie You're so clever, Ellen. I've never met anyone like you. (*Pause.*) So clever. So clever at the games.

Ellen Mmmm hmmm. Games. Ellen's games. Ice-cream. Ninety nine. Want *two* flakes in mine.

Rosie (*laughs*) Yes. You always had to have two, didn't you? But you deserved them.

Ellen (*becoming quite animated*) What date?

Rosie Another one?

Ellen Yes. Ice-cream. Give over. Two flakes mister softee.

Rosie (*laughs*) Okay. Fifteenth of August 1966.

Ellen Robert Thomas. Tyne pit. Brown shorts. Green T-shirt. Sandals. Blue plastic. (*Sniggers.*) No underpants.

Rosie What did he have in his pockets?

Ellen Pockets. Nowt. Holes. Bottom of sandals. Holes. T-shirt. Holes.

Rosie And what did Lesley say?

Ellen Lesley said, 'Must be holy.' (*Sniggers.*)

Rosie You thought that was funny, didn't you?

Ellen Must be holy. (*She laughs to herself.*)

Rosie I think . . . That's enough for now. I've got work to do.

Ellen   (*anxious*) Alright? Mmmm?

Rosie   Yes. Of course. It's alright. You've kept your promise, I've kept mine. (*Pause.*) When you've had breakfast, we'll finish the window.

Ellen   Had breakfast.

Rosie   You *are* keen. (*Pause.*) I've got to get ready, Ellen. You'd better go and help your mother until I call you.

Ellen   Help you.

Rosie   Soon, Ellen. Now, go on. Help your mother.

Ellen *lingers, then exits.*

Madeleine *remains crouched behind armchair, her head resting on her arms, her face hidden.*

Silence.

Madeleine   You took her with you.

Rosie   Yes.

Madeleine   Did she . . . ?

Rosie   She never realized.

Madeleine   There's a word for this . . .

Rosie   A mnemonic device. That's what you're looking for. She was our mnemonic device. Not a word we had ever encountered at the time, but . . .

Madeleine   It must have been so . . . calculated . . . I didn't think . . .

Rosie   Spontaneous mass murder? Maddy!

Madeleine   My God.

Silence.

Rosie *changes into her clothes, brushes her hair.* **Madeleine** *leafs through cuttings.*

Madeleine   She's the girl. The girl you were with. The one recognized by the boy who got away. That was Ellen.

Rosie   Yes. Clever. Her memory was our saviour, but also our Armaggeddon. She always had to do her party piece. Birthdays. It was her special treat. (*Scoffing.*) Of course the boy didn't recognize her. We were too careful for that. But he remembered her talent. (*Pause.*) She was famous for it round here. The police asked round. Everyone knew we were forever taking her out in the car . . .

Madeleine   Didn't anyone realize her role in . . .

Rosie   No-one . . .

Silence.

Madeleine *leafs through cuttings.*

Rosie   You said we were kindred spirits. You know why I was put away. You've accepted that. What difference does the finer detail make. Maddy. Maddy.

Knock on door.

Ellen's voice   Ellen ready. Steady. Go.

Madeleine   The others. The ones remaining on file.

Rosie   You know everything now. (*To* **Ellen**.) You haven't been gone five minutes.

Madeleine   Tell me . . .

Ellen   Mam 'ooking. Haddaway Ellen. Mam 'ooking.

Rosie   There's nothing to tell. (*To* **Ellen**.) Oh, alright then. Come in.

Enter **Ellen***, with scissors. She doesn't see* **Madeleine***, still behind chair.*

Ellen   Ellen's window. Nearly finished. Be-oo-tiful.

Rosie   Have you brought the scissors, Ellen.

Ellen   Yes. Scissors. Snip, snip. Fringe's a bit long, luv.

Rosie   Very witty, Ellen. When I need my hair cut, it'll be a case of don't call us, we'll call you.

Madeleine   Second of February, 1966.

Ellen   (*gleefully*) Nancy Donald. Yellow dress. Two yellow ribbons. Knee socks. White. One up, one down. Diddle diddle dumpling my son John. Frilly frillies. White with teddy bears.

As **Ellen** *is reciting this,* **Rosie** *marches behind armchair, grabs box from* **Madeleine** *and lifts her to her feet.*

Rosie   How dare you?

Madeleine   How dare you?

Ellen *looks worried, holds herself, rocks backwards and forwards.*

Ellen   No. No. Sing Morey Chapel. Not Ellen. Ellen promise.

Rosie   Be quiet Ellen. (*To* **Madeleine**.) How fucking dare you.

Madeleine   A little girl.

Rosie   How fucking dare you?

Madeleine   How many others?

Rosie   Give me those back.

She snatches boxes from **Madeleine**.

Madeleine   You lied to me. A little girl.

Rosie   Little boys . . . little girls . . . what's the difference?

Madeleine   You know the difference. You let me believe there *was* a reason. There was no reason, was there? When it comes down to it. No reason. You did it . . . you did it . . . because . . .

Rosie   I enjoyed it? Yes.

Madeleine   You enjoyed it.

Rosie   Yes. I've told you.

Madeleine   No.

Rosie   Yes. You should have listened.

Madeleine   Peggy! I've listened to everything you told me.

Rosie   It happened. It was intended. I wouldn't have achieved so much if it wasn't . . .

Madeleine   (*shouting*) I found her grave.

Rosie   What?

Madeleine   That first night. Lesley's grave. I found it.

Rosie   Why didn't you tell me?

Madeleine   I was trying to spare you.

Rosie   Spare me what?

Madeleine   It was daubed with paint. Scrawled with obscenities, the turf dug up.

Silence.

Ellen *is oblivious to the other two.* **Madeleine** *watches for* **Rosie***'s reaction.* **Rosie** *stands expressionless, card index boxes in her hands. She picks clippings at random and throws them in the air over herself and* **Madeleine***.*

Rosie   They'll find out. They'll learn. Some things can't be changed. However much they try. We did it. We did it and they can't alter it. However much everything else may change, they can't change *that*.

She tips contents of the two boxes over herself and **Madeleine***, turning in circles beneath the falling cuttings, her head held up to them as if taking a shower, her face triumphant, bathing in the evidence of her past.* **Madeleine** *first cringes beneath the fallen paper, then grabs at her belongings and makes a move to exit.*

Rosie   Wait! Maddy! You are better than the others. The answer is yes. And do you want to know why? Because you want to be better than everyone else. Because you fuck each time like it's the last fuck you'll ever have. That's what I like. That's what matters. All this (*She gestures at fallen clippings.*) can be locked away. As if it never happened.

Madeleine *hesitates, her hand on the door handle. Knock on the door.*

Barbara's voice Rosie!

Madeleine *turns away from door, begins to tidy away cuttings into boxes.*

Rosie Yes, Barbara. Come in.

Enter **Barbara** *carrying brown paper parcel. She seems agitated.*

Barbara Hello Rosie. Madeleine. Ellen! (*To* **Rosie**, *noticing* **Ellen**'s *worried attitude.*) Has she been . . . ?

Rosie We're just about to finish off the window. Only a few more touches and it's ready.

Barbara Oh. It's lovely. It's . . . the room seems somehow . . . holy.

Ellen Holy. (*She looks at* **Rosie** – *almost seems on the verge of laughing.*)

Rosie Ah – it's a holy day today. He died to save us. Took away our sins completely. Washed us clean. 'Though your sins be as scarlet, they shall be white as snow.'

Barbara You think it's possible . . .

Rosie Not just possible. True.

Barbara I would like . . . (*Pause.*) Do you mind if I . . . ?

Barbara *gestures towards bed.*

Rosie Of course. Ellen. Pass me those scissors, would you, please?

Barbara *is about to sit on bed, then changes mind. She kneels on floor among pieces of tissue paper, clasping her arms in front of her, around parcel.*

Rosie Would you like to paste these up, Ellen?

Ellen No paste pot, oh dear.

Madeleine Here it is, Ellen.

Madeleine *has finished replacing clippings in box. She hands* **Ellen** *glue from floor near table then returns to kneel next to* **Barbara**.

Barbara It's beautiful, isn't it?

Madeleine Hmmm.

Barbara She loved that window at St Mary's. But that photo – it's one of the last times she ever went there. After that, every time I asked her if she wanted to go she just said no. An Ellen no. And that means no. No tantrums, no tears, but neither heaven nor hell can move her, when she's got her mind made up.

Ellen Sing morey chapel. Fave-rite. Here. Sing morey chapel.

Barbara I haven't been to church for . . . coming up for thirty years. Since before Ellen was born. (*Pause.*) I felt I couldn't . . . (*Pause.*) (*To* **Rosie**.) What did you say? . . . 'Though your sins are scarlet . . .'

Rosie 'Though your sins be as scarlet, they shall be white as snow.'

Barbara I thought of myself as a scarlet woman . . . (*Pause.*) Ellen! Ellen! Go and get your music, eh? You can sing for us – for the window.

Rosie Go on, Ellen. It'll be ready when you come back.

Ellen Hmmm. (*Relucantly.*) Okay.

Exit **Ellen**.

Barbara (*agitated, handing* **Rosie** *parcel*) Here you are. I picked it up last night from the framers.

Rosie Thank you, Barbara. (*Unwrapping it.*) Perfect.

Barbara (*quickly, as if in confession*) I thought it was my fault. A punishment from God. Because I hadn't wanted her. . . . You know you hear these things . . . about hot baths and gin and so on . . . When we realized she wasn't a normal bairn, I thought it was my fault. Took me twenty years to pluck up the courage to ask the specialist if it could've been something I'd done when I was expectin', to cause it. He said not. With a smile. (*Pause.*) I've felt like a murderer. All these years. As if I must've killed a bit of Ellen in the womb.

She hangs her head, as if in prayer.

Rosie Don't you think that God would forgive you even that?

Barbara I don't know.

Rosie Oh but he would. You see it's all part of his plan. Take Judas, for example. God needed Judas to betray Jesus, in order for Him to be crucified, and save us from our sins. Really Judas was blessed . . . 'Blessed above all men' . . . Without him . . .

Barbara Maybe. I want to believe . . .

Enter **Ellen** *with cassette player.*

Ellen Finished?

Rosie Just this one piece.

She pastes tissue paper into place. Silence as everyone but **Madeleine** *admires it.* **Madeleine** *moves across to bed, picks up frame.*

Madeleine (*reading, shocked*) Peggy Bow. Your degree!

Barbara   (*to* **Rosie** – *very agitated*) I'm sorry. So sorry. I never knew . . . But you asked me . . . I didn't look at it till after the framer . . . he realized . . . I'm sure he realized . . . I'd given him my address . . . I never met you . . . when Ellen was a bairn . . . too busy . . . working, working, always working, no time for me own bairn . . . auntie Bella told me about the two lovely lasses down the road who took our Ellen out . . . never met you . . . never . . .

Madeleine   (*frantic*) Why, Peggy, why? You know what will hap . . .

Rosie   (*to* **Ellen**) Switch on the music, Ellen. Sing for us. Like you used to sing for us in St Mary's.

Madeleine   Peggy! Peggy! Why . . . ?

Rosie   No need to hide. I am forgiven, protected . . . 'Yea, though I walk through the valley of the shadow of death . . . Thou art with me, Thy rod and Thy staff comfort me . . . I will dwell in the house of the Lord forever.'

Music comes on – same music sung by **Ellen** *at the beginning of the play. She sings.* **Barbara** *and* **Madeleine** *are still kneeling.* **Ellen** *stands at one side of window,* **Rosie** *at the other, her hands pulling her hair up from the nape of her neck, her head flung back – an attitude of sexual, rather than spiritual ecstasy.*

Suddenly brick is hurled through window. Stifled screams from all of them. Music continues to play, but chaos in room. **Ellen** *becomes silent and rigid* **Barbara** *and* **Madeleine** *get up, shaking fragments of glass from themselves.*

Shouting from outside   (*ad lib*) Bitch, bitch . . . come out . . . murderer . . . Peggy Bow . . .

Rosie *stands looking out onto street, in front of window, her arms held out against frame, as if to replace the now shattered image of crucifixation.*

Madeleine   Get away from the window.

Barbara   Come away. Please. Come away.

Madeleine   You're cutting yourself.

Banging on front door. Shouts continue.

Rosie   (*without turning to face them*) Answer the door.

Barbara   No. No. I can't.

Rosie   Maddy?

Madeleine   No . . .

Rosie   (*interrupting*) Ellen. (*Caressing tone.*) Ellen. (*She turns to look at her.*)

Ellen *does not make eye-contact. She starts to sing again.* **Rosie** *turns around. She runs her hands through her hair, sensuously, then holds her arms out, as if stretching. The palms of her hands, and her arms, are cut and bleeding. The banging continues. She smiles, walks to bedroom door.* **Barbara** *and* **Madeleine** *seem frozen with fear.*

Blackout.

Foreign Lands

At the same time as I was growing up in the North East, and not so many miles away, an eleven year old girl called Mary Bell was found guilty of the murder of two little boys. At six or seven years of age, I was a little too young to absorb more than the vaguest of details, but obviously something of the horror of the case lingered stubbornly in my subconscious. Periodically my memory would be jogged by an article in the press. Often Mary Bell would be linked with Myra Hindley, who had been responsible, several years previously – along with her partner Ian Brady – for an even greater number of child murders. As I got older, I became familiar – whether I'd intended to or not – with every last detail of what the media dubbed *The Moors Murders*, as newspapers and magazines lovingly resurrected the story on the slightest pretext, year after year after year. Ian Brady was left languishing in his secure unit in Broadmoor, while journalists grubbed around for the latest prison developments with Myra Hindley – snapping open their cheque books for dubious first hand accounts from other ex-prisoners. *Hindley laughs with Lord Longford. Hindley converts to Catholicism. Hindley in lesbian love shock with prison warder.* In the meantime, Mary Bell had been released from prison, with a new name, and a new home. She married and had a child. It seemed that unlike Myra Hindley she had successfully shed her previous life, emerging reborn into a life of anonymity and ordinariness.

These swirling, half-digested tit-bits of information became the basic ingredients of *Foreign Lands*. The question to which I kept returning was why, if we accept that some people are intrinsically good, we cannot accept that others are just naturally wicked? No-one feels the need to examine Mother Theresa's family background and formative childhood experiences in order to find justification for her acts of altruism. We just accept that she is a *good* woman. Why, therefore, shouldn't someone be bad – if you can excuse the pun – just for the hell of it? Because they *enjoy* it. This is where Rosie made her entrance.

When I was reading transcripts of the Hindley/Brady trial, one particular aspect of the case embedded itself in my memory. The couple kept a checklist of every item worn by their child victims, down to the last button, so that after the murder had been committed they could ensure that they had left no evidence behind. I found this unbelievably chilling. Turning it over in my imagination, I wondered what would have happened if the recording device had been, not a book, but another person. I was reminded of the autistic brother of a friend of mine. A first meeting with Johnnie Gathercole is memorable. He insists on telling you the day on which you were born, after having been supplied with the date, month and year. His delight in dates is only exceeded by his pleasure in recounting tales of his favourite doors. He makes no concessions to those who aren't attuned to his obsessions, leaving the hard work of explaining and interpreting to Maggie, his sister. His world is utterly complete and self-contained, with him as lord and master, allocating doors to his subjects, like regal favours, graciously, if somewhat on a whim. Ellen grew from my experiences with Johnnie.

I could see a basic similarity between Ellen and Rosie. They are both detached from reality, have both created their own worlds, around which everything else is foreign and unnecessary. Also they both have – for entirely different reasons – a functional view of other people, seeing them as characters to flesh out the games they play. Ellen's amorality is almost a benevolent mirror image of Rosie's psychopathology. Realising this, Rosie is capable of showing a genuine affection to the only true *kindred spirit* she recognizes – a stark contrast to the cynicism she expresses when Maddy tries the title for size.

The relationship between Rosie and Maddy received some criticism after the first production of *Foreign Lands*, because of the association between lesbianism and deviant, anti-social behaviour – a linkage I strongly oppose. Rosie is a murderer, not because she is a lesbian, but because she enjoys having power over other people. Rosie's sexuality was important to me – however naïve it may seem to those critics – because I wanted to write a play in which men played no major role in the lives of the four main characters. Where the female characters are the driving energy for everything that subsequently happens. I also wanted to avoid the parallels with Hindley and Brady. Such murderous male/female pairings are inevitably complicated by spurious gender assumptions – in this case that Hindley was the most evil of the couple, because she was contradicting her 'natural' feminine instincts. With Rosie and Lesley as the perpetrators there could be no passing the buck. An equality – however terrible – exists. Above all, although the play uses characters like Myra Hindley and Mary Bell as a starting point, it is not a biopic. The characters – as they are prone to do – developed lives of their own.

It took almost six years from completion of *Foreign Lands* to its first production at the Finborough Theatre, London. On the way it received a lot of interest from other theatres, but for one reason or another, never saw the glimmer of a stage curtain. I was beginning to feel it was a case of *always the bridesmaid, never the bride*, and that perhaps it would be best to consider it as lining material for my bottom drawer. For that reason, I must offer my most special thank you to Jessica Dromgoole for believing so strongly in the script that she actually asked if she could direct it in a real, live production! I couldn't have asked for a better guide to the strange foreign land of theatre in which I found myself. Thank you also to Dominic Dromgoole at the Bush theatre for passing the script on to Jessica in the first place, to Cathryn Horn for producing it at the Finborough Theatre, to Celia Bannerman who chose to direct the play in a rehearsed reading at Croydon Warehouse as a runner-up in their annual playwrights award and has offered help and encouragement ever since, to Maggie and Johnnie Gathercole for their inspiration, and to a long-suffering Stephen Mears for sharing me uncomplainingly with a word processor ever since he's known me.

Karen Hope
July 1994.

Karen Hope was born in Gateshead, Tyne and Wear. She won a number of literary awards as a child, including the W. H. Smith Children's Literary Award and the Barclays Bank Essay Writing Competition. She won the 1991 LBC/GLA New London Playwrights Festival with her radio play *Lotus Blossom*. Her stage play *Ripped* was highly commended in the 1992 Verity Bargate Award and was performed at the Cockpit Theatre by the Soho Poly Theatre Company in October 1993.

Hurricane Roses

David Spencer

Hurricane Roses was presented on 25 March 1994 as *work in progress* at the Royal National Theatre Studio, with the following cast:

Tyler	David O'Hara
Judith	Ruth Lass
Jean	Jenny Lee
Harold	Richard Butler

Directed by   John Burgess
Designed by   Jackie Brooks
Assistant Director   Sarah Frankom
Voice Coach   Jeanette Nelson
Fights by   Terry King
Video Production   Nicola Baldwin & Richard Hodson
Stage Management by   Jude Wheway and Jaun 'Arsenal' Escandell
For the RNT Studio   Sue, Martyn, and Harry.

Author's Note

Hurricane Roses was a RNT Studio commission.

From April to September 1992 I enjoyed an *Alfred Doblin Aufenthaltsstipendium* (Senatsverwaltung für Kulturelle Angelegenheiten / Akadamie der Künste, Berlin). Much of the early work on *Hurricane Roses* was done during this residence.

There are a vast number of people and things that helped during, and with, the writing of this play. I have them all to thank and I hope they *know* who, and what, they are. The following played a special part. My Mum and Don, Wendy Langford, Max, The Girls, Bones and Bones' Mum, David and Jose Colmer, Tony Musgrave, Bill Leahy, Hilary Irving, Edward Bond, Pete Dollins, James Hamilton, David Tushingham, Mickey Ott, George Sydney, The Boyze with E status. Marcus, Bernd, Andrea, Helen, Karen, Beau, Klaus and Gee. Anne Marie Brannon's child care, The Kinderladen on Seeling Strasse. The Lightning Seeds' CLOUDCUCKOOLAND, U2's ACHTUNG BABY and the ZOO TV thing! The Wooster Group's BRACE UP. BFBS, my Amstrad 9512 with Locoscript 2, and my Panasonic 270 with Microsoft Word 5.

If not for John Burgess, and his continued spiritual and material assistance, it is highly unlikely this play would exist at all.

Characters

Harold 61, Yorkshire *born, bred an' t'be buried.*
His heart and lungs are totally fucked.
His optimism and generosity of spirit are almost as painful as his occasional stupidity. That said, by any analysis, he's a fucking brilliant bloke.
He chain smokes.
He's white.

Jean 56, Derry born. She's not *lived* in Ireland for thirty five years.
She's subject to a strong suicidal drive, so each smile's a triumph of will and self affirmation. For someone in *Shit Street*, Jean smiles often.
At the play's start Jean's well on the way to becoming the cripple she is before her death.
As a *hallucination*, she's mobile.
She is is white.

Judith Mid 30's, Northampton born. She has a Londonish *for der kids* twang.
She's a well qualified and highly motivated Social Worker whose working methods are a fine balance of theory, common sense, and experience.
Judith's weary glamour, with the right light on or in her eyes, can

easily become beauty. It's this beauty that has written its name in Tyler's skin.
She does not have to be white.

Tyler   30ish, his Yorkshire accent was slightly softened by Education.
He has a University Degree, in Applied Biology.
He works for the Pollution Control Department of the local Area Water Company.
He is white.

Where and When

Jean and Harold live in Halifax, West Yorkshire.
Judith's house is in a Midlands New Town.
The *counter* is under Judith's stairs, and in Tyler's head.
The rest happens in a *kinda theatrical cyberspace* hotlined to Tyler's *grey matters*.
The Tyler – Judith elements, plus Harold's arrival, take place on a *thunder-stormed* evening, during the autumn of 1990. There's a fictionalized power workers' strike going on: think of it as protest against that epidemic of Eighties Privatization.

Lights and Sound

Lightning, candles, *the lot really*, and all those TVs too: it's going to be a nightmare to light; and that's exactly how it should look on occasions, nightmarish.
Good sound! Essential! Vital! This piece should have a good *Sound Track*, just like a movie.

Design

The characters, like *real-world* people, are shaped by, and shape, their environment; so they must interact with objects. But for the play's purpose, only as far as the objects support the play's action. This play is *not about two flats, sinks, furniture, etc.*
My conception is a *projection of the inner landscape of Tyler's mind, his vision of the World.* Clutter, chill, depression. As the play develops, there should be a mood of *growing disorder and chaos.*
The set will provide different levels and enclaves to play in. One area is Harold and Jean's home and will have a TV, Jean's chair, a music player, and a *looks-like-jade* lamp. If a real lamp is logistically hard, do one on a TV. Another area is Judith's home and will have a TV set and a telephone. *Jean can use the same phone.*
The Electricity Meter can be a large revolving disc, or it can be *numbers on the TV screens.*

The Tellies

A number of TVs should be placed and built into the set. They can be of different sizes and makes: at least one, the main screen, should be large. Some TVs should look as if they've been abandoned and not all the TV's need to be operational. I hope to draw attention to the network of images and information that the characters live among.

John Burgess's RNT Studio Production used electronic red and blue when the TVs were not transmitting pictures, but still turned on. The colour was useful in creating mood and atmosphere, as well as allowing the audience to follow the more formal aspect of the play's action.

The function of the TV sets are as follows.
1. Real TV.
2. To import images from the World: that is, the World outside the physical World of the characters. These should contrast and strengthen the action. They shouldn't be over-considered but best not entirely random either.
3. A medium for transferring information simultaneous to the *formal theatrical* action.
4. As a guide to the *real area action*, eg. the Hospital.
5. A medium for transferring information from the inner World of characters.
6. As a sort of sub-title.

Recorded telly and some live shooting will be necessary. There's scope for more TV than I've scripted and *praxis will show how much can be used before it ceases to be effective*: that is, image overload.

Use news items, and other images, from the decade 1980–1990. If a *viewpoint* is required to *select*, then try to see through the eyes of Tyler, then Judith, and lastly Jean and Harold.

Watching the meter/counter

Tyler watching the meter, the *counter*, is both literal and metaphorical. Once the literal is established, a *freer* attitude to the speechs will help. As written, the first few speeches could certainly be read as if Tyler's running to the meter and talking to himself. But we gradually learn that this is not the case. And it should not be acted as if it is. The main thing is that this activity of *watching the meter* began on the day of Jean's funeral and continues until the night of Harold's visit. The order of speeches is certainly correct, but they could have occurred at any point since Jean's death.

Text

No commas, semi-colons; oh yeah and no colons: just full-stops. That means getting a sense of how to say the line will come before knowing which full-stops are just that. And which can be ran over.

Silence is a quiet where it's not certain who will speak next.

/ means a change in tack, switch in emphasis, or sometimes pause; use them as they're useful.

. . . the line runs out, or is cut into by the next speaker, (*Cuts in.*)

(*Cuts in.*) Means just that.

(*Overlap.*) Sometimes it's just carrying on the thought from a previous line: that is, parallel voices. Sometimes it's just talking over another character's speech. And sometimes it's kicked in as a reaction to something the previous speaker said, the second speaker picking up before the first has finished. Look at it, work out what the speaker has to hear to react, and cut in . . .

Italics is an emphasis, sometimes a quotation.

CAPITALS are usually rag lost.

David Spencer
Berlin 1994

15,000,000 children under the age of five die each year from the combined effects of infection and malnutrition.

1,250,000 every month.

47,600 every day.

1736 every hour.

29 every minute.

Every 2 seconds a child dies, their eyes full of dust, their faces covered in flies, their tongues bloated and stuck to their lips. Dying slowly, painfully. Alone except for those dying around them. Too weak to stand, usually too weak even to sit. Unable to piss; unable to shit. Unable to cry. Their hair no longer growing, or lying as powder around their listless heads. Still able to think.

Every 2 seconds the thinking stops.

From *Millions* by Bill Leahy
(Published in *Panurge 17.*)

TV screen. Rest states. Blue and red.

Sound: The Cowboy Junkies, *'Blue Moon Revisited'.*

Tyler, **Harold** *and* **Jean** *take their start positions.*

TV screen (Cont.) Famine & War stuff. Starving screaming babies, heads stomachs swollen, babies, dead babies.

Tyler *watches the counter spin.*

Tyler   Fourteen Million a year Mum. Fourteen Million. / Give a tek a few thousand that's. Forty thousand a day. Thirty a minute. One every two seconds. / Think about the time it teks me t'say this. Just this. A lotta dead babies Mum. / Sometimes a. A sense it but. Remote. It's all so remote. / A dunno. / I think about those Babies. Think about 'em. Like it's more important than owt. Owt I can do. And it pisses me off! I watch the eleccy meter g'round and I'm frightened. Frightened. / There must have been summat y'cudda dun Mum! Change't subject eh? / It's a fuck off World Mum. And all the fuck off things in it.

Tyler *pulls the main fuse.*

Lightning.

Sound: storm intensifying.

Jean *at a grave.*

Harold *remotes on his TV, looks across to* **Jean** *and lights a fag.*

Jean *steps back from the grave and lights a fag.* **Jean** *covers her ears as a war helicopter passes overhead.*

Tyler *drinks.*

Judith, *with Sainsbury's bags, crosses against the storm.* **Judith** *exits.*

Sound: storm peaks.

Jean'*s pained journey to her chair causes* **Tyler** *pain.* **Tyler** *shakes his attention free from* **Jean**. *He turns on fuses, one by one.*

Judith *enters with bags and a basket.*

Judith   *(different rooms. Calls)* Tyler? / Tyler! / I need y'help get stuff from the car! / Tyler! It's pissing down! / My house looks like a bomb hit it!

Tyler   *(Different rooms. Calls)* It's only Harry coming.

Exit **Harold**.

Judith   *(different rooms. Calls)* / Has he phoned yet?

Tyler   *(different rooms. Calls)* Just a minute luv.

Judith   *(different rooms. Calls)* / Tyler!

Judith *pauses.* **Judith** *exits.*

Jean *smokes, a glass of brandy on her chair arm, beside her chair a claw device at the end of a long stick.*

TV screen close-up: **Jean***'s mouth.*

Jean   I want the softness of then. I'm fifty-six and I want my Da back. And t'go home. One more time. Christ. Jesus. Home. The farm's not there. The fucken Brits fly over Da's grave. Rest in Peace? Why rest in peace when yer no livin in it! / Y'know my idea of heaven? A big Supermarket and a fist-full a found money. / When your Heaven stinks Earth has t'be rotten. / Christ I'm tired. Y'hear me now? I'm tired!

Jean *can't turn on her music player.*

TV screen (Cont.)

Jean   Good songs bring back then. Then the better. Then the bright. Then the before. / When I hear a good song I wait for my favorite bit. It's where I wanna be. Forever in the moment of my favorite bit.

Jean *remotes on the TV. No sound.*

TV screen (Cont.) Sport. Sex. Royals. Famine. Madonna. Natural Disaster. War. Politicians.

Tyler *watches the counter spin.*

Tyler   Rite now Mum. A starving woman is unfolding an old pouch she's had hung over her back for a week. Inside's a small-skin-sack. And this small-skin-sack-thing has a swollen head. And legs no thicker than a finger. And this thing opens its dry-fish-mouth to scream. But no sound comes out. / And this woman. The Mother of this thing. If she is lucky. This one-year-old-starved-from-birth-skin-sack-baby-thing. It will die now. And if her one-year-old-starved-from-birth-skin-sack-baby-thing dunt die now. Then in a few years. One of a thousand sicknesses will take to death this one-year-old-starved-from-birth-skin-sack-baby-thing. / A know this picture. You know this picture. *For Christsake Mum the World knows this picture!* But change the World? / *Send 'em a tin a beans? A packet a crisps? A Mars bar?*

Tyler *drains his bottle and puts it down on or near the counter.*

Tyler   Tell you what I do! I have a wank! Watch TV!

Lightning.

Sound: storm.

Judith *enters with Sainsbury's bags.*

Judith   Where's the paper?

Tyler   Y'can read ten papers a day n'still not know what's going on!

Judith   *I asked you to get me a paper!*

Tyler   (*overlap*) And why? Papers in this country aren't fit t'keep chips warm! Some give a rough idea a what happened.

Judith *tries to ignore him.*

Tyler   But none of 'em's interested in how things come about.

Judith   I wanted a paper.

Tyler   I forgot.

Judith   *I phoned you!*

Tyler   Honest. A forgot.

Judith   Did you put new towels in the bathroom?

Tyler   (*reads*) *Plastic bags use less energy to make than paper bags. Reuse this bag and conserve World Energy Resource.* / The Rio Rule? Concerned with depleting Kilo Joules? Kill an American!

Judith   Did you put the new towels in the bathroom?

Tyler   (*candles in the bag*) We've got loads a these.

Judith   Power cuts? Y'know. Might come in handy!

Tyler   O? (*Dildos.*) I've no idea what you get up to!

Judith   Your mind's a cess pit.

Tyler   Good n'organic! And a muddy mind meks wanking more exciting!

Judith   The chocolate's in the wicker basket. / Did you put new towels in the bathroom?

Tyler   For fuck's sake a . . .

Judith   (*cuts in*) *I want towels in the bathroom. Harry's bed made. And y'go get me a paper!* I WANT A FUCKING PAPER!

Tyler   (*enjoying her lost temper*) Whoooo! Pre menstrual tension? Look at the bright side! Not just headaches and rows. Sex without contraception. Y'remember . . .

Judith   (*overlap*) I WANT A FUCKING *CHRONICLE*!

Tyler   Ok. I'll run up shop! Get a paper. (*Candles.*) You wank yoursen inter feverish readiness. And I'll be back before you come!

Judith   Get some natural yoghurt.

Tyler   (*overlap. Walter Brennan*) *Cuz I ain't seen a woman in years!*

Judith   And some free range eggs.

Tyler   O? Emma cumin? Not Harry's type y'know. Likes girls, Emma.

Judith   And that makes you nervous?

Tyler   Not content with eating out Judith brings home a *Take-Away*!

Judith   What's that supposed to mean?

Tyler   It means I wont be running. S'keep yer knickers on. A dunt suppose Emma likes y'sweaty!

Tyler *exits.*

TV screen. Cash, a young Alsatian.

Jean   (*to Cash*) There my wee babee. My wee babee. Come t'Mummie.

Harold *enters.*

Harold   Dunt have 'im up on't chair luv.

Jean   My wee wee babee.

Harold   E gets hairs all ova't bloody place.

Jean   My wee luv. Wont do no harm. Will yee my wee love?

Judith *tidies, finds the bottle.*

Harold   Cash! (*Cough.*) Get down!

Jean   Dont you be shoutin at him now!

Harold   E is luv. (*Cough.*) Wi'the greatest of respect. E is. A dog.

Jean   What did the vet say?

Harold *coughs.*

Jean   Harry?

Harold   (*TV*) D'we 'ave t'ave that on luv?

Jean   Am waitin' t'see sumthin!

Harold   We've a clock luv. A mean. It's. What. What d'yer want t'see?

Jean   Just sumthin! / A just wanna see sumthin!

Harold   (*cough*) A've left me cigs in't bloody car!

Jean   Have one of these. / What did e say?

Harold   It were that young lass. Y'know. Nice lass. (**Harold** *sparks up one of* **Jean***'s.*) She reckons Cash is underweight like.

Jean   We give him plenty t'eat.

Harold   She reckons e's got summat up we his stomach.

Jean   (*to Cash*) There's nothing a'matter we you.

Harold   She took blood. T'mek some tests. We'll know in a couple a weeks. /
Luv it's . . .

Jean   (*to Cash*) My wee babee. My wee babee.

Harold   Are y'listening luv?

Jean   (*to Cash*) My wee luv.

Harold   We mite have t'put Cash down.

Jean   What d'yee mean?

Harold   That's why she took them tests.

Jean   What d'yee mean?

Harold   If we cant afford the treatment like.

Jean   What's wrong whit him?

Harold   She called it an *enzyme deficiency*.

Jean   Harry!?

Harold   A mean you'll know more than me.

Jean   I shudda gone'we yee. / What's a operation cost?

Harold   Tint really a case of an operation.

Jean   We could sell that lamp.

Harold   (*cough*) That were yer retirement present!

Jean   I didn't retire!

Harold   Y'cant just flog everything!

Jean   I went on't sick! / I didn't retire!

Jean's *stare begs confirmation.*

Jean   Tisnt certain? Those tests could show good?

Harold   It's daft. (*Cough.*) To get your hopes up!

Jean   May be they'll show up good?

Harold   If e's got it. Which Vet thinks e has. E'll tek tablets.

Jean   I take tablets.

Harold   Everyday!

Jean   You take tablets!

Harold   For the rest of his life!

Jean   He'll take tablets then!

Harold   She rekons on twenny quid a week at the start!

Jean   We'd find that!

Harold   Then a tenner from six months in!

Jean   We'd find it!

Harold   She rekons even then it miten't work!

Jean   We'd find it!

Harold   She sez all't signs are.

Jean   We'd find it!

Harold   Cash won't get better!

Jean   (*repeats*) We'd find it! We'd find it . . .

Harold   (*cuts in*) I love Cash as much as you!

Jean   (*to Cash*) We're not having you put down.

Harold   Why you allus mek me out a sod I dont . . .

Jean   (*cuts in*) We'd find it.

Silence.

Harold   We still owe for that bloody Microwave.

Jean   Just like you t'blame me.

Harold   Once an'fer all. We cant afford it! / We've t'pay yer Muther back. (**Harold***'s wanted to bring this up for some time.*) Which reminds me. She phoned. She thanked us for the fifty. And said to send t'rest as we can.

Jean *continues to pay Cash attention.*

Jean   She'll not mind.

Harold   Where did y'get fifty pound from?

Jean   Mum'll not mind.

Harold   N'gud luccin at me like that! Yew've only wun fa'ther. Y'burry him only wunce. An'as far as am concerned it's only rite fer us t'pay us bit. A just wanna know . . .

Jean   (*cuts in*) A'll pay it back when a get me Mobility.

Harold   A just wanna know where y'got yer fifty pound from.

Jean   A'll pay it back when a get me Mobility.

Harold   If y'get it!

Jean   Ye'got it and I canny move for Christsake!

Harold   Y'cud hardly move last time an'they refused yer!

Jean   I'll get it!

Silence.

Jean   I'll get it!

Silence.

Jean   They're in the telly again.

Harold   What? Oo?

Jean   (*overlap*) Tyler sez so many die. It's more than the whole a London and Leeds dying every year. / The babies. They're on the telly again!

Harold   You and Tyler speaking then?

Silence.

Jean *tries to stand. She's in pain.*

Harold   Wer y'going?

Jean   As gettin' Cash somethin' t'eat.

Harold   Vet sez we'them injections e wont be wanting owt. Sit down. I'll get you a cup a tea.

Jean   Y'cud sell yer car!

Harold   It's bloody Mobility's.

Jean   They cant do nuthin to us.

Harold   It dunt bloody belong t'me!

Jean   We've nuthin tew loose!

Harold   Dunt be bloody stupid.

Jean   What if we send the TV back?

Harold   We'll probably do that anyway. Color licence is t'costly.

Jean   Am not watchin that black'n'white thing. I'd rather do without than watch that old junk.

Harold   (*cough*) Not workin' knackers me.

Jean   Linda had you at your best.

Harold   Past is past and that's all it is.

Silence.

Jean   It wasn't like going home.

Harold   This is yer home luv.

Jean   I always said one day I'd go home t'live. / I kept expecting I'd see Da. / We'll not have you put down my wee babee. / You don't understand.

Harold   Course a do luv.

Jean   Get me a brandy!

Harold   No point in taking your tablets and drinking on top ov it!

Jean   GET ME A BRANDY!

Harold   Luv. Me Mobility plus y'bit a pension gives us seventy four pounds thirty five pee a week.

Jean   You're just tight.

Harold   What we ampt got is what we ampt got. Twenty seven a week goes on rent.

Jean   Twenty five pounds thirty.

Harold   Till we pay back what we owe. Twenty seven pounds fifty seven pence t'be exact. Minus a fifty two pence rebate. Which they send us we a twenty four pence stamp!

Jean   Judith understood. She lent me the fifty.

Harold   What you doing borrowing from Judith?

Jean   Me and Judith are a lot alike. / We wrote to Alice Mahon. About me Mobility. Alice phoned me next day. She sez she'll talk t'Kinnock. And he'll talk t' . . .

Harold   (*Cuts in*) Pigs fly.

Jean   Alice's 'n M.P. now.

Harold   I know that!

Jean   When she wer at the Hospital she always liked me. She wanned me t'be shop steward! She'll take me case up in Parliament!

Harold   Luc luv. Y'werked all them years an' you dont even get a proper pension. Tell Alice the house can debate that whilst they're at debatin!

Jean   A'll get it!

Harold   Awrite. Suppose y'dew get it! We've still only just ova an'undred.

Jean   Get me a brandy.

Harold   You want brandy. (*Cough.*) Get it yourself!

Jean   All the time a was there. / I kept expectin' I'd see him.

Harold   I'll just go tert car.

Jean   Get me a brandy.

Harold   Sit down.

Jean   Cash is my dog!

Harold   I'll just get me cigs!

Jean Home's nuthin t'dew with where yew are. It's cuz y'get older.

Harold *exits.*

Jean It's time! Time goes! Y'lose time. That's why y'cant go home!

Jean*'s pain stabs her. She pours out tablets, takes them.*

Jean Come on here my wee babee. We'll not have you put down.

Tyler *watches the counter spin.*

Tyler Put a man in a cage. Shock him every ten minutes. At first he'll rage and spit and condemn his torturers. He'll scream and shout and try to jump away. But in the end Mum. He'll just sit there. And take the pain. Habituation. / Stop shocking him when he sleeps. He'll try to sleep all day. He'll *dream of how in a few hundred years. Life on Earth will be unbelievably beautiful. A life he can't have. But a life he has a vision of.* He'll dream away the cage. Dream away the electricity. The pain! And you know what Mum? We live a lot like that. Shocked and dreaming. Whilst filth. Pain. Disease. Needless dead. Whilst they pile up. We dream our good and harmless normal lives. / But imagine Mum. Imagine a man dreams of the World as it really is. Not as it cud be. Shud be. But as it really is. What'd happen t'that Man? / He'd beg for ignorance. Crave for innocence. But it wunt return. And in't end his dream'd drive him mad. All because he dreamt of the World as it really is.

Lightning.

Judith *cuts up food.*

Tyler *enters, strips to the waist, dries himself down.*

Tyler (*James Cagney*) *Y'know kid?*

Judith (*the bottle*) That was under the stairs.

Tyler (*overlap*) *I'd like t'stop running myself sometime.*

Judith (*overlap*) On the electricity meter.

Tyler (*James Cagney*) *But there's something driving me.*

Judith (*overlap*) I'm talking to you!

Tyler (*overlap. James Cagney*) *Always driving me. In here. Won't let me go. But just now.*

Judith You've been drinking!

Tyler (*overlap. James Cagney*) *Walking around out there. I was OK. Seemed there was just me an'Ma. Y'know what . . .*

Judith (*cuts in*) You've been drinking!

Tyler Hardly drinking like I've been drinking tea all day. *Or I'll have ten pints and three triple vodkas.*

Judith *Meals. Out with me. Never on your own.*

Tyler One beer just one . . .

Judith (*cuts in*) *Never before seven. And mid week only on special occasions.*

Tyler Special occasion.

Judith *I gave up smoking!*

Tyler Y'know how many women died last year of respiratory ailments?

Judith (*overlap*) I don't know.

Tyler (*overlap*) Smoking related!

Judith (*overlap*) And I don't want t'know!

Tyler (*overlap*) Twenty thousand!

Judith *carries on with the meal.*

Judith Y'didn't go to work today. *Y'said you'd go t'work.*

Tyler The water gets poisoned whether am there or not.

Judith Go on like y'goin on an'you'll lose your job!

Tyler *is taking his pants off.*

Tyler Forty eight minutes to go.

Judith I don't want y'drunk when Harry's . . . What y'doin?

Tyler Does it make y'nervous or something? / They're damp.

Judith You are going to put some pants on?

Tyler When does Emma arrive?

Judith Seven.

Tyler The Witching Hour! Tyler turns t'Mr Hyde! Judith's new town home to a coven. (*The candles.*) Sure y'not having a seance.

Judith I should think you're the one who's . . .

Tyler Go on.

Judith The difference between you and me is . . .

Judith *carries on with the food.*

Tyler Go on.

Judith You think you're funny all the time. I know I am not.

Silence.

Tyler   According to *your paper*. Last year. In the UK. Two hundred and sixteen women choked to death on their food. But before y'think of going to bed without any tea. Three hundred and five fell down stairs and died! / Thinking of not eating and then sleeping down here? Well dont. A hundred and twenty four died from excessive cold. / *But!* And this is *the but!* F'women between sixteen and forty. Only sixty five were murdered by their husband or lover. / So? What's *our* conclusion? / You eat carefully. Climb stairs carefully.

Tyler *embraces* **Judith** *from behind.* **Judith**, *softened by* **Tyler**'s *humour, reluctantly accepts.*

Tyler   And let me keep you warm!

Judith   This is soaking! And I wanted a *Chronicle*!

Tyler   That's one a the brainy ones. What you wanna *Chronicle* for?

Judith   (*parental*) *Local* paper. *Local pow-er cuts?*

Tyler *tries to kiss* **Judith**. *She shifts and he tries again. He tries to palm her breast.* **Judith** *stiffens.*

Tyler   I remember the first time I touched your tits. In my room. I took hold. Softly. But I wanted to grip real tight . . .

Judith *twists and pushes* **Tyler** *away.*

Judith   *The first time.*

Tyler   (*overlap*) Like I was climbin' a mountain.

Judith   (*overlap*) Was in the *Market Square.*

Tyler   (*overlap*) But. I.

Judith   (*overlap*) And you grabbed hold like a crab!

Tyler   I remember you reaching up. (*Fiddling with his balls.*) Your arm coiling me neck. How warm you . . .

Judith   (*cuts in*) You're turning into something really pathetic!

Sound: Telephone.

Tyler   It'll be Harold.

Judith   Then answer it.

Tyler   I feel funny talking t'Harry we no kecks on!

Judith   Answer the phone.

Tyler   Am puttin' some kecks on.

Judith   *Tyler!*

Tyler   You answer it. / Go on! / Please.

Judith   (*overlap*) Typical! You can't even answer a phone. This weekend's gonna be great. You both wanting to say something. Neither of you having the guts. (*Telephone voice.*) Six four eight four. / Hello? / What d'you mean you can't? (*Professional care.*) Yess. / Yess.

Tyler   (*overlap*) What's he say? What's he say?

Judith   (*phone*) Just a second Emma. (**Judith** *covers the phone.*) Emma!

Tyler   O?

Judith   She's at the Center. / Put your pants on.

Tyler   (*reclines*) Live art. Man in repose. Sexy and nonchalant.

Judith   More a dead fart. Tyler in no clothes. Sweaty and not so nice.

Tyler   (*standing*) My my oh well! (*Claps.*) One nil!

Judith   (*phone*) Sorry Emma. Just Tyler.

Tyler   (*for Emma*) *Can women give up the deep pleasure of the penis? Like they might give up chocolate?*

Judith   If y'must quote Emma. Get it right. Relinquish. Not give up. Relinquish. And this? A device t'carry a voice over a long distance. Y'wanna say something. Don't shout. Speak to her.

Tyler   Tell her to call back later.

Harold *mends a portable TV.*

Judith   Harry can arrive at any minute.

Jean *smokes and drinks brandy.*

Tyler   Whatever she wants. Say no. / I want you here tonight.

Harold *bangs his TV.*

TV screen. All TV's go on temporary blink.

Judith   Put some pants on!

Tyler *exits.*

Judith *curls up with the phone. She remains there until her next scene.*

TV screen (Cont.)

Jean   Forty years. Forty years I worked. Not even a fucken pension. Wont even give me my Mobility. Instead I get a stick we'claw on the end. And handles t'turn the taps on. If a can get in't bath at all. / And I loved my work. Loved it. / When I couldn't go back. The other nurses. My friends. From their own pocket. They gave me a party. And bought me a lovely lamp. Made a jade. / A fucken jade lamp! As useless t'me as I am t'the World. I'd far rather roses in me garden. / I wasn't always like this. When. When then was

now and me a girl. I'd pedal ten miles t'dance six hours. Bike back ten too.
But that was then.

Harold *bangs his TV.*

TV screen (Cont.). All TV's go on temporary blink.

TV screen (Cont.)

Jean   Now my bones whit even the thought of bending burn. Petrification.
Take a dictionary t'the word. I did. Petrification. I'm turning t'stone.

Harold *bangs on his TV, coughs.*

TV Screen (Cont.) All TV's go on temporary blink.

Jean   Do you know what yer doin?

Silence.

Harold   Just needs cleaning.

Silence.

Jean   A cant stand black n'white.

Harold   It wer give the color back or go t'jail!

Jean   They wunt a put n'wun in jail!

Harold   Well they wunt a put yew in jail no.

Silence.

Jean   We shud have wunna them there pitbulls.

Harold *coughs.*

Jean   That fella wudn't have been so cocky then. *Redifusion! Come to repossess
your television. Non payment of H.P.* If we'd wun a them there pitbulls. It'd a took
the smile off his face.

Harold   O'aye. Along wi'his bloody face.

Harold *coughs.*

Jean   Am tellin yee. Y'shudda have let me hit that fella with the iron! They
can put me in jail for all I care. Three meals a day and good company!

Harold *coughs.*

Jean   Holloway's awrite. Judith said so!

Harold   No doubt she knows a rite lot about it!

Harold*'s work on the TV has tired him.*

Jean   She was wunna them *Greenham Common Women*. She was in for a month. / *Redifusion*? I shudda knocked his fucken teeth out! Iron! Wham! Teeth down his throat! No bloody smile then.

Harold   Do you want it on?

Jean   Cash'd have sorted him out!

Harold   (*cough*) Do yer?

Jean   Bloody vicious e wer when e wanted t'be!

Harold   Dont you even want t'try it?

Harold *leaves the TV off, sits, waits, coughs and takes three small pills.*
Jean *kills a brandy, re-fills, checks the time and drinks.* **Jean** *cries.*

Jean   I keep seeing him!

Harold, *disquieted, tinkers with the TV, coughs; he can't get a very clear picture but the sound is fine.*

TV screen: Adverts – include one for dog food.

Silence.

Jean   I keep seeing him! / It'll be soon. / His birthday. / Soon. / I keep seeing him! Looking at me!

Silence.

Jean   Leave it alone!

Harold *stops tinkering with the TV.*

Silence.

Harold   We would go owt for a run in't car.

Jean   You've no heart!

Harold   Oh cum on Jean. (*Cough.*) We'd t'put him outta his misery. A wish things w'different. They're how they are. That's that!

Jean   Did Linda think you were heartless?

Harold   Did Tom think you were cruel?

Jean   Tom made good money. He still does!

Harold   / How long have we been married?

Jean   You don't know?

Harold   A wonder if you do? / Eight years. And in eight years. A doubt there were a full month where life we you were easy. But it dint bother me. Cuz a luved yer. *Now you listen t'me!* When I had me first heart attack that were n'more my fault than't moon is square. And there was nub-dey. Nub-dey

more put owt than me. / If a cud work now then a'd be there! (*Cough.*) A
know what's what. Not being able t'werk. A know how y'feel. But there's nowt
t'do but mek best of it. / An' if after eight bloody years all you can think t'do
is t'get at me threw my Linda or your Tom. Well I think it's a rite bloody
poor show.

Silence.

Jean   Instead a drivin 'round we cud dew the garden. I'll help yee.

Harold   Yew'll just stay here.

Jean   I dont want to be on me own!

Harold   Y'not on yer own. You'll see me through't window.

Jean   I WANT TO HELP YOU! I WANT TO HELP! (*She's in pain.*)
THOSE FUCKEN GOLD INJECTIONS ARE NO FUCKEN GOOD!

Harold   Supposed t'be (*Cough.*) The best money can buy.

Jean   I get them on the National Health.

Harold   You've hold a the wrong end a the stick there.

Jean   I'm not sitting in here like a lemon. / If you go in the garden. I'm
going too! I dont want you making a mess of it! / First of all we're going up
town. And get some roses!

Harold   An' what are we gunna use as money?

Jean   Our Trish sent me some money for me birthday.

Harold   Yew sold yer lamp!

Jean   She's still guilty about Andrew.

Harold   It's not yer birthday.

Jean   It's broken!

Harold   I know what y'told me.

Jean   We've the money.

Harold   What did y'go sell that lamp for.

Jean   I'm not bothered for a posh bloody lamp anyway.

Harold   It's what it stands for.

Jean   Rather roses in me garden! / A snooty bastard that Andrew!

Harold   He's just quiet that's all!

Jean   So bloody quiet he'd not told his lot Trish was pregnant! The day I
called his mother! (*Mimics.*) *Thompson Residence.* Her cunt thinks it's the Queen

Mother's! *Thought you'd like to know* sez I. *Trish is pregnant! And your Andrew's the father!* No Thompson Residence then!

Harold   / Are we going for a run in't car?

Jean   Y'dunt believe me about that lamp? / There's our Trish's letter! / She's fine she sez. Little Andrew's fine. And the house is fine. / Nuthin else. No photo. Just a twenty quid note! / I'll bet the Queen Mother's cunt's a photo!

Harold *coughs.*

Jean   / All the time our Trish was pregnant that cunt never wunce asked her how she was. A cunt like that! If she was on fire I wuddn't cross the street t'piss on her! / We'll see rite for your baby. I teld our Trish. Have your baby. And fuck the Thompson Residence. Have your baby and fuck 'em!

Silence.

Jean   Do you think I did the right thing? / Do yer? Do yer?

Harold   E wer banking on it goin't same way as first 'en. Am just not sure these days y'build a marriage. (*Cough.*) With a shot-gun.

Jean   They aren't married.

Harold   Y'know what I mean.

Jean   She could have her baby whit or whitout him. *We'll see for your baby,* I told our Trish. *Have your baby and fuck the Thompson Residence.*

Harold   I know you miss her luv.

Jean   Have your baby!

Harold   I miss her too.

Jean   And fuck 'em.

Harold   Let's just drive up there and see her! Eh?

Jean   I'll not be snubbed by the likes a that Andrew!

Harold   But yew'll tek his money?

Jean   When Trish goes back full-time she'll make more than him! / And she'll get it all back when I get me Mobility!

Silence.

Harold *coughs.*

Harold   Lets go a run eh?

Silence.

Jean I don't wanna go no run. / I see him. / His little blue jumper. The lovely yellow rings. / I see him.

Harold Who luv?

Jean I KEEP SEEING HIM!

Tyler *drinks and watches the counter.*

Tyler You wanna know how the World is really? Sadness Mum. Sadness arrives and y'look the other way. Sadness taps y'shoulder and y'run. And y'keep runnin. Til yer breathless. And Sadness? He's waiting the kettle on. Y'slippers by the fire. / To beat yer sadness y'have t'run at it. Strike its centre. Site the *Sad Pole*. A station where every sign says *happiness this way*. / May be? / F'sure y'cant outrun it.

Tyler *has a final swig.*

Tyler It's bullshit. Mum.

Lightning.

Judith's *phone conversation is no revelation,* **Tyler** *knows what's between her and* Emma.

Tyler (*repeats*) It's bullshit.

Judith (*overlaps*) Just try an get here! / A told you. I can't. His stepfather. / Just some bloody support. / Of course I'll tell him. / It's a big step for me. / I know I need to. / Soon as I can. Don't hang up! *Please*! / Soon. / I love you but. / I do.

Judith *hangs up.*

Tyler BULLSHIT!

Judith *Who you talking to?*

Tyler Mum. / Mum.

Judith / Emma's gotta g'down the *Cop Shop*.

Tyler O naughty? What's she done?

Judith Evelyn's pregnant. The Law caught her boyfriend. He ripped off a chemist's. He's claiming Evelyn did it. She was pregnant when she absconded.

Tyler Absconded?

Judith Run off.

Tyler And no one at the Centre knew?

Judith Shut up! I don't know how I didn't notice. I don't know how I . . . (*Chastises herself for excusing herself to* **Tyler**.) Oh God!

Judith *gets her paper and ignores* **Tyler** *completely.*

Tyler   Do y'remember when I met Eve? At the Guildhall *Wimpy*? Y'must remember cuz Eve n'me got on well? And you gotta monk on cuz I got her a beer from the *offie*? / So Emma's not coming eh? Just me you an' Harry then eh? / Steak n'kidney pie chips n'beans? / Y'know am heartbroken. / A nostalgic blast of *Never Mind The Bollacks?* / Or *Tracy Chapman*? The sugary end of Dink Guilt. / Got it! *The Cowboy Junkies*!

Judith *doesn't want a record on.*

Judith   It was one hundred and forty seven! One hundred and forty seven women murdered by their husbands or lovers.

Tyler   Yeah but sixty five between sixteen and forty.

Judith   Hard for a misogynist to believe older women have lovers?

Tyler   I dont hate all women.

Judith   Y'trying to tell me you hate me?

Tyler   Beautiful women intimidate me. / Beautiful women intimidate me? / All systems go on sexist sub-text. Judith misses the compliment completely.

Judith   One of a number of little things. That pisses me off about you. Is how y'comment on a conversation at the same time as y'have it. Childish. Puerile. Point-scoring. / And for your information. Septic flattery's all part o'the same sub-text.

Tyler   OK! *Older women wi'lovers*. Tina Turner. Jill Tweedie. Er. That Irish woman. With the red hair. She wrote that novel about the girl who came from Ireland to England to . . .

Judith   Edna O'Brien.

Tyler   Than-Q. / And. And. Raisa Gorbachov. The rest rot t'menopausal treacle. / Wat d'yer think a think? / A think if y'spent less time tuned t'the trivial. Yer'd notice wat were going on around you.

Judith   *(overlap)* Er. What did you say? / What did you say?

Tyler   Oh? Deaf now?

Judith   Since when has the death of one hundred and forty seven women been trivial.

Tyler   *One of a number of little things that pisses me off about you*. Is that every time someone says something that's not strictly party line. You fake deafness.

Judith   Since when has the death of one hundred and forty seven women been trivial?

Tyler   You wanna talk death. One hundred and forty seven anythings is a piss in the ocean. OK?

Judith   Typical.

Tyler   If anything is (*He hates 'typical'.*) *typical*. It's typically you t'behave this way. Whilst you'n Emma are flirting over manifesto gospel. A lively little girl of barely fifteen gets pregnant in front of you. Very slack!

Judith   (*rushes him*) Get out of my fucking house. (*Rpt.*) Get out!

Judith *drags* **Tyler** *by his hair. Her attack amuses him. He frees himself and, enjoying his power, grabs her chin.* **Judith** *thrusts a self-defence nose-punch through the block.* **Tyler**, *eyes-a-water, steps back, no blood.* **Tyler** *flashes a V.*

Judith   Bastard!

Judith *delivers a neat, but telegraphed, gut-kick.* **Tyler** *catches her foot and forcefully pushes her away,* **Judith** *doesn't land well.*

Judith   Get out! Get out! (*cowers.*) Get out of my house.

Tyler   This is our house!

Judith   It's my name on the mortgage.

Tyler   And both of us on my rent agreement.

Silence.

Tyler   Did I hurt you? (*Genuine.*) I'm sorry. I said I'm sorry.

Judith   I'm good at what I do.

Tyler   I'm not saying you're not.

Judith   I want you to take back what you said. Take it back. I see it as a serious professional error. / I'm shocked at myself.

Tyler   Y'not shocked. Y'went straight to your paper. Something's up here. But it's not Eve.

Judith   *I'll tell you what's up here Tyler!* If not for what Harry meant t'your Mum! I would go down the *cop shop*. And come back with a couple a big rozzers for the joy a seeing 'em carry you outta this house!

Judith *resumes preparing food.*

Tyler   *Leave that!* I'll cook it. / *I said leave it where it is.*

Judith   Oh you gonna assault me again are you?

Tyler   I don't say two wrongs make a right but I plead self defence.

Judith   Surprised you don't plead *special occasion your honour.*

Tyler   I've told you before. When you hit me you hurt me. Which means am likely to hit you back. I don't wanna hit you. But you fucking hit me a lot Judith. You even hit me in public. And you can't expect me not to react.

Silence.

Tyler   EVERY TIME THIS HAPPENS IT'S ME. That ends up feeling shit. / Do y'follow me? D'yer? / I don't wanna say this again!

Judith   (*overlap*) If you don't want raw food. Get it in the oven. / The power cut is in one hour.

Tyler   Thought you needed a *Chronicle* for the power cuts? Y'dont read the papers. Y'just do the crosswords.

Judith   Instead a talking shit!

Tyler   Admit it!

Judith   You want something t'think about. You think about that last number. *Suicides.* Four thousand that article says. Four thousand suicides.

Jean *in her seat.*

TV screen.

Jean   At seventeen I was pregnant to a man I didn't wanna spoil my life with. I spoiled it with a different man. But that's another story. And a simpler regret. / Mother gave me money and I *went to London.* But I didn't kill my baby. I didn't kill my baby.

Silence.

Jean   Da would have been alrite. Da would have been alrite. Da was the only one who ever understood me. / When Doctor Bullshit told me. *Your desire to die is deep. As if a long time ago you did something bad. Something you'll never let yourself over!* Da just said *That's rubbish my wee Jean. Just rubbish.* (*Laughs.*) Da was the only one who ever understood me. / See! I can smile!

During the above **Jean** *tries to stand. At last she manages to push herself up, laughs, balances, then falls.*
Harold *enters.*

Harold   Jean!

Jean *can't stop laughing.*

Harold   Jean!

Jean   Am all rite.

Harold   Jean!

Jean   Am all rite.

Harold   Wat's up luv?

Jean   Am all rite. / It's all all rite.

Harold *helps* **Jean** *up.* **Harold** *coughs.*

Harold   Are you bloody drunk or what?

Jean   D'you love me!

Harold *helps her to her chair.*

Harold   Let's go to that doctor.

Harold *and* **Jean** *go simultaneously for their cigs; seeing the humour, they exchange cigs.*

Harold   Cum on luv.

Jean *shakes head 'no' and begins to control her laughter.*

Harold   Cum on. / A'll call him. Get him to cum 'ere.

Jean   D'you love me!

Harold   Cum on. It's not long due anyroad yer check up.

Jean   No!

Harold *coughs.*

Harold   See sense luv!

Jean   No! Not a day sooner! No!

Harold   Cum on luv. Let's go to him now!

Jean   Do you luv me?

Harold   A dunt bloody understand yew.

Jean   Just answer me.

Harold   *I bloody luv you we all me heart luv. I bloody do! You know a bloody do.*

Jean   Then we dont go to that bloody doctor.

Harold *coughs.*

Jean   Not one second sooner.

Harold   (*crying*) It's bloody stupid. Let's go.

Jean   Harry. If I'm t'have me legs off. Y'know what'll happen. Y'know now.

Harold   OH THIS FUCKIN' COUNTRY! / Y'cant stand and they wont give her y'Mobility.

During the following **Harold***'s crying turns to coughing.*

Harold   A wer a live n'let live man me. Never Militant. Never a push over. Allus sed *Harry! Be a nice fella. Nice fella?* Tint *nice fella time* this. *Sharktime* this. If I'd a bloody gun I'd go up that Town Hall. And I'd bloody shoot someone.

Jean   Some days are better than others.

Harold   (*overlap*) A bloody would!

Jean   (*overlap*) I was just thinking on me an' McDee. Ten miles t'dance. And back we'd bike. We drove the boyze wild with our lipstick and our ciggies. / Not one second sooner? Eh? / Not one second sooner.

Harold   (*choked up*) A'll luc out for yer luv. Y'know a will.

Jean   / Fetch me me music. I wanna listen t'me music.

Harold   (*he's beaten back the tears*) Tell you what luv. We'll g'get them roses. And bugger what it costs.

Tyler *watches the counter.*

Tyler   Sympathy. Waste. Guilt. Pity. Failure. Feelings we dunt show n'more Mum. Even though us senses spin forever inward. We cant find us conscience. May be cuz those very senses are shrunken. Or maybe. Maybe cuz a World grown Evil's got n'need a'conscience. / *Thirty a minute.* / Each turn o'that red wheel. *One every two seconds.* All the things that happen.

Lightning.

Judith   (*reads*) *In England and Wales. The number of adults who die by their own hands is around four thousand a year.* Trivial? Piss in the ocean? Is that what you *really* think?

Tyler *snatches the paper.*

Tyler   You'll like this. Suicides. (*Reads.*) *Men outnumber women by near three t'one. / Which means. For every one man who kills his wife or lover. Forty two men kill themselves.*

Judith   What sort of an equation is that?

Tyler   Easy! Y ratio X. Where X's the yearly rate of male suicide.

Judith   (*overlap*) NO! NO! NO! NO! NO!

Tyler   (*overlap*) An' Y the rate of males who murder wives or lovers.

Judith   NO! Not another nutso night talking nutso equations with you!

Judith *rushes the food into the oven.*

Tyler   Okay? Twenny thousand women die from fags. *A small secret network of misogynistic tobacconists involved in genocidal assassinations! / Five thousand women die in traffic accidents. A not too tiny team of homicidal chauvinists drive up and down the roads of our fair land! Or better still. One hundred and forty seven women are murdered by their lovers. All men are brain dead thugs! /* I'll tell y'why you and your lot keep painting the Forth Bridge! Ground problems in a rancid system! A world of economic and spiritual poverty. Neck deep in blood guts shite poison. And you rant on about domestic crime.

Judith   *No such thing* as domestic crime. It's just crime.

Tyler   Crime here?

Judith   Crime.

Tyler   Crime there!

Judith   *Just fucking crime!*

Tyler   You come on like Bible-belt evangelists. It's a wonder I've a liver left.

Judith   *You're so smug!* With your beer and your *nihilism! (Silly voice.) The World can't be changed!* It's a lie! That we don't know how to do it! That we don't have the power to do it! *That don't alter the basic truth! We can change the World in which we live! And by helping people. We change it for the better!*

Tyler   Thank God for social work. The ambulance of capitalism trundles along. / *You're flying a kite in a fucking hurricane!*

Judith   *You just listen now gobshite.* One women at the Center was assaulted thirty five times before she called the cops. *Listen!* She said she realized *things were going wrong as he began to threaten the kids. Listen!* She lost an eye in one torture session. And not to some stranger. But to her husband. Her living partner. That's attempted murder.

Tyler *turns on a cassette.* **Judith** *turns it off and takes it from the machine.*

Judith   *I've got something to tell you!*

Tyler *unspools it as . . .*

Tyler   I AM A SLOB! A MACHO! A FASCIST! YOU DONT LOVE ME! AND YOU WANT ME OUT! I KNOW! YOU TELL ME EVERY WEEK!

Silence.

Tyler   Apart from your affection. And the obvious consequences of double X chromosomes. What's Emma have that I don't?

Judith   It isn't Emma I wanna talk about.

Tyler   Is it your curiosity? Your vanity? Your fem cred?

Judith   Emma and I talk. We *can talk.*

Tyler   What d'you talk about?

Judith   All sorts of things.

Tyler   *What!?*

Judith   *Brookside.* Where t'buy the best cheese and spinach pie. Split ends. Sexism. Patriarchy. You even. Emma . . .

Tyler   *(overlap) A set of social relations between men. Which have a material base. And although hierarchical. Establish or create an interdependence and solidarity among men that enables them to dominate women.*

Judith   *(overlap)* Alright point proved.

Tyler   *(overlap) Patriarchy's material basis lies in men's control over women's labour.*

Judith   *(overlap)* You've proved your point.

Tyler   (*overlap*) *In capitalist societies that's jobs that pay living wages. And by restricting women's sexuality.*

Judith   How come y'can remember things like that.

Tyler   And now the best bit!

Judith   But you can't even remember a paper when I phone you?

Tyler   (*overlap*) *Monogamous heterosexual marriage is a relatively recent and efficient form that seems to allow men to control both these areas.* Lucy Bland.

Judith   (*overlap*) How come?

Tyler   (*overlap*) Another bag in the bin!

Judith   How come?

Tyler   Because *y'gave it* me. And me thinking it was important t'you I read it. But did you ask me what I think? Did you fuck?

Tyler *goes for a beer.*

Judith   (*calls. Different rooms*) I didn't give you that stuff to read as some kind of disguised smack in the gob. / I hoped you'd want to know what I do. Why I do what I do. How I do it. I thought if I could interest you in something. Anything. You might get back from wherever it was you'd gone.

Tyler *returns.*

Y'think I'm a bitch don't you? A cold heartless bitch. Y'think I've no sense of loss. No pain? There are times I'm damm near impotent with pain but I don't just accept things as they are. No! Becuz as soon as you do it means you're working for the machine. / Something you said y'never wanned t'do. / Come here. / Please.

Judith *reaches for* **Tyler**.

Tyler   Oh? We gonna do it are we?

Judith   Just come here. Hold my hand. And talk to me.

Tyler *stares at her.*

Tyler   When the gods wanna punish us. They give us what we want!

Judith   Meaning?

Tyler   To little. Too late.

Tyler *in pathetic defiance gulps beer.*

Judith   I know it can't be easy after what hapened to Jean. But it's not as if it started then. It's been going on for ages! / I could probably have helped you. But you don't want it.

Tyler   *The Lord helps those who help themselves.* Very Old Testament. The World doesn't need *justice* Judith. It needs *mercy*.

Judith   Mercy?

Tyler   How many social workers does it take to change a light bulb? / Not many. Just a small well trained team. Sometimes even one. But the light bulb . . .

Judith   (*cuts in*) *Has t'really want to change!* / Fuck! You've no idea! / Last week. We asked that woman who'd lost her eye. We asked her *would she ever go back?* Quote. *Sometimes I miss him.* / We've women with burnt and broken arms. Jaw n'cheek bones destroyed. Horribly beaten. Tortured. I know they're not all bad men. I know that. But fuck! Sometimes I wanna do 'em harm. Real harm. If it weren't for Emma. I don't think I would have stood work.

Tyler   Oh? Politically sound rumpy tumpy! Fuck off! / D'yer laugh with Emma?

Judith   It's you who forgot how to laugh!

Tyler   So you do?

Silence.

Tyler   When I helped Mark E move in. From his window you could see in windows across the court. There were two women on a bed. They were there as we started. And there as we finished. It took us five hours to move in. / Not cuz we were watching. He lives on the fourth floor. / One woman had a blonde bob and pale thin arms that kept wafting up. Tugging down the dark haired woman. Arms like swans necks. / Every so often their heads bobbed up. As if for breath. It was passionate. And at the same time totally silent. In that way beautiful things are silent. I thought of you and me Judith. I felt sad. No. Not sad. Narked. I couldn't watch anymore.

Judith   The sexual part of our relationship. If we must separate it off. Which I hate doing. Has always been honest! *For Christssake leave that!*

Tyler *stops cleaning the mess.*

Judith   I have never made love with you when I didn't want to. I have never faked an orgasm! And OK. Since I have to spell it out. I have never been oppressed by penetration by you.

Tyler   Thought it was *enclosure?* What we did.

Judith   Don't be childish.

Tyler   Not penetration.

Judith   (*overlap*) Not now.

Tyler   Enclosure! Historically speaking I mean.

Judith   DON'T BE CHILDISH! / I don't know how we got like this.

Tyler   You have used me as a rubbish dump for your bad ideas.

Judith   *Meaning?*

Tyler   Robin Morgan? And her brilliant. *All sexual contact that is not initiated out of a woman's desire or affection. Constitutes a rape.*

Judith   Just what exactly is so wrong with desire or affection?

Tyler   *Desire or affection?* Feelings a'd gladly show yer. But me. Not being a woman. Am supposed t'wait f'your desire or affection to initiate something. / Am lonely.

Judith   And I got lonely being pumped into by someone who forgot I was there. / All you wanted was to unload. And mainly your balls. For you sex is now an extension of your toilet habits.

Tyler   Sometimes a good shit is better than a bad fuck!

Judith   BAD FUCK!

Tyler   (*overlap*) But right now.

Judith   (*overlap*) GOOD FUCK?

Tyler   (*overlap*) I'd rather be constipated.

Judith   (*overlap*) YOU FUCK ME. I FUCK YOU. WE FUCK EACH OTHER. WHAT THE FUCK HAPPENED TO MAKING LOVE.?

Tyler   (*overlap*) I CANT CARRY ON PULLING ME PLONKER AND SCREAMING AT THE CEILING.

Judith   GOD KNOWS WHAT YOU GET UP TO WHEN I'M NOT HERE. BUT FOR MOST OF LATE TYLER. YOU'RE EVEN TOO DRUNK TO WANK.

Silence.

Tyler   You don't like Harry do you?

Judith   Please don't drink!

Silence.

Tyler   Wud'it a made a difference if we'd have had that kid?

Judith   Why do you ask that?

Tyler   May be we'd have had more to be together for.

Judith   Why now?

Tyler   If we'd changed the stakes?

Judith   Changed the stakes?

Tyler   I cudda gone full time at the lab.

Judith   Shit!

Tyler   I cudda got another job.

Judith   You're a fucker!

Tyler   I cudda got another job.

Judith   A fucker!

Tyler   I cudda looked after it.

Judith   You're a fucker!

Tyler   Y'cudda kept your job.

Judith   A fucker!

Tyler   We *cudda*. We cudda. We cud.

Silence.

Judith   A don't think Harry's coming.

Tyler   You know in Africa. Every two seconds. A baby dies.

Silence.

TV screen

Jean   I kept my wee baby for two weeks. Called him John. / Then came the day. I dressed him. A lovely blue and yellow jumper the Salvation Army gimmie. And some red socks. And pants. I can't remember the pants. What color wer the pants? / I lay him out on a sheet. I give him a little kiss. And I said. Bye bye John. Bye bye wee boy. / A man came in. Took John through a door. And shut it. A never saw . . . / I've forgotten the pants. / Our Trish would have been awrite. I'd a stood to her. She could hold her baby. She could hold him.

Harold *enters with a letter.* **Jean** *tries to stand.* **Harold** *hands* **Jean** *the letter.* **Jean** *can't open the envelope.*

Harold   I'll open it.

Jean   I'll open it.

Harold *coughs.*

Harold   If you're nervous.

Silence.

Jean   You're right. You do it!

Harold *opens it, he coughs.*

Harold   I'll get me glasses.

Jean   No. Give it to me.

Jean *has difficulty unfolding the letter.*

Jean   Me Mobility. / I've got it!

Harold   Congratulations luv!

Jean   I've got it!

Harold   (*cough*) Only bloody decent thing Kinnock's done.

Jean   It wasn't Kinnock! It was Judith. Judith wrote to Alice. And Alice wrote to those poxy gits at the Town Hall.

Harold   I'm bloody delighted luv.

Jean   / I've got it!

Harold   I. I. A.

Jean   I'm phoning Judith!

Harold   A knew y'stood a good chance the way y'crawled them stairs.

Harold *coughs.*

Jean   I'VE GOT IT!

Harold   Y'should a got a bloody Oscar!

Jean   I'VE BLOODY GOT IT!

Jean *fights against her pain.*

Jean   I'm phoning Judith.

Harold   Wait 'til after six.

Jean   Am phonin her!

Harold   It's cheaper after six.

Jean   If it wasn't for you. Cash'd be alive. I told you we'd have the money. I told yee.

Jean's *dialled.*

Jean   (*phone*) I've got it! I've got it!

Harold *coughs.*

Jean   (*phone*) Never mind what Tyler. I want t'talk to Judith. / Well as soon as she gets in you tell Judith. I've got it!

Harold   I'll mek a cup a tea.

Jean   (*phone*) It's too bloody expensive t'be arguing! Harry! I'll have a brandy! (*Phone.*) Soon as I've seen that doctor Harry'll drive me t'see you. / Trish and baby can come here any time they like.

Harold   We can go up and see her if you like?

Jean   Shut up you. And get me a brandy. (*Phone.*) Don't you be calling me mad!

Harold *exits.*
Jean *moves slowly towards* **Tyler**.

Jean   If that doctor tells me I'm to lose me legs. You won't be seeing me! / That's no threat. That's a fact. / Am tellin yee. Y'wont be seeing me. Ever. You hear me?

Tyler *turns from* **Jean**.

Jean   Have you been drinkin?

Tyler   *Have I been drinking?*

Jean   Have you been drinkin?

Tyler   (*laughing*) Have I been drinkin?

Jean   Have you been drinkin?

Tyler   *Have I been drinking?*

Jean   (*overlap*) The bloody image of your father.

Tyler   Tell me news.

Jean   (*overlap*) Now listen to me!

Tyler   News?

Jean   (*overlap*) Have you been drinkin?

Tyler   *News!*

Jean   (*overlap*) Tyler!

Tyler   And here. Two hours too early.

Jean   (*overlap*) Have you been drinkin?

Tyler   Cuz a'll be pissed by nine.

Jean   Tyler . . .

Jean *slowly into darkness as . . .*

Tyler   The Nine O'clock News. / Millions starve as Amiland gobs half the World's food. Juicy Flesh do Death Burgers for less than the price of a pack a recycled bog roll. Economic rationality! And *has Tyler been drinking?* Utopian Socialist vision crammed down wi'owt a dying belch. (*American accent.*) *Told you Reds Central Planning won't work. See son. Force's the thing. Market force.* / Self esteem pissed at n'longer being a super power. The British ruling class indulge in a bitta bullying a' Thick Micks an' assorted Wogs. / Germany says t'the EEC. Wall up Life Boat Europe. And if niggers. Slant eyes. Or any other non-Aryan gook tries to get in. Shoot the bastard. / And tonight's summary. Is Body Earth Terminal? Lungs fucked. Fluids poisoned. Skin punctured. And *has Tyler been drinking?*

Jean, *claw-handed, palms pills she swills down with brandy. She conceals the brandy and the pills.*

Tyler   And now a funny at the end. Earlier this morning a plane crashed into Buckingham Palarse. / Wait for it! / A Palarse Spokesperson said the four hundred passengers died. *Almost.* Instantly. / *Our* Princess McDee. Wearing a tasteful blue coat with a tasteful white lace trim and a tasteful orange hat. Was visiting the Palarse on a recently obtained Westminster County Council care order. *Our Tastefulness* finished her *Cornflakes.* And before walking tastefully away. Spat in *Charley's* dead eye. / I miss you Mum! I miss you Mum.

Jean *can't turn on the music player.*

Lightning.

Tyler   I remember that clinic waiting room like it were yesterday. All those couples holding hands and talking in low voices. All smiles and togetherness. Like we were in some airport lounge. Waiting to go on a mass honeymoon. And that fish tank. Do you remember that fuckin fish tank?

Judith   *You drain me!*

Tyler   I couldn't get the idea owtta me head. That the embryo in you had gills too. And the fish in that tank were water-cherubs wi'wings n'gills. I shudda screamed my fucking head off. *No! Don't do it! Don't do it!*

Judith   Look at it from where we are now.

Tyler   That's when I started crying. And you said.

Judith   (*overlap*) It would have made things a lot lot harder!

Tyler   (*overlap*) *I shudda come with Emma. / I shudda come with Emma.*

Judith   I need someone to care for me sometimes.

Tyler   Oh very good Judith. You're very good at saying. *This is what Judith wants. This is what Judith feels.* But do you ever show me what you want. What you feel?

Judith   You're talking about yourself!

Tyler   Oh am I? Am I really? You were empty Judith. Empty but for a great big howl. And if I did pump into you. If I did just empty my balls. It was because I wanted to fill you up with me. Just fuck away the loss.

Judith   Why didn't you say anything?

Tyler   Why didn't you?

Judith   I did what was right.

Tyler   And that's what really hurt.

Judith   It was right. For Christssake Tyler. It was right.

Tyler   I know it was right! Judith's choice I said. Judith's right. Tyler's a fuck up. / All that rational shite about *wrong time. Something to cling too.*

Eventually we will. / I felt like every thing we'd been up to then had come to a leap you didn't trust to take with me. / You say you want someone to care for you. But do you don't mean me!

Judith   If I ever did reach out to you. You were either busy with your own need. Drunk. Or worse. Dragged my arm out at the socket!

Silence.

Tyler   Did Mum tell you about John? Grandma wanned Mum to have an abortion.

Judith   *She gave her the money to go to London.*

Tyler   But Mum had him anyway. My Uncle said. *Shud she bring that bastard home. I'll drown it!* And me Grandma? *Give him away or dont come home. Pure Patriarchy there?* / Y'suppose that wudda scarred me Mum?

Judith   You can't just haul out the past. If . . .

Tyler   *(cuts in) Well Mum? Seems y'can't haul out the past. We will all be forgotten. Such indeed is our fate. Nowt we can do about it. What we find serious . . .*

Judith   *(cuts in swiftly) Significant highly important. The time will come when it's all forgotten.*

Tyler   I'm sorry I taught you that.

Judith   *Can you just drop the Jesus Christ act? Can you?* / *What I mean is. If all you do with the past is carve yourself up. It's useless to you. Sooner or later you've to live for* the future.

Tyler   It's the present we live in.

Judith   Philosophical bullshit!

Tyler   Life is a lot harder than *cheer up.*

Judith   Yeah. And Jean knew that as well as anybody! But despite all the crap. You make the future mean something to you. And you live for it! / It was her work. Not becuz she couldn't move. May be not *even* the pain. It was her work. It was . . .

Tyler   *(cuts in)* She O.D.'d whilst she were at work! Me and ower Trish scraped enough *Valium* out of her mouth t'kill an army. A ten year old boy. A seven year old girl? There were times I wished her dead!

Judith   You didn't. I know you didn't. And I'm sure Jean didn't either.

Tyler   What are you at Judith?

Judith   I'm trying to help you.

Tyler   Mum dint mean it?

Judith   Trying to share an insight.

Tyler   *(overlap)* That it was a mistake? / She took her own life.

Judith   And how does that make *you* feel. / FOR CHRISTSSAKE TYLER WHAT THE FUCK DO YOU FEEL!

Tyler   FUCKED OFF! AND WHEN I'M FUCKED OFF ENOUGH. I'D GO AS FAR AS T'SAY. THIS POXY STATE THIS POXY COUNTRY. IT FUCKING MADE HER MANGLED HER AND IT FUCKING MURDERED HER!

Silence.

Judith   What I was trying to say was . . . I was just saying. / *Tyler.*

Judith *inclines to touching* **Tyler** *but does not touch him.*

Judith   After Jean's first stomach pump. She was in hospital a few days for treatment.

Tyler   Likely more drugs.

Judith   *Listen.* Y'know it wasn't her first attempt. But the others were *cries for help.* Her words. Anyway. She wouldn't go home in an ambulance. *The neighbours.* She got a taxi. But only rode 'round the corner. / It was spring. I know from how she said. *The light green buds all opening on the trees.* / A woman stopped Jean and asked. *Can I help?* She noticed Jean was embarrassed and said. *I had to ask you looked so dead sad.* Jean never forgot how a total stranger stopped in the street. And asked. *Can I help you?*

Tyler   She told me the same story!

Judith   (*choked up*) I remember her face as she said.

Tyler   It's the *why I wanted to be a nurse story.*

Judith   (*overlap*) *That's when I decided to be a nurse.* / (*Choked up.*) It's vivid because she said. *You'll be the only one who'll understand. You're like me. It does y'good to help other people.*

Tyler   *You'll be the only one who understands me. You're like me. It's why y'do all that political stuff. Isn't it?*

Judith   So she repeated herself? / At the party the nurses gave. When she couldn't go back. Alice the MP. Alice said when the arthritis set in. Though Jean was still at work. She was in the most pain ever. The pain killers were low grade. Every move was an act of faith. She clenched and smiled and kept on.

Tyler   (*overlap*) Romantic bullshit. Cleaning arses.

Judith   (*overlap*) It was really central to her.

Tyler   Stripping corpses n'stiching up drunks. Does not bring fulfillment. She worked for money!

Judith Oh I know she worked for money. And I know that the demands of that kind of work brings its own dangers. But I also think helping other people brought Jean meaning.

Tyler Self justification *Judith*!

Judith Empathy *Tyler*! / I think right up until . . .

Tyler (*cuts in*) She was depressed!

Judith *I think right up until the* . . .

Tyler (*cuts in*) She was always depressed!

TV screen:
No smoking. / Hospital video surveillance.

Judith *I think* . . .

Tyler (*cuts in*) This time she had something to be depressed about.

Harold *on the waiting room bench. He'd like a fag but . . . He coughs.*

Judith *Right up until the last moment.* She hoped she'd get back to work. When she saw she wouldn't . . .

Jean *enters very very slowly.*

Harold What did he say luv? What did that doctor say?

Jean I'm not being pushed around in any old wheelchair.

Harold Here luv. (**Harold** *gives her his seat.*) What did he say? What he say?

Jean He said. *If I don't stop smoking. I'm gonna lose me legs.*

Harold Just like that? / *Rite. I'm off to see him!*

Jean *Dont!*

Harold I've always thought he were a rite ignorant sod anyroad!

Jean *Dont do that.*

Harold *goes far away from* **Jean**. **Jean** *tries to take a cig from her packet.*

Harold (*calls*) Hey up you! / Never mind five bloody minutes!

Sound: A war helicopter passes overhead.

Jean *drops her fags, covers her ears.*

Harold (*cough*) A dont give a shit how many sick patients you've t'see. A've me wife owt ere in tears! Am next on that list! No ifs. No buts. / Y'just tell him Harry Norman'll have words we him. / Aye. And thank you very much and all.

Harold *returns to* **Jean**. *He sees her cigarettes and picks them up.*

Harold   Y'come on back in we me! We'll sort that bloody fella owt! If it costs me another 'artattack. (*Cough.*) I'll belt his nose 'til it opens up like a bloody purse.

Jean   I need a by-pass.

Harold   Don't cry luv.

Jean   Those things only last a few years at best.

Harold   We'll get us a second opinion.

Jean   A mean if a did stop.

Harold   There'll be summat we can do.

Harold *coughs.*

Jean   They dont last.

Harold   A promise y'luv.

Awkward but profound, **Harold** *embraces* **Jean***, him standing, her sitting.*

Jean   A few years then that's it!

Harold   They said you wunt get (*Cough.*) Your Mobility. But y'got it!

Jean   I dont wanna go on we no legs.

Sound? 'Mr Harold Norman. To F2 Room F417. Please.'

Jean   I dont wanna go on we no legs.

Silence.

Sound: 'Mr Harold Norman. To F2 Room F417. Please.

Harold *coughs.*

Sound: 'Thank-you.'

Jean   There's no way I'm going on without legs.

Lightning.

Judith   In England five percent of men. And *ten* percent of women. Are at some time depressive. *Fifteen percent* by some definitions.

Tyler   How's it your theories have to stake claim to everything.

Judith   They're not my theories.

Tyler   Do a feminist analysis of elephant hunting. Be a laugh that!

Judith   (*overlap*) They're something I do my work with. It's like you bringing acid home from the lab to clean the kettle.

Tyler   Lime scale equals suicide? And y'don't wanna talk nutso equations. *Fucking marvellous*. Go off up the Center n'save the World.

Judith   Bit uncomfortable?

Tyler   Or fuck Emma.

Judith   Bit emotional.

Tyler   (*overlap*) Or whatever y'do do up there!?

Judith   Tyler gets afraid! Wants to run away. Typical.

Tyler   When *typical* means common or normal. It's normal to want t'run from what y'fear. *Fear flight fight*! But since it's *typical you* to use *typical* t'mean *typically male*! Tell me this. If women are so good at talking emotion. How come more get depressed?

Judith   I don't know.

Tyler   *You dont know*.

Judith   But as you say. The first thing to do with what you fear is get away from it. But women. Quite neurotically. Are socialized to cope with fear.

Tyler   (*overlap*) *What are you on about?*

Judith   And if they do need to fight are they taught to hit back?

Tyler   (*overlap*) WHAT ARE YOU ON ABOUT?

Judith   (*overlap*) No! They're taught to turn agression in on themselves. And *that's depression*.

Tyler   WHAT THE FUCK ARE YOU ON ABOUT!

Judith   Tom!

Tyler   / Mum's been away from Dad for years now.

Judith   Not really.

Tyler   Years!

Judith   You said yourself *Mum's still in love with Dad*. At first I thought it was cuz you wanned that. But now I think you were right. Y'dont just walk away from twenty years. You were there. Your Trish . . .

Tyler   You're talking like Harry didn't exist.

Judith   Harry's one of the best things ever t'happen to your Mum. A sweet simple ordinary bloke. But precisely because he is sweet simple and ordinary. He wasn't equipped to help her. Not in the end. It takes a special kind of person to go that far.

Tyler   You maybe?

Judith   You maybe? / Harry couldn't cope.

Tyler   You dont know what it's like to live we someone who every second week tells you they're gunna do themselves in.

Judith   Nothing like every second week. Often I grant you. But on a scale of years and not weeks.

Tyler   She drove Harry himself to an'overdose.

Judith   In a relationship with someone like Jean. *Attempted suicide becomes a means of communication.*

Tyler   / When me and our Trish were kids we called it. *The Suicide Game.* We used to think she played it for attention!

Judith   She probably did. Probably saying. *Look. Look at me.* I'm trapped in this horrible relationship! And I stay because *I love you kids. Help me!*

Tyler   Y'mek it sound s'one sided. I loved me Mum! But she could be bloody evil. Me Dad worked his balls off! Sent us on 'oliday every year. Put me and Trish through college. An' for what? Money for bosses n'taxes to a state that dunt give a fuck about workers at the end of their working life!

Judith   Why do you think your Dad worked so often away from home?

Tyler   To get away from me Mum! / Dont look at me like that! He said it often enough!

Judith   It is certainly true that when someone causes stress in a relationship it often comes back on them.

Tyler   *You just drop that fuckin tone. You just shut the fuck up now. Cuz you dont know what you're talking about.* / Yer so fuckin judgmental. It's a wonder you can do the kind work you do do.

Silence.

Judith   Your Mum wanted to leave for years *but thought she had to stay for the kids.* She probably thought by sending him away he could work and drink.

Tyler   There was no work in Halifax!

Judith   And she could try to protect you all from the worst of it.

Tyler   And the money was better!

Judith   Was she happier if he wasn't there?

Tyler   Me Mum loved me Dad.

Judith   Just ask yourself.

Tyler   There were times he cud be a bastard.

Judith   Were you happier?

Tyler   But he was always a very lovable bastard. And Mum loved him.

Judith   If y'love someone it's hard t'stop loving no matter what they do. That's the trap! Women start to see where they are as normal. In extreme cases they cease to struggle because they're exhausted by fear.

Tyler   He wern't one a these beating her every week types.

Judith   There often are long quiet periods. Your Mum probably believed it wouldn't happen again. Trouble is it always does.

Tyler   An' odd slap in a row that mostly she'd start. It was always him who felt shit. He'd be guilt ridden for months. And she'd grind him. Grind him! Cuz she had him where she wanted him.

Judith   He kicked her whilst she was pregnant.

Tyler   Who told you that?

Judith   Jean told me.

Tyler   / Wun night. *He were drunk.* It wer late. But he were singing. *Happy Birthday.* An he put a bottle a brandy down on't coffee table. And Mum said. *Tom I told yee not to bring drink in the house.* And he kept on singing. *Happy Birthday.* Just singing. And she picked up the bottle. And she hit him in the head we it! Did she tell you this one? / He sat there on the couch. Blood pouring off his face. Blood tears and brandy running down his face. And he said. *The brandy was for you Jean.* And she said. *It's two o'clock Tom. My Birthday was yesterday.* Me and our Trish hant given her owt. We'd forgot. / Me Dad put his wage packet on the coffee table. And he went tert bathroom t'clean himself up. And Mum turned to me. And she said. *There yee are now Tyler. There yee are. Now you see what he's really like.* She tell y'that did she?

Judith   He kicked her more than once.

Tyler   My Dad was a hard man.

Judith   And he tried to strangle her.

Tyler   If he'd wanted to beat someone up. They'd not get up again.

Judith   Just listen to yourself.

Tyler   *Never mind me listening t'meself.*

Judith   That's the reality of the threat.

Tyler   *You listen t'me* / She would demand the impossible. I feel terrible talking about her like this. But look at the way she were wi'Harry. She'd only ever want what he cunt give her.

Judith   That's not true.

Tyler   The time with the decorating. She went on and on and it lucced OK. But whilst she were out. A man we two heart attacks. Got on a step ladder t'wall-paper. / It weren't a brilliant job. But instead a seeing he'd done his best. She just telled him it wern't good enough. Worse. Teld him *me Dad were good at decorating!* She knew who's side I were on there. I'll tell yer. She wunt talk t'me for months!

Judith   I'm not saying y'Dad was the ultimate thug. But Jean was a victim. Once violence enters a relationship. It becomes a currency. And it's very very difficult to eradicate.

Tyler   *Where's this going?*

Tyler *goes for a bottle.* **Judith**, *aware of the risk, follows and keeps on.*

Judith   If you've a drunk who's trying t'crush your neck.

Tyler   She is dead and she meant it!

Judith   Then you've an event! A woman in a violent relationship is in a jungle of such events. A squabble about washing up. What time someone comes in. The sexual act even. The dynamic's always the same. And everything is defined by the clearest manifest. In this case the murder crazed drunk. Living twenty years with that threat will scar!

Tyler   Y'know we're not talking feeling here Judith. This is anatomy. Y'expect me t'hack out vital organs n'take a detached look. It hurts! *It hurts me!* / And you can turn that last lot on its head! Y'live with a suicidal woman who y'love very much. But cant cope with her continual threats of self destruction! Watta yer do? Leaving isn't easy! An' even if y'do. You've the feeling you can't out run it. So watta y'do? Amateur anatomy Judith. Y'destroy the threat. Perhaps Dad was just desperately trying to help her along a bit.

Judith   (*Not accusatively*) Is that why you told her she should do it?

Tyler   / You bitch!

Silence.

Jean, *claw-hard hands, downs tablets and brandy and hides the remainder.*

Tyler   I told her. I told her she should stop threatening people who loved her. I mainly meant Harry. And then I told her. That if she really meant it. Then it were her decision. That I loved her. And that I would miss her!

Silence.

Harold   Lucs real that garden now. Dunit? / I were never really one for gardens. / Not til I met you. / Lucs rite real dunit?

Jean   I want yee t'look after it when am gone.

Silence.

Harold   A'd trim't (*Cough.*) Hedge if a thought me heart'd stand it. /
Anyway. It'll be dark before am halfway. / Ow were Trish? / Little Andrew? /
It's a nice new motor Big Andrew has?

Silence.

Harold   Nice motors Fords.

Jean   I want you to take the music player upstairs. And put it in the little
room.

Harold   May be y'shudda kept up we them *Samaritans*.

Jean   Och Harry. That was a one off.

Harold   That woman teld me (*Cough.*) You were right good on them phones.
She were right behind yer. They'd give y'training an'all. / A'd drive y'there
whenever y'want.

Jean   Y'do know I'm not gonna get better.

Harold   They've a wheelchair entrance.

Jean   Harry. Please. I want that music player upstairs. And then I want you
to go and get me a half bottle.

Silence.

Harold   Yew should get out more. You like it when you get out.

Silence.

Harold   D'you think you'd like to have another dog?

Silence.

Harold   If you're still upset about Tyler. Phone him. / Go on. / Only dont
stay on it too long.

Jean   I held little Andrew for two hours.

Jean *considers the fag in her hand*.

Jean   I didn't have one.

Tyler *drinking*.

Harold   If we got you another dog luv . . .

Jean   (*cuts in*) You wanna dog. Get a dog. It'll be your dog. / Put the music
player upstairs. Then go out and get me a brandy.

Harold *coughs*.

Jean   Tyler was drunk but he knew what he was saying.

Tyler   Am knackered!

Jean   No need to say it all again.

Harold   A can't mek head n'tail a yew. One minute e's the only wun oow understands yer. And next minute yer finished we him.

Jean   I didn't say I was finished whit him. I said I said good bye to him. / Harry. Will yee please do as I ask yee?

Tyler   Am just knackered!

Harold *picks up the music player, coughs and heads off up stairs.*

Jean   / I only wanna listen t'me music.

Tyler *crosses to* **Jean**. *He hands her a cassette.* **Jean** *smiles, pockets it.*

Lightning.

Judith *considers the fag in her hand and stares at the cold food.*

Tyler   Its her loneliness gets me. I'd ov liked to ov kissed her. Held her as she died. Like she held me as I were born. Does that sound mad? does it? / I used to imagine what I'd do when she died. / Set fire to a tree. / Walk into water? / I just watched TV.

Harold *gives* **Jean** *a last look before going for the brandy.* **Harold** *exits.*

Tyler   Am a fake. / Am a fake.

Blackout in **Judith**'s *flat. Darkness in* **Harold** *and* **Jean**'s *house.*

Jean *goes upstairs clutching her pills and her brandy.*

Judith   Oh shit!

Tyler   It's just the eleckie.

Judith   That's all we need.

Tyler   I'll get a torch.

Judith   I've got it.

Tyler *lights candles.*

Tyler   When yer up the Center. A watch the meter. A watch it spin. All night. Like a've forgot how to sleep. And I panic. I *panic*. / I panic in case the bill's too high. An'you get annoyed. / I turn off the fuse box. It's like the house dies. I turn it on. Fuse by fuse. The fridge whirs up.

Judith   You turn the fridge off?

Tyler   And I think. It's OK. It's not dead!

Judith   You turn the fridge off?

Jean *reaches her bathroom.* **Jean** *and* **Judith** *light their fags simultaneously.* **Tyler***'s look is enough.*

Tyler   You're not afraid of me being annoyed.

Judith   Do you want me to be afraid?

Tyler   When yer annoyed a ask myself. *Will it always be like this?*

Judith   If you want t'leave. Leave.

Tyler   Great! I try to describe something. A doubt. A fear . . .

Judith   (*cuts in*) Just what profound doubt . . .

Tyler   (*overlap*) And you go.

Judith   (*overlap*) Or exactly what fear.

Tyler   (*overlap*) Ah ha. Well fuck off then.

Sound: The Cowboy Junkies, '*Blue Moon Revisited*'.

Judith   (*overlap*) Are you trying to express? You panic about the electricity bill being too high!

Tyler   I'm tryin! I'm tryin t'describe. / If you were going through something. And I didn't notice. For hours never mind months.

Judith   *Oh you!*

Tyler   *Mum going put me owtta joint.*

Judith   *I waited and waited.*

Tyler   *You act as if grief is some verbal process.*

Judith   *But you wouldn't tell me how y'felt.*

Tyler   *Pushing me to talk all the time.*

Judith   *She was in pain.*

Tyler   *You think cuz you name a feeling you control it.*

Judith   *It can be a release.*

Jean *swallows the last of her tablets.*

Judith   *You couldn't help her!*

Tyler   You're the one wi'the megalomania for helping people. Y'professional pride is injured.

Judith   You feel guilty. Guilty because you feel you abandoned her!

Tyler   If anyone abandoned anyone.

Judith   *You couldn't do more.*

Tyler   You abandoned me! And now by doing something like your professional duty. You are trying to absolve yourself before you throw me out into the street!

Judith *stubs out her fag.*

Judith   Harry's not coming.

Harold *enters.*

Harold   (*calls*) *Jean?*

Tyler *blocks* **Judith**'s *exit.*

Tyler   A cunt think.

Harold   (*calls*) *Jean?*

Judith   I'm going for a take-away.

Harold *walks to the bedroom.*

Harold   (*calls*) *Jean?*

Tyler   A cunt . . .

Harold   (*calls*) *Jean?*

Tyler   A cunt . . .

Harold   (*calls*) *Jean?*

Judith   I'm starving.

Harold *Jean?*

Tyler   YOU ARE NOT STARVING!

Tyler *grabs* **Judith**'s *T-shirt.*

Judith   (*repeats*) I AM STARVING.

Judith *slaps* **Tyler**'s *arms.*

Tyler   YOU ARE NOT STARVING! YOU ARE NOT STARVING! MILLIONS OF PEOPLE AROUND THE WORLD ARE STARVING. THEY ARE DYING . . .

Harold *Jean?*

Jean *dies.*

Tyler   . . . OF STARVATION. BUT YOU.

Judith's *T-shirt rips open. She is naked beneath.*

Tyler   YOU AT WORST. ARE HUNGRY!

Stunned, **Judith** *steps back.*

Harold *Jean?*

Tyler   It's Harry. Harry's at the door!

Harold   YOU AWRITE LUV?

Harold *shoulders open the door to find* **Jean** *bent over.*

Harold   JEAN!

Tyler   It's Harry! Harry! Harry's at the door!

Blackout. Candlelight

Sound: The Cowboy Junkies: *'Blue Moon Revisted'* fades.

Tyler *exits to the toilet.*
Judith *tugs on a jumper, straightens her hair and invites* **Harold** *in.*
Harold *enters.*

Judith   So. Hello. How are you Harry?

Harold   Oh am fine luv. Y'know (*Cough.*) Y'self?

Judith   / The road was no trouble then?

Harold   Last bit wer tricky. Lights gone n'that. Wunce a wagon man allus a wagon man. / Nice motors Fords.

Judith   And the rain? / And the rain?

Harold   Rain or fine. Dunt bother me luv.

Judith   I thought you wern't coming.

Harold   A tried t'phone yer a few times luv. But you youngens. Allus on't bloody blower.

Judith   He's not any better. He's . . . / A just can't . . . He's. He's been drinking so . . . / He's . . .

Harold   You've only got wun Mum luv.

Silence.

Judith   Thanks for coming.

Harold   Wer long ova'due anyroad luv. It wer just. Well a wern't rite meself. / Have y'still that (*Cough.*) White *Datsun* luv?

Judith   I've a green 2CV Harry. I've had it two years now. / You saw it last when I drove up to Jean's funeral.

Harold   Oh that's right. Y'know a dunt remember much about that luv. / A never thought motors like them 2CV's (*Cough.*) Were up t'much. But they reckon there's lots who swear by 'em.

Tyler *enters. A look passes between him and* **Judith** *that would boil lead.*

Tyler   Ay up Harry.

Harold   Ay up lad. 'Bout time yew learnt t'drive.

Tyler   Immoral cars. Unnecessary strain on't environment.

Harold   (*cough*) Y'lazy bugger.

Tyler   Yew hungry?

Harold   Nay lad. A stopped by an old haunt. A'd steak n'kidney pie . . .

Tyler   (*cuts in*) chips n'beans!

Harold   Can't beat it lad!

Judith   (*to* **Tyler**) I wanna talk t'you!

Tyler   A'd offer yer a cuppa Harry but leckie's gone.

Harold   A've a flask in't car.

Judith   I was just going to go out.

Harold   Have a cum at a bad time then?

Judith   No. It's just . . .

Tyler   Trouble at mill Harry.

Harold *coughs.*

Tyler   Wun ov'em's run off we a bun in't oven.

Harold   Tell yer what lad. A'll go out an'get that flask. An'yew an't lass can 'ave a chin-wag . . .

Judith   *Harry. Am thirty-four!*

Harold   Oh my God a ampt cum on yer birthday have a?

Judith   All a wanna say is am not a lass.

Harold   Oh. Er. Rite you are luv.

Harold *exits.*

Judith   Y'think that's funny do yer? Y'think it's funny? / Well. I shall stay and have a cup of *Harry*'s tea. Then I'm off. Harry can stay but I want you out! If yer not by the time I get back. I'll get the police. / Go to one of y'friends. Whatever. I'll send your stuff on. / Is that clear: *Is it*? IS IT!

Tyler *goes for a beer.*

Silence.

Tyler   I remember us kissing. Kissing 'til we were only lips and tongue. *Kissing til we were the kiss.*

Judith   *This isn't real.*

Tyler   *We were one animal.*

Judith   *Life is not as simple as having something to suck on.*

Tyler   (*sucks on his beer*) Famous Czech exports. Milan Kundera. Semtex. And *The Sadder-But-Wiser*.

Silence.

Harold *enters.*

Harold   It's terrible out there. / Shift yerself lad. Get bloody cups. (*To* **Judith**) A wunt gow owt unless y'have tew luv. / Yew'll hatta put yer own sugar in. A dunt tek it. Me bloody heart. / (*Calls. Different rooms*) How long dew't cuts last down 'ere?

Tyler   (*calls. Different rooms*) Four hours. Sometimes eight.

Harold   (*calls. Different Rooms*) S'long! 'Bout time you southerners got the sharp end of it!

Tyler   (*calls. Different Rooms*) This is the Midlands Harry.

Harold   (*calls. Different Rooms*) Dunt cum it lad. (*Cough.*) A can smell London from 'ere. (*To* **Judith**) 'Ere 'ave wun a mine luv.

Harold *lights* **Judith**'s *fag.* **Tyler** *returns with tea stuff. Another look passes between* **Tyler** *and* **Judith**.

Harold   How's werk then?

Tyler   Same twats pour't same poison in't same water. Only this new lot in charge have a new set of excuses for letting the same poisoners off. So it amounts tert same. Dead fish. / They've even found dead birds. Only a matter a time now 'til its all dead. / Water authority used t'say cant come down too hard. *Only leads to closures and redundancy.* / A dont remember a business going down for dirty water fines.

Judith *stubs out her fag.*

Tyler   (*to* **Judith**) Am I boring you?

Judith   It's a bit too strong for me Harry.

Tyler   Now it's *cant fine 'em. They'll take their custom elsewhere. Job losses for us.*

Harold   Surely they've t'get their watta from yew lot?

Tyler   On paper they can buy it from any company they want.

Harold *coughs.*

Tyler   A wiff a water cummin owtta them factories'd kill a bear.

Harold   Y'wanna sling y'lot in wi'this bloody power-workers strike.

Tyler   A've had it. A just mek up me results now.

Judith *swallows down the wrong hole.*

Harold   Supposed t'be in arms about this nuclear waste?

Judith *coughs.*

Tyler   They're not against it Harry.

Harold   You awrite luv?

Tyler   They just want more cash for handling it. If they'd a been any kinda union they'd a gone owt we the nurses. / You alrite?

Harold   Get a glass a watta lad.

Tyler   Yew alrite?

Harold   *Get some watta!* / Put yer head back luv.

Judith   Am alright.

Harold   (*calls. Different rooms*) Shift yerself lad! (*Cough.*) Put yer head back. / Put yer head back luv.

Tyler   Here. Take some.

Judith   A feel a bit dizzy.

Tyler   For Christssake drink sum water.

Harold   Watch what yer dewin lad!

Judith's *coughing slows.*

Harold   Y'dunt luc well yew dunt luv.

Tyler   Judith's alrite.

Harold   Y'gimme a fright there.

Tyler   Aren't you luv? / Guess how many dead sheep they found in the reservoir this year?

Harold   Ay up! Dunt be a daft bugger lad.

Silence.

Judith   Am OK. The tea went down the wrong hole.

Silence.

Harold   It's hell owt there luv.

Harold *coughs.*

Tyler   Some like it hot! Don't they Judith luv?

Judith   Tell Harry about the hand and wrist. Tell him. Go on tell him.

Tyler   It was just something that happened at work Harry.

Judith   Tyler was sitting at his desk. Writing.

Tyler   I shunt a told you.

Judith   And then he suddenly saw that he wasn't holding a pen. But a wrist. And a hand. And in the hand was a pen.

Harold   Wer yer on't beer then lad? / No? (*Cough.*) A'd have anuther heart-attack if a saw owt like that.

Tyler   Seeing it wasn't scary. I thought it were there. It were when it went away it scared me. Cuz a knew it weren't.

Silence.

Harold   Nice tea this. Not as nice as Jean used t'mek. But nice tea.

Silence.

Harold   Your Trish swears by that bottle water.

Tyler   You would Harry if y'worked where I do.

Silence.

Harold   Yew were allus a great one for yer tea wernt y'lass?

Silence.

Harold   Y'cud stand up yer spoon in't tea Jean used t'mek. / Am not as bad as a were. Y'learn t'say. *Oh am awrite. How are you?* (*Cough.*) If a need t'be on me own wi'her a shut all't doors and play her music. A like Jean's music. / That little player runs on batteries. Rite useful these days. / An a see me own family a bit. Them and Jean never got on. So a wunt have 'em in't 'ouse. (*Cough.*) But now well blood's thicker than watta in't it. / There's allus a home there for yer though lad. Y'know. Not that you. A mean. Well. Y'know what a mean.

Judith   I can't . . .

Harold   It's just . . . Me an' Jean. We'd us families behind us. So us. Well. It were just about us. Us being t'gether. Like we you two. You've yer other things.

Judith   A can't really drink this.

Tyler   I'll walk you to your car . . .

Judith   No.

Tyler   Just t'the car.

Judith   *No!*

Tyler   Judith.

Judith   I meant what I said.

Harold *coughs.*

Judith   Hopefully I'll see you later Harry.

Harold   Rite enuff lass.

Tyler   Judith.

Judith   No!

Judith *exits.*

Silence.

Tyler *lights more candles.*

Harold   Wern't a light bulb in ower house 'til a wer eighteen. (*Cough.*) Me Father'd eleckie fert farm but e wunt 'ave it in't 'ome. *Electricity? Nuther daft invention by brilliant minds.* / Funny fella me Dad. Wer a pilot in't First World War. Got wounded and walked we a stick. Only a little fella but a saw him crack a few 'eads we that stick. (*To a beer.*) A'll stay we tea lad. Anyway me Mum said *Walter. You get me a washing machine or yer on yer own.* Bloody eleven of us. S'we got eleckie. (*His own Mum.*) You've only wun Mum hampt yer? / A've a photo ert grave 'ere lad. A planted the roses. Stone sez it all dunt it. *So Sadly Missed.* / Y'Grandma wanned an upright stone but kids up ower end just brek 'em down. (*Cough.*) Y'Grandma's still upset. She phones like. A allus call her Mum. Meks her happy that. / What we her husband and her daughter. (*Sparks up a fag.*) A suppose it's hard for her.

Tyler   (*a shade cruelly*) How's yer heart then Harry?

Harold   These things dunt give it much of a chance d'they? / A remember Nye Bevan me. A remember him as Health Minister.

Tyler   (*amused*) Ow d'yer get t'Bevan Harry?

Harold   *Government Health Warning* and that. Just thinking. / They go on about Kinnock losing elections cuzza his Welsh accent. Bloody Welsh accent dint harm Nye.

Tyler   Kinnock loses cuz e thinks Socialism is summat smelly e'd got stuck in. Judith an' me saw Kinnock's first speech as Party Leader. A CND rally in Hyde Park.

Tyler *goes for a beer.*

Tyler   (*different rooms*) He went on about unilateral disarmament to half a million people. Pissed off t'Parliament. And e'd changed his mind in a week.

Silence.

Harold   (*different rooms*) A wer ten when Nye brought in't National Health. Iron Curtain lasted longer. It wer a funny time then. Like Bevan wer Prime Minister. Why not eh? If yew've yer health y'dunt want more. If Jean'd had health well . . .

Silence.

Harold   As a stopped in fer Steak an'Kidney. There were this fella. Sed e wer ova in Germany we a load. E wer out one nite fer a whatever. An' all over't pavement were banana skins. More than leaves in autumn. An' e sees this queue. An everybody in it's scoffin bananas. Some speak English so e gets talkin. Turns' out they're East Germans. E said they swopped Russian Champagne fer cans a *Coke.* Anyway it's about three in't morning and they're queuing outside a bank. Apparently. On their first vist. They've only t'show their passport at a bank. An't West German Government gives'em thirty quid *Welcome Money.* The fella sed it's a fortune t'them. Real cash instead a *Monopoly* stuff. (*Cough.*) So there's thousands queuing. But what they think is a bank turns out t'be a *Sex Shop.* In't morning when it opens up. They sell out a banana flavored johnnies within seconds. / Thousands ov'em. / Am ramblin lad aren't a? Am just a bit starved f'company.

Silence.

Harold (*Fag packet.*) It wer hard t'grasp what Nye'd dun fert like ov us. *Bevan's heaven.* We cud get sick an not lose all. / A remember Nye on me auntie's Ada's radio. Ada n'me Mum cried. A teacher me auntie Ada. And that at a time when there weren't many lasses. Not from where Ada started. A lot like Judith Auntie Ada (*Cough.*) In her own time.

Harold catches **Tyler**'s *stare.* **Tyler**'s *goes to speak but stops, he does know what* **Harold**'s *saying, or why.*

Harold Even me Dad's eyes wer wet. E'd drink on him but e wer clear. An e grabbed me an lifted me and e sed. *Now then Harry. Nowt in't World t'fear. Not now Nye's dun what e's dun.* / Different country then. War ova. All t'hope fer (*Cough.*) Nowt t'fear. A rite bloody turn 'round these days.

Tyler (*cuts in*) Harry. Eh . . .

Silence.

Tyler As a kid a thort lightning rods wer like fishing rods. That they caught eleckie and it wer used elsewhere. / A used t'love t'sit upstairs by't big window and watch the *lightning.* / Mum were allus nervous when it rained. She claimed thunder scared her. It dint. She got nervous cuz when Dad were rained off. E went tert pub. Wunday watchin't rain a remember Mum sayin'. *Wouldn't it be great. If you could bucket up time. / Big plastic buckets of days that bore you. Ones you'd waste. And pour them in a pool. So as when you need time. You could just dive in. Get soaked in time.*

Jean (*overlap*) *Big plastic buckets of days that bore you. One's you'd waste. And pour them in a pool. So as when you need time. You could just dive in. Get soaked in time.*

Harold I'd got yer mum a couple a buckets full.

Tyler Did people believe that? Nowt t'be afraid ov?

Harold Oh aye. They believed it lad.

Tyler Nowt t'be afraid of eh? / A feel a bit sick.

Harold *coughs.* **Harold** *gets* **Tyler** *a drink.*

Tyler   A were on a train rite after I'd heard 'bout Mum. A'd a voice in me head *Oh Jeanie Jean. Oh God Mum Jean y'did it.* A wer racked but a smiled. Sure sumwun'd ask *what's up we you?* And a'd start howling. *Oh Jeanie Jean. Oh God Mum Jean y'did it.* / Thoughts snowed outta me head. Drifting back against trees. Walls. Houses. All were white and . . . And suddenly.

Jean *lights a candle.*

Tyler   *Mum were there.* Arms out t'me. Floating behind't train. I dint want anybody t'see her. She were dead. It were embarrassing. (*To* **Jean**.) *Her being there. Like when she met me at school. And there'd be no other Mums there. An' a felt daft.* / A looked away. And when a looked back. / She were gone.

Harold *puts down a Coke.*

Harold   You've supped enough f'tonite lad.

Tyler   Coke! The ultimate Socialist drink! So Warhol said. *Y'know the President drinks it. Y'know Liz Taylor drinks it. And you can drink it too!* / Surely the same's true of water?

Tyler *slugs a toast of beer.*

Coke? Six spoonsful of sugar in every can! / When a see a black with a can a *Coke* I think. *Idiot. Don't you know the History of Sugar?* / *Go away! For Christssakes go away!*

Jean *recedes.*

Tyler   It's alright. I don't mean you Harry. / I don't mean you.

Harold   Drink (*Cough.*) Dint do yer Mum n'good.

Silence.

Harold   A found her on her knees bent over't bed. Her heart give up. Her face blue. Like she'd had her head in a *pola'thene* bag. / A told yer Trish she'd died in her sleep. Dunt say eh? / I loved y'Mum. A thought she wer bloody marvelous. / A'd cum downstairs four in't morning. She'd be doin't laundry and a'd wanna get riled. Wun look n'ad see she were in a trance.

Silence.

In't room wer she did it. A ampt touched much. There's a brass ashtray we a drunk clung to a gas lamp. *Have a swinging time* it sez. In't tray are t'butts ert last two fags she smoked.

Silence.

Harold   Y'Gran'ma wer rite mad that y'dint cum tert funeral.

Silence.

Harold   What did y'do lad?

Silence.

Tyler A wer on for a London Weekend we sum old college mates. Friday a went from work straight tert station.

Harold *coughs.*

Tyler A rung Judith just ter . . . *Pills* she said. *Y'Mum's dead. Pills.* Then she ranted on about *how much she loved her. How hurt. How shocked she was.* / I felt like reachin up the phone and grabbin' her throat. Tellin' her to *shut the fuck up!* And the pips went. A just got on't Euston train. Seventy five hour bender. / A wer back late Monday. Judith were gone. A'd few more drinks. (*Points.*) Collapsed there. Tuesday when't funeral wer a cum too. I'd shit meself. Been sick. A sat in't dark an'we watched meter g'round. Just me and Mum. We talked an'*it was like I was dead too.*

Harold *coughs.*

Tyler *And it was kind of a good feeling.*

Harold Y'were wrong not t'cum lad.

Tyler Funerals aren't my thing.

Harold All't same.

Tyler A'd a rather had a wake.

Silence.

Tyler Do y'believe that *Godstuff?* Do yer?

Harold Buggered if a know what I believe in. Work. 'Artattacks. A believed in y'Mum. / An' sumtimes nowt at all. A feel ashamed a meself when a think about that. Sumtimes nowt at all. A. / A dunno lad. A wer werked tert knackers yard. / Yew and Judith know more ert World than we did. Y'can go about things n'gud luk t'yer. Put back the live into the let live.

Tyler Look Harry. That time a talked to her on the phone. Well a were drunk and I.

Harold It med n'difference lad.

Tyler I told her *she shud do it or she shud shut up.* And I . . .

Harold She'd med her own mind up.

Tyler I?

Harold Fatal bloody disease *Rheumatoid Arthritis* (*Cough.*) It just chiseled her down. / On bad days a'd t'tek her tert toilet. /

Tyler Y'know a find it hard t'remember her smiling.

Harold She wer brave Jean. Very brave. Then she said *nowt I can do. Enuff's enuff*. That Justice Turnbil fella at Post Mortem. Well he said. *It seems*. It allus gets me this. He said. / *It seems Jean felt she just had enough of pain. Suffering. And trouble*. If life hadda bin a. (*Cough*.) Bit softer who's t'say.

Tyler Don't cry Harry!

Harold Now a know Jean died ov a disease. And ov her own hand. But first and foremost lad. She died a pauper! / Y'remember that report thing wer't government sed y'cud live on ten quid a week. They'd recipes we half a fish finger and a bit a bacon.

Tyler Harry! Dont . . .

Harold Oh God!

Tyler Dont cry.

Harold Am awrite! / Bastards though! / It's awrite. / They'd condemn Jean for her cigs an'brandy. (*Cough*.) Aye they'd condemn her f'cigs an'brandy. Them we their bloody official bloody banquets. Sod 'em! / Tint the lie that gets me! Everybody knows it's a bloody lie. It's the smugness. The *Untouchables* that mob in Downing Street. And one set's as bad as the next. I tell yer. If yer Mum's lot blew up Parliament a wunt care.

Tyler You dont mean that.

Harold If a think on that rent rebate office. Or that Mobility. Or the snotty way that Doctor teld her she'd lose her legs. They cud kill 'em all lad an a wunt give a damm!

Tyler Y'don't mean it Harry.

Harold (*overlap*) Fellas like me. We'd this country in ower hands. An' we let it slip for the like ov a bloody tax cut. / The miners' pay strike. The one that put t'Ted Heath's mob. My firm wer wagoning coke outta Birmingham t'Elland Power Station. N'one driver did a full run but we knew't score. Double time. Delivery bonus. Scabbin'. / When a got t'Saltley. There were thousands a pickets. Yorkshire Scotland Wales Kent. Y'cunt get in't street never mind t'depot gate. / God-nuz-why but a parked up. A wern't round't corner when a young lad cum up t'me n'spat rite in me face. A decked him we wun clout. Next thing a wer decked. A forest a boots and legs 'round me. (*Cough*.) A thort *a were a dead man* but a heard this. *Hey up Harry*. And a hand reached down. Pete Archibald. A fella a'd dun me National Service we. The lad 'ad decked 'd got tew 'is knees. Pete teld him. *Harry's wun of us*. And a shook the lads hand. *Hell of a clout you've got there Mr Harry* he said. *Nice t'have you with us*. / Scargill stood on a (*Cough*.) Public piss house t'talk tert crowd. He'd a big thick head a red hair them days. *When we stick t'gether as wun class* a remember him shoutin. *We can put Parliament on the Pannel*. Those men loved Arthur. Spoke their language. Anyroad as things died down. Pete asked if a fancied a jar. A sed a'd ter get back tert wife. *Truth is Harry* he said. *Am a bit short.* A'd a tenner in his hand before he could say (*Cough.*) *Oh no. A dunt need that much.* / As a wer gettin in me cab Pete rounded the alley. The tenner held out. *Dunt spend it all on booze* a sed. *Save some fer't wife.* We wer eye t'eyeball when e sed. *Yer not a scab are yer Harry?*

Tyler *opens another beer.*

Harold   *Soon as a get back* a sed. *A'll be handin in me notice. And a'll need that tenner.* A pushed it in his hand an' drove off. Corse a dint hand me notice in. A'd a bin a fool to wunt a? / Lately though. We Jean an'that. A thort abowt that look.

Harold *lights a fag.*

Harold   The way Pete held out that tenner. *Yer not a scab are yer Harry?* My God! Can a tenner can buy yer soul? Damm you Pete Archibald. / Now you asked me. (*Cough.*) What I believe in. Well a'll tell yer! I believed that wen the likes a me and yewer Mum. Who'd werked all their lives. I believed that wen we cum t'collect ower rites. I believed we'd get em! That's wat a believed. / It's taken me this long t'see. Nubdey gives yer owt! Yew've t'fite fer it all. Even yer rites. And that's wrong lad! *It's all bloody wrong.* / And the wer a time you bloody stood fer that! I remember you as a *young punk.* Y'wer a cheeky sod lad but a admired yer. (*Cough.*) *Got it up there young Core! A wish my lads wer a bit more like him.* / When you and big Steve went t'University it wer like they'd sent whole bloody Estate! They used t'say *they'll cum back we a fortune.* And *good luck t'em* I used t'say. / But y'went other way. *And I admired y'more.* (*Cough.*) That eighty four eighty five miners strike. You an'Judith were every bloody where. Three times we hauled you owtert *cop shop.* My God y'spouted some stuff. A thought a'd met bloody Lenin! Remember y'wer a week in jail before yer't'go t'Bow Street. Jean wer rite proud. *My son's bin jailed fort miners.*

Tyler   That wer South Africa Harry.

Harold   Exactly. South Africa. The Miners. The IRA. That fella outta't PLO. The Printers. The Poll Tax. The *this six.* The *whatsit four.* Am n'communist but I admired your spunk! Afraid a nowt!

Tyler   A wer often afraid Harry.

Harold   Nay lad there wer a time yew'd tek on owt. For some reason y'threw up yer arms an y'went under! Well am tellin y'lad. Start swimmin! If only for your bloody (*Cough.*) Mum. You never give up. / What the bloody hell happened t'you lad?

Silence.

Harold   *What the bloody hell happened?*

Tyler   A just got tired Harry. A stopped thinking about what wer right and started t'feel what wer wrong.

Silence.

Tyler   A just got tired Harry.

Silence.

Tyler   When my train got t'Euston Station. I went for a pint. They'd the telly on. The Berlin Wall. Millions a people in a small space and every eye in the World on it. But . . . Something about those East Germans. They lucced like Northerners. Same smiles clothes. Same way of holding their fags. Same range a possibilities in their faces. Marching through the Wall.

Harold *coughs.*

Tyler   And after forty years of Socialism what did they march for? To shop for jeans and Japanese radios. / One young lad. Y'cud tell e'd never been tert West. E walked through that wall like e were scared it'd close. When e wer sure e were thru e looked back east. Looked forward tert West. And e pushed his fist in the air and screamed. *Wahnsinn! Wahnsinn! Wahnsinn!* / Right then I heard tears lopp in me lager. / I knew I'd stopped thinking about what wer right. Felt only what wer wrong. / But I wern't me. Not my cryin'. Not my beer. I wasn't me. I was a fake. / I dont think. I haven't thought in years. And this not thinking. It didn't come in a moment. But the knowing I'd stopped. The realizing. That came *just like that*. Tears in me beer. / Flowery as it sounds. I saw that boy look at the West. His fist in the air. And scream. Crazy-Crazy-Crazy. / It's all just crazy . . .

Harold   I don't suppose yer the first t'think that lad but . . .

Tyler   Let me finish Harry! / I fucked off into an *underground* station. And on the platform were this one black guy. It was London so there must have been other blacks. But I didn't see any. An e wer running up to people we kids. Kids in prams even. Chanting. *We will kill your babies. You have killed our babies. We will kill your babies. We will kill them all.* Most people played like they were letting it go cuz e wer mad. *You have killed our babies.* But they let it go cuz they *were afraid. We will kill your babies.* An' when a looked him in the eye. *We will kill them all.* A cunt tell if e were mad or not. Dead clear e sed *What you afraid of White Boy? You ain't starving.*

Harold   Just because yer not starving dunt mean y'dunt 'unger.

Tyler   Not the point. He's right Harry! Am afraid. A believed in the good a'human nature. Human needs. A thort it wer rite t'try and build sumwhere wer that med sense. But it fell apart an' that made me sad. Wasn't a political thought. I felt it. But not just sad. Afraid. / *This white boy ain't starvin'.*

Jean *appears.*

Tyler   E's afraid. And part of why am afraid is. That black bloke wasn't just about justice or food. He wants *revenge*. And I don't blame him. *Revenge*. I want it. *Revenge*. I want *revenge* an' there's millions on this planet who die before the age of one? Millions that state nothing more articulate than need.

Harold *coughs.*

Harold   Aye and may be that's why they need sumwun t'talk for 'em!

Tyler   O I told myself that bullshit f'years!

Harold *coughs.*

Tyler   They've got someone. The Black on an all White platform screaming *you have killed our babies we will kill your babies.*

Harold   Nay lad that's not politics. That's some nut case raving!

Tyler   That is politics t'day!

Harold   (*overlap*) A well fed baby's as innocent as a starvin one.

Tyler   (*overlap*) Just nut cases raving.

Harold *coughs.*

Tyler   When it's not Nationalist shite dressed as democracy. Pure *Swastikas and greed* like the Krauts. Or oily profit like the Yanks and their Gulf. *Then it's not necessarily Justice either. Eastern Europe. Middle East. Even Ireland. It's Revenge. WHEN THE WORLD REALLY NEEDS MERCY.* EVERYONE'S HAULING OUT DEAD AND SCREAMING *REVENGE!* / THAT'S YER NEW WORLD ORDER!

Harold   (*overlap*) TYLER!

Tyler   (*overlap*) *THE POLITICS OF REVENGE.*

Harold   (*overlap*) TYLER!

Tyler   (*overlap*) *ONE BIG BLOODY ORGY OF IT!*

Harold   (*overlap*) TYLER!

Tyler   (*overlap*) WHAT DO I CARE IF ALL N'EVERYTHING JUST FUCK'S OFF!

Harold   (*overlap*) HEY LAD!

Tyler   (*overlap*) JUST FUCKS OFF AND DIES.

Harold   (*overlap*) TYLER!

Jean   All I ever wanted was the moment of my favorite bit!

Harold   Are y'awrite lad?

Jean   And Roses in my Garden!

Tyler   (*to* **Jean**) JUST FUCK OFF!

Jean *recedes into darkness.*

Harold   Look lad. Y'cant starve yerself t'death outta sympathy. And drinkin yerself bloody stupid. That's a bigger waste than any!

Harold *coughing, rpts. 'Get on yer feet!', as he drags up* **Tyler**. **Harold** *strains himself.*

Harold   *You get on your feet. Get on your feet. Get on your feet.* OR I'LL DRAG YER T'YER FEET! *Get on yer feet!*

Tyler   (*overlap / Ad Lib*) *What y'doing. Harry.*

What began as combat has ended with **Harold** *embracing, even kissing,* **Tyler**. **Tyler***, shocked, steps back.*

Harold   *You stay on your feet. You hold yer head up. And if y'wanna know what the first step is. Its ova yer own doorstep!*

Tyler   You alrite. Harry? / Harry?

Harold   Am awrite. / You should go t'sleep now.

Tyler   You go up if y'want. Go on. / Am alrite. Am just a guilty-idle-self-pitying-bastard who scams at work and claims *grief* for his *Mum* is an *act of global dread*. (**Tyler** *finds laughter, so he laughs*.) Anyway. Me girlfriend's leaving me. *Sorry Bob and the Band Aid Boyze.* It seems Sudan'll have to wait. / Go on t'sleep Harry.

Silence.

Tyler   Go on Harry. Am goin meself soon.

Silence.

Harold   Nite nite lad.

Tyler   Nite nite Harry.

Silence.

Tyler *gulps the last of his beer.*

Tyler   (*sings*) *He who would valiant be. Gainst all disaster. Let him in constancy. Follow the Master. There's no discouragement.* (*His voice breaks.*) *Shall make him once relent /* (*Speaks.*) *His first. Avowed intent.* (*Laughter.*) To BE A PILLOCK!

Jean *is visible.*

Sound: A war helicopter passes overhead.

Tyler *stabs his hand with his bottle and smears blood over his face.*

TV screen. Close on **Tyler***'s face.*

Tyler   Some Russian sed people box into four. Those too stupid for *what's the meaning of life?* Those who find the question a downer n'get pissed. N'those who tek the question t'heart find no meaning an' *hari-kiri. / It's a fuck off World*

Mum. / Then we've the Club of the Fourth Sort. *Nothing new nothing true and nothing matters.* But f'suicide they're t'gutlesss. / Anyway Mum. Tint like meaning's sold in *Sainsbury's.* Is it?

Tyler *puts on a cassette.*

Sound: The Cowboy Junkies: *'Blue Moon Revisited'.*

TV screen (Cont.). A frenetic montage of things seen (including **Jean***) to indicate where* **Tyler***'s head is at.*

Tyler, *in a kind of macabre dance, smears blood on his upper body.*

Jean   All I want. Is the moment of my favorite bit.

Tyler   (*to* **Jean**) There must be more.

Jean   And Roses in my Garden!

Tyler   More than.

Jean   And Roses!

Tyler   More than the moment of y'favorite bit.

Jean   And Roses!

Tyler   SHIIIIIIIT!

Jean   (*rpt*) Roses!

Tyler   (*self involvement, rpt*) I love you. I love you. / A luv yer.

Judith *enters and switches off the music and all electronics stop instantly.* **Tyler** *turns to* **Judith***.*

Judith   (*flatly*) What happened?

Tyler   Cut me hand on a bottle.

Judith   And your face? Your body?

Tyler   I was born with it.

Judith   Fantastic!

Tyler   Flattery will get you everywhere.

Judith   Five minutes.

Judith *tosses him his clothes.*

Tyler   (*sings*) Gonna wash that man right outta my hair! Am gonna wash that man right outta my hair . . .

Judith *has the bottle.*

Tyler   *Take the Toys from the Boys.* Eh? / How's Emma?

Judith   I can call a taxi. Or the police?

Tyler   Blood can be difficult to get out.

Silence.

Judith   I've some numbers you can call. But for now. For all we ever were. Please go.

Tyler   The odd regret but never doubt. As long as the World cries. Loud and often. *Good Girl Judith.* / I hope nothin' ever clogs the cogs o'your confidence.

Judith   Get dressed.

Tyler   In all the years ov being with you. I've felt like I was on probation. Inside of two days. Apart from that stain on the carpet. It could look like I never lived here.

Silence.

Tyler   What are these numbers then ? Sumwun gunna give me sumwhere t'live are they? / It's pissing down out there!

Judith *picks up the phone.*

Judith   I cant do for you the things you need to do for yourself.

Tyler   I don't ask you too.

Judith   You do.

Tyler   I can't hold myself!

Judith   I will call the Police.

Tyler   It's too fucking late.

Judith   You are going!

Tyler   And I'm too pissed.

Judith   GO NOW!

Tyler   *I love you.*

Judith   I don't love you. / I don't love you.

Tyler   / Where you going?

Judith   Emma's waiting in the car.

Tyler   That's it is it! *You and that cunt. You cooked it all up.* And now you're gunna play happy families.

Judith   She came to make sure I was alright!

Tyler   *Cunt.* Phone the cops. I don't care! They can put me in jail! Three meals a day. Good company. *Cunt.* Sticks and stones eh.

Judith *begins to call.*

Tyler   *Cunt!* CUNT! *CUNT!*

Judith   (*phone*) Hello. I'd like an officer sent to . . .

Tyler *charges.* **Judith** *alters stance and maces* **Tyler**. **Tyler** *coughs. sneezes and doubles over.* **Tyler**'s *hands come up to his face. He stumbles, falls and tries to suck in air in great hacking sobs.* **Judith** *puts a hankie over her mouth, so she can breathe.*

Harold *enters.*

Harold   What the bloody hell's going on here?

Judith   Tyler was drunk. He fell into something.

Harold   What's that smell?

Judith   What he fell into.

Harold, *coughing, helps* **Tyler** *to his feet and walks him to* **Jean**'s *chair.*

Harold   Yer awrite lad. Yer awrite. Yer awrite lad. Yer awrite. Yer awrite lad. Yer awrite. Yer awrite lad. Yer awrite.

Judith *goes to the door.*

Judith   (*calls*) Emma? Emma?

Blackout.

TV screen. Babies, swollen heads, stomachs, starving babies, screaming babies, dead babies.

Harold *watches the TV.*
Tyler *in* **Jean**'s *chair.*
Silence.

Jean *covers her ears.*

Sound: A War-Helicopter passes overhead.

Tyler *decides on a drink.*
Harold *lights his fag.*
Silence.

Judith   Emma? Emma! / *Emma!*

Judith *looks around and tugs up her shopping bags.*
Tyler *remotes out the TV.*

Harold   Y'dunt want it on then?

Tyler   D'you?

Harold *gestures a no.*

Harold   (*cough*) Music?

Tyler *gestues a no.*

Harold   Cup a tea?

Tyler   In a bit. / Imagine Harry. / Imagine one man has a dream. A dream of the World as it really is.

Harold   I allus thought yer dreamt t'get yer away from things.

Tyler   *It's not as it could be. Or shud be. But as it really is.* What'd happen t'that man?

Silence.

Tyler   He'd beg for innocence. But it wunt return. And e'd b'run t'ground we'sadness. And in the end his dream'd drive him mad.

Harold   I've never thought of it like that. But a. I suppose yer rite.

Tyler   And all because he dreams of the World as it really is.

Harold   I'll tell y'wun thing (*Cough.*) Yer a miserable bloody git lad!

A rum moment of shared amusement.

Tyler   Yeah. I suppose yer rite Harry.

Silence.

Tyler   D'yer still keep yer shears in't cubbie 'ole?

Harold   Aye.

Silence.

Harold *coughs.*

Harold   It looks like rain t'me.

Tyler   It's allus raining sumwhere in the World.

Harold   Is that so?

Silence.

Tyler   Cubbie 'ole y'say?

Harold   Aye.

Silence.

Tyler   *I think I'll make a start we those Roses!*

Fade out.

Hurricane Roses

And I knew that I was born with too many feelings. If I didn't find somewhere to put them, I'd just die of them.' The quotation comes from an earlier play by David Spencer, *Killing the Cat*, and I don't know a better or simpler introduction to his work and to what is important about it – namely its ability to portray (and to provoke) emotion.

I think too in this connection of what Seamus Heaney said about Ted Hughes:

Hughes' voice, I think, is in rebellion against a certain kind of demeaned, mannerly voice. I mean, the voice of a generation – the Larkin voice, the Movement voice, even the Eliot voice, the Auden voice – the manners of that speech, the original voices behind that poetic voice, are those of literate English middle-class culture, and I think Hughes' great cry and call and bawl is that English poetry is longer and deeper and rougher than that . . . It's a form of calling out for more, that life is more. And of course he gets back from that middle-class school the emnity that he implicitly offers. Ted may be accused of violence . . . but there is tenderness and reverence and seriousness at the centre of the thing.*

The unmannerliness, the calling out for more, the hostility that the work arouses, the fundamental tenderness, all these are features of *Hurricane Roses*.

Yet for all its power to move, there is nothing sensational about this writing – in the way that, say, the crowding atrocities of a Howard Barker are sensational. Jean's pain and her poverty are real things, as Harry's love and power to endure are real. They affect us because they are so directly, so honestly and so intimately created. When Tyler cries out against the circumstances of his mother's death, they have been demonstrated for us in all their actual injustice, their cruel grinding down and destruction of a human spirit.

There is nothing mean or pinched about these characters either, despite everything they have to bear. Here is one of Jean's inner monologues as she sits in her chair, crippled with arthritis:

I wasn't always like this. When. When then was now and me a girl. I'd pedal ten miles to dance six hours. Bike back ten too. But that was then. Now my bones with even the thought of bending burn. Petrification. Take a dictionary to the word. I did. Petrification. I'm turning to stone.

There is a grandeur and intensity here which makes the character truly *life-sized* – which is to say larger-than-life, as we all feel ourselves to be, looked at from our own perspective. This is what Raymond Williams meant when he spoke of 'a theatre of ordinary feeling raised to intensity and community by the writing of ordinary speech'.

It is this same mixture of ordinariness and intensity that characterises the writing for Judith and Tyler:

Judith   Tyler gets afraid! Want to run away. Typical.

Tyler   When *typical* means common or normal. It's normal to want t'run

from what y'fear. *Fear flight fight!* But since it's *typical you* to use *typical*
t'mean *typically male!* Tell me this. If women are so good at talking emotion.
How come more get depressed?

Judith   I don't know.

Tyler   *You don't know.*

Judith   But as you say. The first thing to do with what you fear is get
away from it. But women. Quite neurotically. Are socialized to cope with
fear.

Tyler   (*overlap*) *What are you on about?*

Judith   And if they do need to fight are they taught to hit back?

Tyler   (*overlap*) WHAT ARE YOU ON ABOUT?

Judith   (*overlap*) No! They're taught to turn aggression in on themselves.
And *that's depression.*

Tyler   WHAT THE FUCK ARE YOU ON ABOUT!

Judith   Tom!

Tyler   / Mum's been away from Dad for years now.

The sheer verve and actability of these exchanges hardly need commenting
on. What is worth noting is how the playwright has stepped clear of the trap
which says that because characters speak in dialect they are incapable of
having an intellectual life or talking about ideas.

Ideas – the play fairly crackles with them: socialism, feminism, male
violence, depression, gender, the New World order, treated not in some
superficial journalistic way, but focused through the burning glass of Judith
and Tyler's arguments. As their quarrelling approaches incandescence we
seem to see not just these two individuals one close and thundery evening, but
behind them the shadowy universal figures of late twentieth century Man and
Woman.

The play's ability to cover a lot of ground very quickly is a result of the
prodigious formal inventiveness that has gone into its making, as it struggles
to hold the balance between the inner and outer worlds of the characters.
There is dialogue, soliloquy, inner monologue, hallucination. There is the
subtle interplay between Jean/Harry in the past and Judith/Tyler in the
present, by which feeling becomes argument and argument feeling in a
mounting wave that finally breaks into the candle-lit encounter between the
two men, where all the themes of the play are drawn together.

There is also the brilliant use of the televisions to braid another strand of
colour through the play, the colour of memory, dream and nightmare, and the
external world returned as dreamscape. The opening image of the play with
the African babies and Tyler's grief and his mother in her funeral black and
Harry's anxious look towards his wife catapults the audience straight to the

heart of a complex web of thought and feeling. It's as arresting a beginning as any I know and in its density, speed and punch it has an unmistakably modern feel to it.

I hope I have said enough to indicate why I believe David Spencer to be the emotionally most powerful writer in the British theatre today. It is not, of course, a particularly comfortable position to occupy, at a time when so many productions have no higher aim than to be animated versions of a Harvey Nichols window display, and so much 'radicalism' (so-called) is nothing more than a middle-class critique of a middle-class view of the world. But with *Hurricane Roses* he has given us something to be grateful for: '*the freedom and power of real and substantial action and suffering*'.

John Burgess
London 1994

* Quoted from *Viewpoints: Poets in Conversation with John Haffenden* (London: Faber and Faber, 1981) and from *Winter Pollen* by Ted Hughes (London: Faber and Faber, 1994); reprinted by permission of Faber and Faber and Seamus Heaney.

David Spencer's first play, *Releevo* (Soho Poly, London 1987), won the 1986 Verity Bargate Award. In 1987 *Space* was given a platform production at the Cottesloe Theatre in the Royal National Theatre, London and a full production at the Soho Poly in 1988. Also in 1988, through the Thames Television Theatre Writers' Bursary, he was made writer in Residence at the Royal National Theatre Studio, where *Blue Hearts* was shown in 1989. *Killing the Cat* won the 1990 Verity Bargate Award and was premièred by the Soho Theatre Company at the Royal Court Theatre Upstairs in 1990. *Land of the Living* was produced at the Royal Court Theatre Upstairs, London in 1993.

The Life of the World to Come

Rod Williams

For Marc and Rachel

Characters

Jay Snyder	Financial Controller of 'New Hope Life Extension'. An accountant. Forties.
Morgan K. Dyson	An elderly suspension-holder.
Dr Kenichi Makoto	Chief Physician to the President. Noted surgeon and pathologist. Forties.
Marilyn Shriver	Head of Closure. A psychotherapist. A dedicated, idealistic woman. Mid-forties.
Mike Kuhn	A medic. Late twenties.
Don C. Strohmeyer	CEO of 'New Hope Life Extension.' Hard drinking, hard smoking, hard-boiled. Late fifties.
Steve Arbeit	Founder and President of 'New Hope Life Extension'. Good-looking, charismatic and naïve. Late thirties.
A Security Guard	

The Life of the World to Come was premièred by Midnight Theatre Company at the Almeida Theatre, London on 29 July 1994, with the following cast:

Jay Snyder	Garrick Hagon
Morgan Dyson	Philip O'Brien
Dr Kenichi Makoto	David Yip
Marilyn Shriver	Dearbhla Molloy
Mike Kuhn	Edmund Lewis
Don Strohmeyer	Stephen Greif
Steve Arbeit	Simon Burke
Security Guard	Robert Kendall
Donna Blumenthal	Frances Guthrie
Yorrick Blumenthal	David Browning

Directed by　Derek Wax
Designed by　Sue Plummer
Lighting by　Jon Linstrum
Sound by　John A. Leonard

Author's note

Cryonics was the brainchild of American Physicist, R C Ettinger, who first outlined the idea in a book called 'The Prospect of Immortality' in 1964. Ettinger proposed that by perfusing a body with glycerol at the moment of death and freezing to supercold temperatures, it should theoretically be possible to hold an individual in 'cryostasis', effectively buying time for medical advances to cure whatever was the cause of death. 'No matter what kills us,' he wrote, 'whether old age or disease, and even if freezing techniques are still crude when we die, sooner or later our friends of the future should be equal to the task of reviving and curing us'.

It was not long before Ettinger's message found followers and the first body (James Bedford, a Californian psychologist) was suspended in 1967. There are currently six for-profit corporations operating in the USA and over fifty 'patients' in suspension.

Act One

A tax haven in the Bahamas.

The Departure Lounge of 'New Hope Life Extension': a luxurious clinic designed for maximum solace and tranquillity in the last moments of the first 'lifecycle.'

Stage Right, French windows usher in the sound and smell of surf. There are doors both up and downstage left. To the rear, a pair of swing doors lead to the cryotorium.

A desk, laptop, printer, two chairs. A couch, drinks cabinet, refrigerator. A bowl of enhanced cherries.

Recessed into the rear wall, in a kind of Plexiglass sarcophagus, is the frozen cadaver of Company President, **Steve Arbeit**. *Unilluminated, he is totally invisible. There is no sign of the complex of engineering that maintains his body heat at absolute zero. In fact, the fixture draws virtually no attention to itself at all.*

Time: the present. Late afternoon.

On stage: **Jay** *and* **Morgan**.

Morgan *is wearing pink-checked golfing trousers.*
Jay *wears a lightweight suit.*

Morgan *is perusing the forecast in his personal suspension plan.*

Jay   . . . So by rolling you offshore, we've already killed income tax plus capital-gains tax. OK? (**Morgan** *nods*) OK – now that's the easy part. The real problem has always been how do we circumvent the rule against perpetuities? You see by depatriating to this particular haven, we get to take advantage of *Nyborg versus Nyborg*. I mean the High Chamber decision that cryogenic suspension does not constitute clinical death, but a 'temporary cessation of vital processes'. (*Pause.*) Three in one, Moe. We just liberated you from the twenty-one year rule against accumulations; the twenty-one year rule against perpetutities – and of course, death duties.

Pause.

Morgan   Because I . . . ?

Jay   Because you are *not legally dead*; you are merely . . . *incapax*. (*He lights a cigarette.*) . . . So: one hundred percent mitigation of tax; no ceiling on growth; no restriction on time; no on or offshore freeze; your initial investment free to compound exponentially. For as long as it takes.

Pause.

Morgan   11.3 per . . .

Jay   11.35!

Morgan   11.35 per cent from a managed currency fund?

Jay   That's correct.

Morgan   (*shakes his head*) It's astronomic.

Jay   It's a win-win arrangement, Moe. Every way you choose to look at it. The longer it takes; the richer you wake. There simply is no downside.

Pause.

Morgan   (*with some trepidation*) One hundred years?

Jay   You'd like an estimate on a hundred years?

Morgan   Would that be . . . ?

Jay   No problem. No problem at all. (*Computes on hand computer.*) We simply compound your initial investment of 99,000 dollars at 11.35% . . . to the power of one hundred . . . equals . . . over nine billion, three hundred and thirty three million, six hundred and sixty three thousand, three hundred and thirty dollars.

Morgan   And this is good for one millenium right?

Jay   No, this is a *perpetuity plan*, Moe. Your accumulator fund just goes on paying the liquid nitrogen costs for as long as it takes.

Morgan   So what if it takes a thousand years? Go on. Indulge me.

Jay   (*pause*) You want me to go mainframe?

Morgan   No, just – in your head.

Jay   In my head?

Morgan   Just a rough idea.

Jay   Mmmm . . . I think the operative concept in that case, Moe, is: 'the meek shall inherit the earth; but inflation is a variable.'

Morgan   No kidding.

Jay   Time *is* money. Moe. (*The phone rings.*) Just a nickel, please. (*He answers it.*) Life Extension. (*Passes phone.*) Your attorney.

Morgan   (*takes phone*) Uh huh . . . uh huh . . . That's great, Louis. You got the account number? (**Jay** *slides piece of paper under* **Morgan**'s *nose.*) Terrific, Louis. Yeah, it's beautiful. Paradise Island. 'Part from the mosquitoes. Pardon me? Voodoo? Now you knock that off or I'm gonna lay one on you! (*Laughs.*) OK Louis, I'm gonna . . . I'm gonna kickback now . . . yeah – love to all your loved ones too – so – so long now. Louis . . . yeah – miss . . . missin' you already too . . . Happy-happy . . . (*Phone down.*) He's wiring it.

Jay   Excellent.

Morgan   He can't see any wrinkles.

Jay   Blue sky, Moe. (*Over intercom.*) Ken, would you join us please?

Pause.

Morgan   It's unreal, Jay. You know? Spend your entire life . . . lookin' ahead . . . planning for the future . . . old age loomin' up over the horizon. And when the future finally arrives . . . what happens then? You plan for the future! It's kind of a joke.

Jay   (*pause*) That's life, Moe.

Morgan   I guess.

Dr Ken Makoto *enters from cryotorium drying his hands on a towel.* **Morgan** *rises to greet him.*

Jay   Doc, I'd like you to meet . . .

Makoto   (*passes* **Jay** *towel, takes* **Morgan**'s *wrist, feels his pulse*) No, no, no please . . .

Morgan   It's OK . . .

Makoto   Sit down . . .

Morgan   I'm OK . . .

Makoto   (*almost forcibly pressing him back into the seat*) Please!

Morgan   . . . Thank you.

Jay   Doctor Makoto is Chief Physician to the President of the Company.

Morgan   I'm honoured.

Makoto   Please. (*Puts out hand for file;* **Jay** *passes it.*)

Jay   He's also head of our cell repair and rejuvenation team.

Morgan   I've read all about your work.

Makoto   You have?

Morgan   In 'Fortune Magazine'.

Makoto   (*looking at file*) I appreciate your interest.

A fax feeds out.

Jay   Would you excuse me, please? (*Goes to fax.*)

Makoto   So how's the tumour?

Morgan   It's . . . it's there, I guess.

Makoto   Any dizziness? (**Morgan** *shakes his head.*) Bright lights? Burning rubber? No foul smells?

Morgan   Not right now.

Makoto   Excellent. I'm so pleased. (*Closes file; to* **Jay**) We're through.

Jay *removes bottle of champagne and three flutes, places them on a silver tray.*

Morgan   May I . . . may I ask a question?

Makoto   Of course.

Morgan   (*with great trepidation*) How long d'you think it'll take?

Makoto   How long is a piece of string?

Morgan   D'you think you . . . d'you think they'll have to tamper around with my genes much?

Makoto   Morgan, your DNA is like a degraded photocopy. To return you to the prime of life, obviously we're going to have to fill in some of the blanks.

Morgan   'Cause you know . . . I don't mind a few defects.

Makoto   Defects?

Morgan   I mean . . . I just don't want anyone to play God with me, you understand?

Makoto   God?

Morgan   Yes.

Makoto   I hope we can do better than that.

Jay   (*holding tray*) All set?

Makoto   Are we ready now?

Morgan   (*faint*) Will . . . will I be getting a pre-med?

Jay   Relax, Moe.

Morgan   I will?

Makoto   We're going to send you out on a good warm glow.

Morgan   Oh thank you.

Jay   Catnap, Moe.

Morgan   (*wiping his eye*) Thank you so much.

Jay   Could we consummate now?

Jay *places document in front of* **Morgan**, *opens Mont Blanc pen case.* **Morgan** *signs.* **Jay** *and* **Makoto** *countersign.* **Jay** *passes champagne.*

Jay   To your life in this world to come.

Morgan   To my life in this world to come.

Makoto (*simultaneously*) To his life in this world to come.

The toast.

Jay How's it feel, Moe?

Morgan A little spacey.

Makoto You're scared?

Morgan I guess . . . a little.

Makoto What of?

Morgan I . . . I don't know.

Makoto Yes you do. You're scared you're going to die.

Morgan (*a whisper*) I guess.

Makoto Don't be. We know what we're doing. OK? (*He downs champagne, checks watch.*)

Morgan Oh, thank you, Doc . . .

Jay (*picks up phone*) Catnap, Moe.

Morgan Thank you so much . . .

Makoto Just remember: fifty years for us; fifty winks for you.

Morgan Bless you.

Makoto *extends hand;* **Morgan** *takes it:* **Makoto** *fastens plastic tag around* **Morgan**'s *wrist.*

Morgan (*clinging*) D'you think I . . .

Makoto (*prizes off* **Morgan**'s *hand*) We *know* what we're doing.

He exits swiftly to cryotorium. As the double doors swing shut behind him we catch a glimpse of a gleaming, antiseptic corridor receding into the distance.

Morgan (*after him*) Thank you so much . . .

Jay (*on phone*) All set. (*Phone down.*) OK, Moe?

Morgan . . . Thank you . . .

He steers **Morgan** *into chair and wheels chair in front of TV screen.*

Jay You comfortable? Excellent. Would you like any cosmetic aid? (**Morgan** *shakes his head.*) I don't think so . . . OK, in a few minutes Dr Shriver'll be here to perfect closure . . .

Morgan What?

Jay For your final analysis – I know she'll . . . (*Phone rings;* **Jay** *takes it.*)

Hello yes . . . he is – just a dime, please . . . (*Phone down.*) Now you know what to do?

Morgan   (*nods*)

Jay   Valediction autocue runs along here OK – you want to fade up and fade out you press this button here . . . (**Morgan** *nods.*) You look great, Moe.

Morgan   I do?

Jay   Billion dollars.

Morgan   You . . . you too.

Jay   (*shakes*) Have a nice trip.

Morgan   Catnap.

Jay   Wiedersehen, Moe.

Morgan   So long.

Jay   'Missin' you already.'

Jay *exits left*. **Morgan** *sits motionless.*

Intercom   Mr Dyson?

Morgan   (*starts*) Hello?

Intercom   I have your loved ones on hold.

Morgan   Just a second, please.

Morgan *removes comb, hastily combs hair. He prepares smile and picks up handset.*

Morgan   (*holding champagne*) Howdy folks . . . hey partytime! Let's pop, let's party! (*Sound of popping corks emanates from handset.*) Go on. Spray it all around. Hey, Magnum force! This is one swell libation . . . Hi Johnny . . . hi Danny . . . Orangello . . . Lemongello . . . Hi Ester . . . pardon me, honey? Oh I'm . . . I'm (*Goes autocue.*) just steppin' along singing my song . . . Honey, believe me, it's the vacation of a lifetime . . . Total care with a capital T . . . hi Tommy boy . . . that's right sweetie, Grandpa's going to sleep now . . . 'cause Grandpa needs some medicine sweetie and sleep is still the best medicine that was ever invented . . . now you be a good boy now – will you promise me that? Will you make me a promise? Will you promise me to stay lucky? 'Cause whatever happens in this life you have got to stay lucky, now will you promise me that? (*His eyes prick tears.*) I know you will sweetie . . . and I believe it . . . hell, what is this: onion time! Put those onions away, you hear me? (*Sobbing can be heard from the handset.*) You promised me no onions . . . now put them away . . . (*Breaking.*) Oh Lord . . . and I love you too – I . . . I love you so much . . . feel so near home I can smell the biscuits baking . . .

He replaces handset, weeps openly.

Pause.

Marilyn   (*moved*) You were beautiful, Moe.

Unobserved, **Dr Marilyn Shriver** *has entered. She is holding a box of tissues.*

Morgan   They were crying.

Marilyn   Because they love you.

Morgan   I don't want them crying over me.

Marilyn   Tears of joy, Moe.

She proffers tissues; **Morgan** *takes one.*

Morgan   You . . . you think so?

Marilyn   I can feel the afterglow.

Morgan   You think I was OK?

Marilyn   You were beautiful, honey; you were very natural . . . you were very spontaneous . . .

Morgan   I was?

Marilyn   Just totally there.

Morgan   Bless you.

Marilyn   I was moved.

Morgan   (*dabs his eyes*) You know, I was dreadin' that moment above all else. 'Cause they was real sore I wouldn't have them come out here. 'Grandpa, you gonna killjoy your own exit party?' I'm no killjoy. I just . . . I just couldn't go through it.

Marilyn   That's OK, honey.

Morgan   Don't get me wrong, now. I love 'em more than words can say . . .

Marilyn   I know you do.

Morgan   I just couldn't go through with it.

Marilyn   I understand.

He crosses to couch.

Morgan   I guess that's about it. (*Pause.*) Besides, 13 air fares . . . adds up to a heck of a lotta dough at 11.35%!

Marilyn   (*somewhat taken aback*) Quite so.

The lighting has assumed a therapeutic hue. **Marilyn** *is holding a remote control to activate this.*

Morgan   Great surf.

Marilyn *turns the volume of the surf down a fraction.*

Pause.

Morgan (*with trepidation*) Are you gonna take me through now?

Marilyn Are you ready to go through now?

Morgan I believe so.

Marilyn Is there anything you would like to share with me?

Morgan I . . . I don't think so.

Pause.

Marilyn I sense a withhold.

Morgan A what?

Marilyn (*with great sympathy*) I think you're still afraid, Moe.

Morgan What of?

Marilyn Your fear.

Morgan My fear?

Marilyn Yes.

Morgan You think I'm afraid of my fear?

Marilyn I think you're so afraid of your fear you probably even fear your *fear* of fear. (**Morgan** *closes his eyes.*) It's OK, honey. We'll disappear it. That's why I'm here. We'll get to the source. Trust me.

Morgan *covers his face with his hands.*

Marilyn I'd like to go back to something we touched on in your penultimate audition. Now I'm going to ask you to download stuff that may be attached to some very painful memories, Moe. (*Pause.*) When Dr Gruber first shared the news of your malignancy . . . did she at any time use the 'C' word?

Morgan (*with difficulty*) She did not.

Marilyn Did she at any time use the 'D' word?

Pause.

Morgan I have no malignancy.

Marilyn . . . Did she prefer to utilise some other expression?

Morgan I have no malignancy, brain tumour, terminus – call it what you like. I'm 100% clear.

Marilyn (*with kindness and sorrow*) I only wish that were true.

Morgan Well it is true. So there is no need to wish.

Marilyn Honey, we all go through denial. And when I stand . . .

Morgan I am not in denial! I'm telling you the plain, unvarnished facts of my medical situation. I'm over the hump. Right now, I'm in pretty much top-notch shape.

Marilyn Morgan, I've seen your medical records. I've seen the X rays!

Morgan Well seeing is deceiving.

Marilyn It's the size of an egg, Moe!

Morgan It is an egg.

Marilyn It what?

Morgan We plugged the X-rays.

Marilyn You what!

Morgan Dr Gruber was a very helpful physician.

Marilyn (*pause*) Oh, my God . . .

Morgan A far-sighted physician.

Marilyn What've you . . . what are . . . !

Morgan A wise and understanding woman.

Marilyn What the hell are you saying! Moe? Why?

Morgan (*pause*) Because the time is ripe.

Marilyn Ripe?

Morgan 'Cause I promised myself many years ago . . . that if the actuaries were wrong . . . I would see them right.

Marilyn (*softly*) But why?

Morgan 'Cause . . . 'cause all my life I have always had a total-life perspective. See, one of the aspects of that was I didn't take pension till '85 – carried on working till I was sixty-eight years old – and believe me, it was not great work, it was not enriching work, it was it was punchin' time. Now we have had near on 6½% inflation the last fifteen years and I don't mind telling you it has nailed me to the wall . . .

Marilyn (*aghast*) You don't mean this.

Morgan Sweetheart, listen. My Medicaid topped out in '89, the last 5 years I have had medical expenses to the tune of a hundred thousand dollars! (*Pause*) So in the total perspective of my life the time has come for choice – as I always knew it would. 'Cause I'm goddamned if I'm gonna throw good money after bad on a no-win bet!

Marilyn This is not a financial decision.

Morgan   It is one of the aspects.

Marilyn   It can't be!

Morgan   Sweetheart, I have reaped. And now is the time to sow again.

Marilyn   But you still have so much to give.

Morgan   Not gonna be a burden on anybody.

Marilyn   You're not a burden, Moe. Honey, you are not! (**Morgan** *shakes his head.*) You're in great shape, you're very spruce, you're very spry . . .

Morgan   Marilyn, I am seventy-seven years old.

Marilyn   That does not have to be 'old'!

Morgan   It sure as hell feels it.

Marilyn   It's a state of mind.

Morgan   Sweetheart, my memory is gone; my thinking's all fogged up; my celltone is shot to shit . . . the death hormones are running wild in my veins. It's cold out here. I've done my dang. And I would like to go out. On a good, warm glow. (*Pause.*) Now will you take me through, please?

Marilyn   (*deeply conflicted*) Morgan, I . . . I don't . . .

Morgan   What?

Marilyn   We have an ethical code here.

Morgan   Ethical bullshine.

Marilyn   You have to be diagnosed terminal before we can admit you.

Morgan   I have been . . .

Marilyn   You're asking me to . . .

Morgan   To keep the faith.

Marilyn   Yes – but . . .

Morgan   You said I could trust you.

Marilyn   But we have this ethical code.

Morgan   I'm only gonna be incapax!

Marilyn   (*weak*) I know you are.

Morgan   You make it sound like I'm . . .

Marilyn   Because I . . . I have to know that somewhere inside . . . you're not about to embark on a one way trip, Moe. (*Beat.*) I have to know that. That this is a vote for life.

Morgan   Isn't it obvious!

Marilyn   Morgan, I don't know . . .

Morgan   Marilyn, I live life. I mean why the hell would I come here?
Because my life has been so goddamn fingerlickin' good! I took the mix every
day, swam, worked out – I musta ridden that freakin' lifecycle twice around
the world. 'Cause I have affirmed life all my life and I'm goddamned if I'm
gonna kick in now! Just lay there and wait? For the bugs and the lice and the
worms to come fetch me out? To have dirt thrown in my face? Hell no! You
can't 'come to terms' with death: you either win or you lose. And it can be
defeated. Because we have the brainpower, we have the technology and we
have turned back that tide of death and I believe in the life of the world to
come.

Marilyn   'Believe'.

Morgan   I sincerely do.

Marilyn   (*pause*) You have to know, Moe. In here. You have to know.

Morgan   (*faintly*) You cannot know.

Pause.

Marilyn   Moe, when Steve was . . .

Morgan   Honey, will you please let me go?

Marilyn   No, listen to me Moe . . . when Steve was dying of leukemia and
he was interviewed for *Time* magazine . . . they said 'Mr Arbeit, do you
sincerely believe cryogenic suspension is any different from death?' Do you
know what he said?

Steve v/o   (*the voice of a sick man*) No, I do not believe; I know. To say 'I
believe' is to confess 'I doubt'; to say 'I know' is to say 'I know'; and either
you know or you don't.

Marilyn   You see?

Morgan   (*shakes his head*)

Marilyn   He knew, Moe.

Imperceptibly slowly, **Steve Arbeit** *is illuminated.* **Marilyn** *activates these effects with
a remote control.*

Morgan   Sweetheart, you cannot know. You have to be lucky. In this life
you have to be lucky.

Marilyn   Don't you see?

Morgan   I'm sorry.

Marilyn   You can know.

Morgan   (*increasingly hot*) Then how? How did he know? How? I'm sorry, it rubs me raw. You expect me to swallow this . . . feelgood bullshine! 'I know'. That asshole. He didn't know squat! Now will you please let me go!

Pause.

Marilyn   I'd like for you to meet The President.

Steve *is now fully illuminated. His handsome features and perfectly preserved body seem luminous with vitality. Even at absolute zero his skin still glows with health.*

Morgan   (*hushed*) This is The President? (**Marilyn** *nods.*) This is Steve Arbeit! How long . . . how long has he been a patient here?

Marilyn   Since 1984.

Morgan   (*shakes head, smiles broadly*) God in Jesus. (*Pause.*) He's . . . very well-preserved.

Marilyn   He's perfect, Moe.

Morgan   (*moves closer*) My God . . . he is too . . . (*Laughs.*) he's perfect. (*Hushed.*) Perfect! (*Exultant.*) He is absolutely . . . He's perfect. Oh my . . . (*Transfixed, his joy now overwhelming.*) Oh my poor sweet . . . ohhh Jesus . . .

Marilyn *embraces him; he clutches her wildly.*

Morgan   (*catharting deeply*) Don't let me go.

Marilyn   I won't let you go.

Morgan   Please don't let me go!

Marilyn   I won't let you . . .

Morgan   Just don't let me go . . .

Marilyn   I won't let you go!

Morgan   Ohhh . . .

Marilyn   I'll be praying for you honey . . . I'll be praying for you every minute of the day.

Morgan's *sobbing eases;* **Marilyn** *sits him on couch.*

Morgan   (*holding her hands*) You have such beautiful hands. Soft hands. So soft and smooth. You know that? (*He touches her face.*) My God you are so young. So young and beautiful.

They embrace again. **Morgan** *rests his head on her breast;* **Marilyn** *looks over at* **Steve**; *she seems almost on the verge of tears herself.*

Morgan   (*finally*) Honey? (*Pause.*) Marilyn?

Marilyn   (*disilluminates* **Steve**) Are you ready now, Moe?

Morgan   (*totally clear*) I believe so.

Marilyn Are you sure?

Morgan I know now.

The lights flicker. They flicker again. An electric hum emanates from the tomb.

Morgan Sweetheart? Is something . . . ?

Marilyn *suddenly looks terrible. Offstage, far away, an alarm sounds.*

Morgan (*with rising panic*) Honey?

Marilyn (*inwardly*) Oh, my God . . .

He clutches hold of her.

Morgan What've I . . . ?

Marilyn No! (*She rushes out.*)

Morgan Marilyn . . . Come back . . . Don't leave me!

Steve *is suddenly reilluminated. A piercing alarm emanates directly from his tomb.*

Morgan NO!

Reeling with horror, he falls down behind couch.

Mike Kuhn *bursts in from cryotorium holding a liquid nitrogen canister. He yanks off panel at based of tomb, attaches it to a nozzle, empties canister and rushes back out.*

Don Strohmeyer, *wearing croquet whites and a panama hat, bursts in via French windows, throws croquet mallet aside, attempts to connect nozzle of empty canister to tomb. Dry ice sprays up in his face.*

Marilyn *re-enters down left with canister, attempts frantically to connect nozzle to tomb.*

The alarm cuts out.

Don (*coughing*)

Marilyn Oh . . .

Dry ice sprays in their faces. **Mike** *re-enters from cryotorium.*

Mike He's cool . . .

Don (*still struggling with nozzle*) Goddamnit this thing . . .

Marilyn (*coughing*)

Mike Guys . . . ?

Don He's cool?

Mike False alarm.

Marilyn (*sobbing with relief*) Oh God . . .

Don (*catching breath*) Croesus, Mike . . .

Mike   I just tanked him.

Don   Are you sure?

Mike   He's absolutely cool.

Don   Did you take his temperature?

Mike   It was only a thirty second out . . .

Don   Take his temperature.

Mike   But it's . . .

Don   Get me his fucken body heat, *now*!

Mike *exits to cryotorium.*

Marilyn   Thank God!

Don   Croesus wept!

They catch their breath.

Don   The hell is Ken?

Marilyn   Don, it's OK . . .

Don   Huh?

Marilyn   I can feel that he's OK . . .

Don *catches his breath. He rolls up shirtsleeve to elbow and slides watch, which has an expanding strap, from his wrist up to his forearm.*

Don   Shit!

Marilyn   Don, please . . .

Don   I'm in the red.

Marilyn   Now is not the time to get hysterical about blood pressure!

Don   (*punches chest*) Fucken kludge.

The phone rings.

Don   Shit! That'll be Breistman!

Marilyn   Will you uncoil!

Mike *re-enters holding thermometer with tongs; it is steaming with cold.*

Don   Read.

Mike   It's frosted over.

Don   Schnell! (*He takes tongs.*)

Mike   Hey, be careful . . .

Don *removes coin from pocket, attempts to scratch off ice.*

Mike   Please – be careful.

Don   (*grabs phone*) Bruce, hi. He's cool – no, it's just a temporary glitch with the thermostat – just 3 degrees – no, he looks great Bruce . . .

Jay *bursts in left, holding a canister, runs to tomb, attempts to connect nozzle;* **Mike** *and* **Marilyn** *intercede.*

Marilyn   He's cool.

Don   He looks perfect . . .

Jay   (*breathless*) Jesus God . . .

Don   Just 3 degrees . . .

Mike   He's cool.

Don   –196! . . . that's nothing . . .

Jay   You're sure?

Don   Uh huh . . . ? (*He is cut off.*)

Marilyn   He's OK . . .

Don   Shit . . .

Jay   He's absolutely cool?

Mike   (*holding case for thermometer*) Could you replace the . . .

Marilyn   Uncoil . . .

Jay   Did you take his . . . ?

Marilyn   He's cool, Jay.

Jay   You took his tempera . . .

Don   He's cool Jay, *cool*!

Jay   Hey, cool it . . .

Don   No, you cool it pal. That was our bankers!

Jay   It was?

Don   Hey, cool it . . .

Mike   Mr Strohmeyer?

Jay   Croesus . . .

Don   The fuck is Ken!

Mike   Could you please replace the . . .

Don   Huh? Where is he? I want my goddamn chief syringe to the President. Now!

Don *thrusts the thermometer into the casing; withdraws his hand; double-takes as he realises the thermometer has stuck to his fingers.*

Jay   Oh shit.

Don *reflexively tries to unstick it with his other hand; there is a hiss as it sticks too.*

Mike   Oh no.

Don   (*finally*) Ahhhhhh . . .

Stunned pause. **Marilyn** *goes to fridge, rummages in ice-box.* **Jay** *grabs a bottle of whisky and pours contents over* **Don**'s *hands. Hissing and steaming.* **Don**'s *face creases with pain.* **Mike** *peels off the thermometer, rushes out to cryotorium.* **Don** *is speechless with agony.*

Jay   Jesus Don, I . . .

Marilyn *returns with cold compress, presses it against his hands; several ice cubes fall out.*

Don   The hell kind of a joke is that! (*Hurls compress to ground.*)

Marilyn   Your hand is burned, Don.

Jay   Don, I'm real sorry . . .

Don   Will someone get me a band-aid?

Marilyn *hastens to exit left; as she passes the couch she suddenly freezes as she sees* **Morgan**.

Mike *re-enters from cryotorium with first aid box;* **Don** *grabs it, applies band-aids.*

Don   Disinfectant.

Jay   (*to* **Don**) Are you OK?

Mike   (*picks up whiskey bottle*) Will 'Red Label' do?

Jay   Can I get you a . . . ?

Mike   Marilyn?

Marilyn *is standing over* **Morgan** *in a kind of silent hysteria.*

Mike   (*rushes over*) Oh no.

Jay *crosses over.* **Don** *continues to apply band-aids.*

Jay   Moe . . . ? (*slaps his face.*)

Don   Gimme a break.

Jay   Hey senior . . . buck up . . .

Marilyn (*still motionless*) Moe . . . ?

Jay Oh shit. (*to* **Mike**.) His face is blue.

Mike Basic life support.

Marilyn Moe!

Mike CPR! Get the oxygen to his brain! (*Rushes to intercomm.*)

Marilyn *lunges in and frantically gives CPR.*

Mike (*over intercomm*) Sus team to O.R.

Jay Attaboy . . .

Mike *reclines chair, whizzes it over to* **Morgan**.

Mike Let's go, let's go!

Marilyn (*to* **Morgan**) Don't go . . .

They get **Morgan** *on chair.*

Jay Easy does it . . .

Marilyn Don't go!

Jay *and* **Mike** *whisk him through swing doors to cryotorium;* **Marilyn** *sits astride, pumping chest like crazy.*

Don *removes pills from side-table, hastily swallows some.*

Voices are heard outside French windows; **Don** *picks up croquet mallet, winces, goes to French windows.*

Don (*as he exits*) Rex, I am so sorry – no, just a temporary glitch with the thermostat . . . (*Inaudible question.*) on a four ball break . . . !

Eventually we hear sobbing from the cryotorium corridor.

Marilyn *enters weeping. She goes to tissue box.*

Jay *and* **Mike** *re-enter grim-faced.* **Mike** *holds two new canisters which he sets about fastening to fixtures each side of tomb.*

Jay *crosses to drinks cabinet, pours himself a shot, downs it, pours another.*

Marilyn He was such a sweet old man. He had such grace . . .

Jay Come on, Marilyn. We got him aboard.

Marilyn You know, his audition was so clear, his illumination was total, he was just like a baby in the womb . . . and I . . .

Jay Marilyn, please.

Marilyn . . . I pulled out on him . . .

Jay   We got him aboard! Yeah, it was tight; but he made the flight. We got the sus-team right in there.

Mike   He's right, Marilyn.

Marilyn   He had so much to give . . .

Mike   There was no anoxia, no hypoxia . . .

Marilyn   (*shakes her head*)

Jay   (*softly*) Marilyn, what are . . . what are you saying?

Marilyn   He was gone, Jay.

Jay   But we got the oxygen to his brain!

Marilyn   He was dead.

Jay   He was not dead! He was merely . . . incapax.

Marilyn   Oh bullshit. I can't stand that bullshit.

Jay   (*softly*) Marilyn, what are you saying?

Marilyn   I just want us to show a little respect is all!

Jay   You want to autopsy? Want us to call the coroner? Hold a . . . a wake?

Marilyn   Yes. Yes, I think we should hold a wake.

Jay   Throw dirt in his face.

Marilyn   Yes! (*she exits with tissues via French windows.*)

Jay   Marilyn? Marilyn? This is out of alignment.

Mike   She's just going through the grief process in her own way.

Jay   Shut up. And tidy up. (*exits left.*)

Mike   Asshole. Asshole!

Mike *picks up spent canisters, etc.*

Pause. **Makoto** *enters from cryotorium. He is wearing a surgical gown plus hi-tech surgical paraphernalia.*

Mike   Jesus, Doc . . . what the hell've you . . . ?

Makoto   (*hypertense*) Close the door. Lock the door!

Mike *shuts and locks door.* **Makoto** *removes paraphernalia. He is drenched in sweat.*

Makoto   Diary.

Mike *fetches recorder.*

Mike   Doc . . . ? We just had a . . .

Makoto   Date.

Mike   Date?

Makoto   Date!

Mike   (*checks desk calendar*) 15th.

Makoto   (*to diary*) 15/7/ . . . (*Presses pause.*)

Mike   We just had a condition red!

Makoto   Get me a sandwich. Peanut butter.

Mike *goes to fridge, makes sandwich.*

Makoto   (*to diary; cross-refers time with his watch*) 15/7/ . . . 15.45 . . . subject removed from storage at zero kelvin; white female, biological age seventy-five years . . . 16.10 . . . we contour the coefficients of expansion and program the microwave . . . 16.30: body temperature stabilised at 30 Celsius . . . we take her out of the oven . . . (*Presses pause.*) . . . get me a Bloody Mary.

Mike   Tabasco?

Makoto   (*to recorder*) Subject sustained severe systemic frostbite . . . though to the naked eye she's looking pretty good . . . 16.45: we begin blood transfusion . . . working in tandem with Bob Borg I restore normal blood-sugar, salts and ATP . . . 18.00: we unblock her metabolism . . . 18.10: CAT scan greenlights critical brainstructure . . .

Mike   (*whispers*) Motherfucker!

Makoto   Get my drink! (*To recorder.*) 18.15 . . . Borg hotwires her heart . . . 18.20: we raise body heat to 36 Celsius and delegate heart–lung back to brainstem – now in basic life-support mode – she's breathing, her reflexes are all there, her heart's there and . . . (*Suddenly emotional.*) I lean over to check her pupils and . . . and all of a sudden she smiles in my face.

Pause.

Mike   . . . Smiled?

Makoto   (*nods*)

Mike   She just smiled at you?

Makoto   She was so pleased to be back.

Mike   (*pause*) Oh, my God . . .

Makoto   It's a cliché, Mike. You know? You get so hooked on the DNA and the ATP and you just completely lose sight of the whole cadaver. (*Takes drink and sandwich.*)

Mike   . . . Unbefuckinglievable! (*Pause.*) You did it. Doc? You did it! You fucking genius . . .

Makoto   Those goddang ethicists are gonna have a hernia.

Mike   Ethicists?!

Makoto   That's right.

Mike   Come on!

Makoto   No Mike, it sucks. That I was forced offshore to do this vital work. The whole medical establishment – it totally sucks.

Mike   Don't you understand?

Makoto   And they come kissing up with a 'Fellow of the Royal' they can stick it right back up inside.

Mike   Doc?

Makoto   Kiss my ass!

Mike   Don't you understand! You did it! You just bought down the fire . . . !

Makoto   (*still in shock*) I did it.

Mike   . . . So what happened then?

Makoto   (*Pause*) When?

Mike   You're leaning over, she's smiling in your face . . . come on!

Makoto   Oh yah . . . she . . . that was when the complications started.

Mike   Uh huh?

Makoto   She went into shock.

Mike   Cold shock?

Makoto   Yah, she started to get the bends . . . we . . . it was . . . basically we had to terminate the operation. Did you put any vodka in this?

Mike   (*pause*) You refroze her?

Makoto   That wasn't a viable option.

Mike   No . . . ?

Makoto   After what she'd just been through? The collateral damage would of been catastrophic. She was too old, Mike.

Mike   She's dead.

Makoto   Her destiny is accomplished.

Mike   Jesus Christ. What . . . what are you going to do with the body?

Makoto   Cremate it.

Mike   Just . . . burn it?

Makoto   Do you have some kind of a problem, Mike?

Mike   I . . .

Makoto   Because you know we have been through this.

Mike   I'm sorry.

Makoto   We've handled the ethical objections!

Mike   (*ashamed*) Genius, Doc.

Makoto   (*sees canisters, etc*) What happened?

Mike   Your microwave oven just blew the main.

Makoto   . . . It what!

Mike   Only for ten seconds.

Makoto   Oh shit.

He takes remote, illuminates **Steve**.

Mike   It's OK.

Makoto   He's cool?

Mike   Plus 3 degrees.

Makoto   (*relieved*) Shit . . .

Mike   It was pretty hysterical.

Makoto   Why do we have to interface with these creeps? I mean, he's going to 'thaw out'? (*He fixes himself another Bloody Mary.*)

Mike   It's a neurosis.

Makoto   Three degrees above absolute!

Mike   Sick culture, Doc.

Makoto   Pathological.

Mike   And you've just blown it wide open.

Makoto   I wish.

Mike   What – you think he'll buy this?

Makoto   (*pause*) Buy what?

Mike   (*indicates environment*) This . . . shit?

Makoto   What do you mean?

Mike   He founded the company, Doc!

Makoto   I realise that.

Mike   He would of hated this corporate shit. I mean he was a regular guy, he never enshrined himself.

Makoto   So what.

Mike   So look at the guy! Does he look like an 'afterlife insurance' salesman! An accountant? He was a visionary, Doc. An immortalist. (*Quiet.*) And when he finds out the way these assholes've treated us . . . My God the suits will bleed.

Makoto   (*amused*) You think so.

Mike   So what are we waiting for?

Makoto   Waiting for?

Mike   Sure.

Makoto   What do you mean?

Mike   What do you think I mean?

Makoto   . . . You mean we . . .

Mike   Why not?

Makoto   We just . . .

Mike   Reanimate. Soon as you're ready. Say the word.

Makoto   He's company property.

Mike   So what are you going to wait'll it come down from the suits? Not in a thousand years.

Makoto   . . . Just take the body . . . ?

Mike   He's your patient, Doc. You're Chief physician; you make the decisions.

Makoto   (*looking at* **Steve**) He's so young. Perfect subject.

The locked door is tried. **Mike** *disilluminates* **Steve**.

Mike   Just say the word. (*He opens door.*)

Jay   Mike, in case you forgot, we have the Governor of the Island coming. Now are you gonna tidy up or what? (*Goes to drinks cabinet.*)

Mike *picks up discarded canisters, etc.* **Jay** *loads champagne flutes onto tray. He ignores* **Makoto**, *who is adding more vodka to his Bloody Mary.*

Mike   (*to* **Makoto**) I'll be in the lab. (*Exits to cryotorium.*)

Makoto   Run me a bath.

A fax feeds out. **Makoto** *finishes mixing drink, starts for cryotorium.*

Jay   (*avoiding his eye*) I think that's for you, Doc.

Makoto *takes fax.*

Makoto   Who's it from?

Jay   Our bankers.

Don *enters.*

Makoto   (*reads*) 19.975 . . . ? What's this?

Don   (*grave*) It's our stockprice, Ken.

He goes to drinks cabinet and pours himself a scotch. He is now wearing a white tuxedo with an embroidered waistcoat. His hands are plastered with band-aids.

Makoto   So what?

Don   (*to* **Jay**) 'So what?'

Makoto   Is this unusual?

Don   Unusual, Jay?

Jay   A twenty million dollar wipe-out?

Makoto   Twenty million!

Jay   Well it doesn't happen every day.

Don   (*pointed*) Then it's not every day the President gets a temperature is it, Ken?

Makoto   (*pause*) I blew the main?

Jay   Condition red.

Makoto   Shit. This leaked out?

Don   That's right.

Makoto   Just 3 degrees above absolute?

Don   Take a look.

Makoto   (*reads*) But it's nothing.

Don   Just cost us twenty million bucks.

Makoto   This is insane.

Jay   Price-sensitive information, Doc.

Makoto   But thermodynamic instability doesn't begin till −85! Come on. You know that. He was in absolutely no danger.

Don   (*beat*) No sweat.

Makoto   Believe me.

Don   I do.

Makoto   He's absolutely cool.

Don   See, that's not really where we have a problem, Ken.

Makoto   . . . No?

Don   No. Our problem is what the fuck are you doing with a twenty megavolt industrial microwave in the first place?

Pause.

Makoto   R and D.

Jay   You need 20,000 volts to defrost a mouse?

Makoto   (*beat*) You know, I came here on a carte blanche basis. What happens in the lab is my responsibility. (*Starts for cryotorium.*)

Don   I need an answer, Doc.

Makoto   What do you think?

Don   That's why I asked.

Pause.

Jay   You've been thawing out the stiffs!?

Makoto   I have revitalised one of the bodies, yes.

Jay   Oh shit.

Don   You've been guinea-pigging with our patients!

Makoto   That's correct.

Jay   This is unconscionable!

Pause.

Don   So what happened? Aren't you gonna tell us about it?

Makoto   We achieved several historic seconds of full vitality before terminating the experiment.

Jay   Oh, my God . . .

Don   'Full vitality.'

Makoto   That's right.

Jay   You fucking . . . !

Don   Shut up. And what happened after you 'terminated the experiment'?

Makoto   We disposed of the body.

Don   Disposed of?

Makoto   Cremated it.

Jay   You cremated it!

Makoto   'That's right.'

Jay   (*pause*) This is culpable homicide.

Makoto   Oh bullshit.

Jay   You just killed one of our patients, Doc.

Makoto   I just gave them life!

Don   You just blew their only chance of it.

Makoto   So the others will now have that chance for real. 'No greater love', Don! Yes, I was prepared to take risks – risks you would never of had the balls – and they've paid off!

Jay   (*pause*) You fucken Nazi.

Makoto   Oh bullshit. Bullshit!

Don   You're fired.

Makoto   (*pause*) I'm having a bath.

Jay   No, you're taking a shower.

Makoto   Don't you understand?

Jay   It's over, Doc.

Makoto   What this means for the business!

Don   Get him outa my sight.

Jay   Would you please vacate the premises?

Makoto   Have you no idea? (*Pause.*) What we . . .

Jay   You're fired, Doc.

Makoto   Don't be ridiculous.

Jay   (*over intercom*) Security, we have a tresspass in the Departure Lounge.

Makoto   What the hell are you doing!

Don   Get this goddamn Nazi outa my sight!

Jay   You're fried.

Makoto   This is absurd!

Jay   (*takes* **Makoto***'s arm*) Now how you gonna go: sunny side up; or hard over!

Makoto *suddenly sends* **Jay** *sprawling, darts for cryotorium;* **Don** *intercepts; there is a scuffle,* **Makoto** *rips* **Don**'s *waistcoat.*

Don   Sonofabitch!

Jay *comes forward and punches* **Makoto** *hard in the diaphragm; he collapses.*

Jay   That's on behalf of our stockholders, Mengele.

A security guard enters, takes hold of **Makoto**, *almost lifting him off the floor*

Guard   Ok, mon . . .

Don   Throw him the fuck out.

Makoto   (*winded*) You idiots . . .

Mike *enters from cryotorium.*

Mike   (*stunned*) Doc?

Jay   Fucking Nazi.

Mike   Stop!

Don   There's a plane at eight o'clock . . .

Mike   What are you doing!

Guard   Over easy, mon . . .

Don   You're still on the island by midnight I'm gonna have you charged with homicide. Understood?

The **Guard** *exits with* **Makoto** *followed by* **Mike.**

Mike   You can't do this! Come back!

Don   Shit.

Jay   You OK?

Don   My waistcoat.

Jay   Oh no.

Don   You handle our guests a minute?

Jay   Leave it to me.

Pause.

Don   Fucken Japs.

Jay   I always thought he was fishy.

Don   Fully fledged Frankenstein, huh?

Jay   You think we should check the lab?

Don It'll wait.

Jay Don't we oughta check what was going on back there?

Don We know what.

Jay I mean, case there's something we don't know.

Don Like what?

Jay Like . . . I mean, in case he was nearing some kind of . . . breakthrough?

Don Breakthrough!?

Jay Well – yeah.

Don (*beat*) You disappoint me, Jay.

Jay (*ashamed*) Don, I'm sorry, I . . . I have these dreams . . .

Don So wise up. (*Exits down left*).

Jay . . . Sorry.

Jay *crosses to drinks cabinet, picks up tray.* **Mike** *re-enters.*

Mike (*near tears*) Assholes! Well he'll be back, pal. Your card is marked, you hear me?

Jay Shut the fuck up.

Mike No, you're fucked. All of you. You're carbon. (*Exits to cryotorium.*)

Jay *exits up left with tray.*

Marilyn *enters via French windows, adjusting her earrings. She is wearing a white ballgown. She looks rather washed out. She picks up remote, illuminates* **Steve***, prays.*

Makoto *appears at French windows. His coat is torn and he has a bloody nose. He sneaks through to the cryotorium, unobserved.*

Don *re-enters, buttoning up a new waistcoat.*

Don (*clears throat*) Marilyn? Marilyn?

Marilyn (*disilluminates tomb, turns to him with a smile: she seems refreshed*) Sorry I'm late.

Don (*beat*) Thought you were gonna to stand me up.

Marilyn This zipper was a killer.

Don Well it was worth the wait.

Marilyn You like it?

Don You look great.

Marilyn   Thank you.

Don   Real vestal.

Marilyn   Get off.

Don   (*attempting to attach button-hole*) Shit.

Marilyn   Let me.

Marilyn *attaches button-hole;* **Don** *ties his bow-tie.*

Don   (*pause*) You know I was thinking . . . when this is over . . . we could drop by the Condo and watch the sun rise over the reef.

Marilyn   (*brittle*) That would be nice.

Don   Shoot some shark maybe.

Marilyn   (*changing subject*) What happened to your waistcoat?

Don   My waistcoat?

Marilyn   With the gold buttons?

Don   Oh yeah. Doc just took a fall. Couldn't bear to let go.

Marilyn   He what?

Don   He just got fried.

Marilyn   What the hell for!

Don   He blew the main.

Marilyn   But . . . but surely that was an accident?

Don   Honey, he just wiped twenty million off our stock!

Marilyn   But what about his work, his research?

The door is tried up left.

Don   What about it?

Marilyn   Flash thaw – I mean his work on genetic clocks . . .

Don   Pie in the sky.

Marilyn   What are you talking about? Don? He's developed a fruit fly capable of living one hundred and fifty years!

Don   No shit.

Marilyn   It's absolutely vital to us!

Don *unlocks and opens door:* **Jay** *puts his head round; sound of party from adjacent room.*

Jay   Don?

Don   Two cents.

Jay   (*nervy*) It's Makoto.

Don   Huh?

Jay   Security think he may of snuck back on the premises!

Don   Have him placed under arrest.

Jay   He's a black belt, Don.

Don   Just deal with it, OK?

Jay   . . . Right.

Jay *closes door.* **Marilyn** *is sitting on the couch; she looks most unhappy.*

Don   (*finishing bow-tie*) OK: our mission this evening; basically, we're gonna eat a plate of prime-cut sphincter and relish every mouthful of it. OK? So don't forget, dances three, five and eight you're booked for the Governor, Finance Officer and Minister of Tourism. So please: no politics, no psychobabble; just look radiant, talk croquet and pray God the deal is in the bag. OK? (*Pause*) Marilyn? Let's party.

Marilyn   (*shakes her head*).

Don   Marilyn?

Marilyn   This is . . . this is not what I had been led to expect.

Don   . . . What isn't?

Marilyn   This.

Don   What are you talking about?

Marilyn   I thought this was supposed to be a ball.

Don   It is a ball.

Marilyn   You just gave me a mission statement.

Don   So?

Marilyn   Kissing up to Rex is not my idea of a ball.

Don   It's not my idea of a ball.

Marilyn   Then why do you . . . ?

Don   Whoa whoa whoa whoa whoa – what do you think I would socialize with these blimps? Play croquet with them?

Marilyn   That's what you do.

Don   Honey, for the love of Croesus, this is a fifteen million dollar development! Half the goddamn island. Get planning permission for this –

we'll be viable for ten million bodies, one hundred million pekinese – and we are gonna make the pyramids look like something out of a Christmas cracker! That means we gotta kiss ass to the local baboons from time to time, that's Hospitality!

Marilyn   (*pause*) I'm sorry, Don.

Don   What are you gonna stand me up!

Marilyn   This is not my job.

Don   You do not have a job; you have an assignment.

Marilyn   That's what I mean.

Don   OK then.

Marilyn   I can't go through with it any more.

Don   Go through with it . . . ? (*Beat.*) Honey, have you got . . . are you in apple time?

Marilyn   No.

Don   Is it . . . is it the zipper?

Marilyn   No!

Don   Then what the hell are you talking about?

Marilyn   (*beat*) It's everything.

Don   What?

Marilyn   The whole culture here.

Don   Culture?

Marilyn   Yes.

Don   (*sitting beside her*) Uncoil.

Marilyn   (*with difficulty*) You know why I came here, Don.

Don   Remind me.

Marilyn   'Cause I was so disillusioned of 'The Lightship'. Of that whole approach.

Don   Uh huh.

Marilyn   'Let go of the body'. 'Go for the light'. When all they're actually doing is giving people an excuse not to fight. And really getting off on it. Goddamnit, I will not be midwife to the Grim Reaper! You can choose life.

Don   You chose it.

Marilyn   There has to be a better way.

Don   You found it.

Marilyn   'Cause I don't care how old or sick you are you can still vote for life. (*Beat.*) So when I found out about Steve it was like the scales fell from my eyes. I mean everything he said was just totally where I was at. That we don't have to let go of the body! And I knew – and this is going to sound absurd, Don . . .

Don   No – no . . .

Marilyn   . . . Because I am not a psychic person, I don't even believe in any of that – but I knew, that in some wierd way I had actually been chosen to continue his work.

Don   And that is what you are doing!

Marilyn   (*smiles sadly*).

Don   Marilyn . . . honey, you are a rock. I mean you're absolutely vital to us.

Marilyn   I'm sorry.

Don   You just gotta get to know the business a litle more is all.

Marilyn   But this is not it.

Don   Not what?

Marilyn   This is not in alignment with Steve's purpose.

Don   What isn't?

Marilyn   The whole way you're running this company.

Don   What do you got – some hotline to the hereafter?

Marilyn   (*evasive*) I have his tapes.

Don   Well I'll be blown – so do I.

Marilyn   And when did you last listen to them?

Don   Marilyn, may I remind you: I have been running this business for over nine years. You only just came aboard the last six months!

Marilyn   Then maybe you've lost sight of it.

Don   No, maybe you can't see just how well we're doin'! (**Marilyn** *shakes her head.*) Well it's a fact.

Marilyn   I'm sorry.

Don   (*hardening*) Marilyn, when Steve went on ice . . . when I took over in 1985, you know where this company was actually at?

Marilyn   Yes, it was early days.

Don   Early days.

Marilyn   It was small scale.

Don   It was strapped for space . . . strapped for cash . . . locked into a tiny Californian market niche . . . I mean it was virtually being run out of a garage! The last nine years we have created this firm one of the greatest success stories of the decade! We've broadened the appeal, redefined the USP: we laid down more bodies the last quarter 'n . . .

Marilyn   Bodies!

Don   Patients.

Marilyn   You see?

Don   . . . So I'm not a people guy, I'm a marketing and operating guy . . .

Marilyn   Don't you see?

Don   Sure I do.

Marilyn   Then where is it?

Don   What?

Marilyn   The prayer.

Don   Prayer?

Marilyn   Yes, where is the prayer?

Don   Well that is one of the reasons we hired you, Marilyn. To bring a touch of feminine spirituality into the organisation.

Marilyn   You expect me to shoulder this all alone?

Don   Not exactly.

Marilyn   Then why don't you pray?

Don   I do pray.

Marilyn   You pay lip service.

Don   Honey, I'm a busy man.

Marilyn   You don't care.

Don   Sure I care.

Marilyn   And why did you just fire our best hope of a breakthrough?

Don   . . . Breakthrough?

Marilyn   Our best hope in ten years!

Don   (*pause*) Marilyn, you have to face the facts . . .

Marilyn You see, you can't answer me.

Don I mean haven't you ever asked yourself . . . ?

Marilyn Just marketing talk . . .

Don (*cutting in hard*) So let's cut the crap. Let's look at some cold hard facts.

Marilyn . . . I'm listening.

Don Since 1975 . . . when our first ever client went on ice, how many patients have been successfully resurrected?

Marilyn That does not . . .

Don How many? (*Forms zero.*) That many.

Marilyn That does not prove anything.

Don Just a ducat. And how many Suspension-Holders worldwide took 'Red Sky' in the last financial year?

Marilyn (*with sudden trepidation*) What are you saying, Don?

Don Twenty five thousand!

Marilyn What do you . . . ?

Don What does that say? What does that say to you?

Marilyn What does it say to you?

Don It says, Marilyn, that our Unique Selling Point is *not* what it would appear to be.

Marilyn (*pause*) I don't understand.

Don Yes you do.

Marilyn (*sickening*) What are you . . . ?

Don What do our patients want, huh? What do they really want? A second Life-cycle? Unlimited wealth? Perpetual wellness? Absolutely. But what do they really want? When it comes to the clinch? (*Pause.*) They want out.

Pause.

Marilyn Are you serious?

Don What do you think?

Marilyn You think . . . this is all just . . .

Don Consecrated Euthanasia.

Pause.

Marilyn (*spinning*) . . . Oh God . . . oh, my God . . .

Don   I'm sorry to disillusion you.

Marilyn   Is that . . . is that all this is for you?

Don   It's the market we're in.

Marilyn   Our whole research program . . . it's just . . .

Don   Pure science fiction.

Marilyn   How can you believe that!

Don   I'll believe it when I see it.

Marilyn   What are you a . . . a vulture?

Don   I don't think so.

Marilyn   Then what?

Don   It's a job.

Marilyn   To prey on the old and sick . . . ?

Don   We give our patients what they want.

Marilyn   You 'invest' their money!

Don   And they get what they pay for! We add value. We take the sting out of it, Marilyn.

Marilyn   You deceive them.

Don   They know the score.

Marilyn   Like hell they do!

Don   Then maybe I'm wrong – hell, maybe viability *is* possible maybe they can repeal the law of gravity – and they can have their compound interest, they can inherit the earth just as soon as it happens – not in my lifetime.

Unobserved, a trickle of dry ice emanates from the base of the tomb.

Marilyn   (*gathering her things*) I have nothing to say to you.

Don   Don't take that moral tone with me. We *add value*. We give our customers a good death. They die well. Club class. That means a lot.

Marilyn   You sicken me.

Don   Quit deceiving yourself, Marilyn.

Marilyn   I can't bear to be in the same room as you.

Don   Yes you can.

Marilyn   You goddamn fascist!

Don   Don't deny the chemistry.

Marilyn   Are you out of your mind!

Don   Listen to your hormones, Marilyn.

Marilyn   You sicken me, Don. You understand? You physically repel me! I can't bear to even . . . !

Don   (*of* **Steve**) It's not me you can't bear to be with – it's him!

Marilyn   What did you say?

Don   That's right.

Marilyn   How dare you . . . ?

Don   Well you can fantasize as long as you like, he's not coming back . . .

Marilyn   (*smashes him in the face*) How dare . . .

Don   He's meat, Marilyn . . .

Marilyn   (*strikes him again*) Say that agai . . .

Don   (*gripping her*) And meat is meat is meat!

Marilyn   Ah . . .

He has crushed her to her knees. **Don** *sniffs, suddenly notices the ice, grabs remote, illuminates tomb: it is empty. Far away, an alarm sounds.*

Don   What! (*instinctively tries to get* **Steve** *back with the remote.*)

The thermostat suddenly explodes with a shower of sparks. Dry ice gushes from the tomb.

Marilyn   (*a whisper*) Alleluia . . .

Jay *rushes in holding a canister.*

Jay   Guys . . . ? Oh shit.

Don   Croesus . . .

Marilyn   (*exultant*) Alleluia!

And as the alarm fills the auditorium . . .

Blackout.

Act Two

The same. Some hours later. The tomb stands empty.

Jay *enters from left. He is carrying a body-bag which would appear to contain a rigormortised cadaver. He heaves it onto the couch, catches his breath. He crosses up left, closes and locks door.*

Don *enters from cryotorium looking ashen-faced. He goes to drinks cabinet, starts to pour himself a shot.*

Jay . . . Well? Did you . . . ? (*Faint.*) Is there . . . Is there any sign of life?

Don *retches, swiftly exits down left.*

Jay Oh shit.

Marilyn *enters from cryotorium in tears. She picks up tissue box and exits via French windows.*

Jay Well that's promising.

Makoto *enters from cryotorium, goes to table, picks up diary, sits at workstation, ignoring* **Jay**.

Jay (*pause*) So how's your new patient, Doc?

Makoto (*in time with fingers*) I'd say the President was coming along . . . just . . . fine.

Pause.

Jay So where are you at?

Makoto We've restored normal blood sugar, salts and ATP . . . begun preliminary tissue repair . . . restored heart–lung back to brain-stem . . .

Jay Brain-stem.

Makoto That's correct.

Jay He's comatose?

Makoto Of course.

Jay So what are his neurological prospects?

Makoto (*prints data*) There will be deficits.

Jay Deficits.

Makoto What do you expect?

Jay What do I expect?

Makoto He's suffering from severe, long-term, whole body frostbite!

Jay Don't say.

Makoto Are you being snide?

Jay Snide!

Makoto Then what do you expect?

Jay Wait, wait, wait, wait a nickel: you break and enter; you burglarize the President; you indulge your . . . necrophilic fantasies . . . and I'm . . . !

Makoto (*prints out data*) I think you should uncoil.

Jay And I think you should get yourself a lawyer.

Makoto The President is coming along fine.

Jay Cop a plea of diminished responsibility.

Makoto Just don't expect miracles. (*Picks up diary and exits to cryotorium.*)

Jay Well you better pray for one, Doc. 'Cause if he doesn't pull through you are going down for murder.

Don *re-enters wiping his face with a towel, returns to drinks cabinet.*

Jay (*after* **Makoto**) Sicksicksick. Are you OK?

Don Oh boy. (*Downs shot.*) Oh boy oh boy. (*Pours another.*)

Jay You look real pale. You need some sugar?

Don Sugar?

Jay For your blood-sugar?

Don Got any blood? (*Downs shot.*)

Jay (*pause*) So? Did you see him? (**Don** *nods.*) Was there . . . was there any sign of life?

Don Just meat.

Jay You sure? (*beat.*) Doc said they got heart–lung going. Says they're getting . . .

Don Jay, they can put in what they like; they can get out what they like . . .

Jay (*anxious*) Brainwaves . . . ?

Don He's deader 'n shit.

Pause.

Jay Well that's clean.

Don Clean?

Jay   Well it's a result.

Don   Wait'll the Dow opens.

Jay   No problem.

Don   It's over, Jay. Meltdown. And if you're about to tell me it's not a crisis it's an opportunity, don't.

Jay   We deny it.

Don   Deny it?

Jay   Absolutely.

Don   (*gestures towards empty tomb*) How can we deny that?

Jay   We have deniability.

Don   Jay, you have a promising career ahead of you . . .

Jay   Listen Don . . .

Don   I were you I'd start thinking CYA . . .

Jay   We have a cover.

Don   'Cause when the suits come wind this place up your 'Financial Controllership' is coming under some very close scrutiny, Jay.

Jay   Would you . . . ?

Don   You wanna squat hot; squat hot: I'm outa here.

Jay   Will you shut up and listen?

Don *pulls up sleeve and slides up watch to check blood pressure.*

Jay   Remember I took that vacation down the Valley of the Kings?

Don   In Egypt?

Jay   That's right. They were past masters. Anyway, I became kind of intrigued by the processes of mummification. Which apparently was a bitch even for those guys. So round about the third Dynasty – this is over 2000 BC, Don . . .

Don   I'd love to see your album . . .

Jay   – Apparently some of their heads started to ask: 'Do we really have to go on pouring away all this food and booze ad infinitum when we could finish the job once and for all with some stone fruit and rock cakes? And that led them on to the thought that maybe they could spare themselves all this anxiety about mummification by commissioning a stone replica of the guy so that if the mummy started to decompose, the soul would like hop out of the mummy and into the backup statue.

Don Well, that's great.

Jay Isn't it?

Don A seminar in Egyptology.

Jay I don't know dick about Egyptology, Don, I'm an Accountant. But this has got to be the oldest insurance policy in the world!

Don So what?

Jay I figured we should have it too.

Don Have it too. Are you out of your mind? What the hell use is that now? Huh? What can these primates teach us now? What did they know, who did they worship? The sun?! Due respect, Jay, there has been some progress in four millenia.

Jay beckons **Don** over to couch. He unzips bodybag to reveal a waxwork replica of **Steve Arbeit**. It looks identical to the frozen cadaver in act one.

Don (speechless) Jesus God. He's . . . he's perfect. He's absolutely perfect. (Pause.) Who the . . . who the . . . ?

Jay Tussauds.

Don (of **Jay**) Goddamn ubermensch!

He unzips bag further, runs his hand further down the torso.

Jay Remember when that came out about Lenin?

Don Lenin!?

Jay He was a waxwork, Don. All those schmucks queueing up in Red Square!

Don No shit.

Jay Anyway, that decided me. (Beat.) You buy it?

Don Is it my imagination . . . or did they downsize his pecker?

Jay I fear they may of. Way of the Greeks.

Don No – I approve.

Intercom Mr Strohmeyer?

They start. **Jay** grabs waxwork, slides it under the couch. **Don** disilluminates tomb.

Intercom Mr Strohmeyer?

Don (pressing button) What?

Intercom Rex would like to know if you're going to join them for breakfast?

Don Absolutely. (Checks watch.) Shit.

Jay   There goes planning permission.

Don   Tell 'em I'll be right with. (*Removes pills from sidetable.*)

Jay   Right. (*Starts for exit.*) We're just going to leave that lunatic at large in there?

Don   He can fry later.

They exit stage left. **Don** *removes key, locks door from far side.*

Steve Arbeit *enters from cryotorium, reeling with shock, pain and exhaustion. He is naked save for a plastering of tubes, tapes, etc. All his extremities are bright red.*

Voices are heard in the cryotorium corridor. **Steve** *stumbles over to locked door, tries desperately to open it. As the voices get nearer, he ducks down on couch as* **Makoto** *and* **Mike** *burst into the room.*

Makoto *picks up length of medical tubing, tries to work out which way* **Steve** *has gone.* **Mike** *tries doors up and down left.*

Mike   This way!

They exit down left.

Steve's *eye falls on phone. He grabs it, speed-dials. Shivering, he notices discarded bodybag, pulls it up to his waist.*

Steve   (*quietly*) Police? Police? Hallo . . . ? (*slams down phone, speed-dials again. He winces as his hand slides over his chest.*) . . . my nipples! . . . the fuck've they . . . (*on phone.*) Hallo . . . ?

Marilyn *re-enters via French windows, halts as she hears* **Steve**; *gasps, turns away, unable to believe her own eyes.*

Steve   No . . . no, spik Inglese? Speak English? What? Look, this is an emergency, pal . . . then speak the motherfucking tongue! (*Near tears.*) I'm being tortured here . . . *now get me the Police!* What credit card!? You fucking . . . ! American Express! Now get me some help! Wait . . . wait, hold it . . . (*His hand slides to crotch; voice emanates from handset.*) Oh, my God . . . I said hold it, will you, just hang on a second! (*drops handset, peers at crotch.*) Oh no . . .

Marilyn   (*still half convinced he is an hallucination*) Steve?

Steve   My dick . . .

Marilyn   (*touching him*) Is it you . . . ?

Steve   I can't feel my dick!

Marilyn   (*joy, shock and repulsion*) It's really you?

Steve   This is not my dick.

Marilyn   Steve . . . ?

Steve   Get my dick back.

Marilyn   You came . . .

Steve   (*screaming*) Get my dick back!

He is weeping hysterically.

Marilyn   You came back?

Steve   My balls . . .

Marilyn   (*near tears*) Oh Steve . . .

Steve   Why? Why have you done this?

Marilyn   (*inwardly*) Forgive me . . .

Steve   I come in for a blood test . . .

Marilyn   How could I have . . . !

Steve   You fuckin' napalm my insides . . .

Marilyn   You came back!

Steve   I can't feel my pecker, my toes, my balls, you fried my nipples . . .

Marilyn   You're alive . . .

Steve   Alive!

Marilyn   You didn't die . . .

Steve   Oh, my God . . .

Marilyn   You came back!

Steve   Help me.

Marilyn   God bless you . . .

Steve   You've got to help me . . . What the hell are you doing . . . ?

Marilyn   (*coming to*) What am I . . . ?

Steve   Stop it.

Marilyn   What are *you* doing?

Steve   You've got to get me out of here . . .

Marilyn   Why aren't you in bed?

Steve   Your hands are so cool.

Marilyn   You're on fire!

Steve   (*holding her hand to his forehead*) Please . . .

Marilyn   Let me get help . . .

Steve   Help?

Marilyn   Let me get a doctor.

Steve   No!

Marilyn   (*trying to get up*) Steve, please!

Steve   No way.

Marilyn   You don't understand . . .

Steve   Shut up!

Voices can be heard.

Marilyn   You're delirious . . .

Steve *clamps his hand over her mouth and pulls her down onto the couch.*

Makoto *and* **Mike** *re-enter left.* **Makoto** *sees another length of tubing, picks it up.*

Mike   (*sees open French windows*) Beach!

They rush out through French windows.

Steve   (*softly*) Now listen close . . .

Marilyn   Steve, please . . .

Steve   Tell me your name.

Marilyn   Marilyn.

Steve   I need your help.

Marilyn   You need medical help.

Steve   No.

Marilyn   You're delirious!

Steve   What I need . . .

Marilyn   Steve, please . . .

Steve   (*gripping her arm*) Are you gonna help me or what?

Marilyn   At least let me get you some pyjamas!

Steve   Are you prepared to . . .

Marilyn   Ouch!

Steve   Are you prepared to help me!

Marilyn   I'd do anything for you.

Steve   Anything?

Marilyn   Anything!

Steve   Are you willing to affirm that?

Marilyn   Yes.

Steve   You are?

Marilyn   Willing!

Steve   Will you get me some clothes?

Marilyn   I can get you some croquet whites.

Steve   Great. I would love some croquet whites.

Marilyn   And a pair of croquet shoes?

Steve   Fantastic.

Marilyn   Uncoil, honey.

Steve   (*taking hand*) Lifepact?

Marilyn   (*kisses him on the mouth*) Lifepact!

She goes out down left.

Steve   What kind of a hospital is this?

Voices are heard outside French windows. He ducks down again. **Makoto** *enters followed by* **Mike**.

Makoto   (*of* **Steve**) Stupid idiot . . .

Mike   Come on, Doc . . . We'd've found the body . . . we'd found the body . . .

They exit to cryotorium.

Marilyn *re-enters with croquet whites, shoes and a tuxedo.*

Marilyn   Steve?

Steve *grabs clothes, speed-dresses.*

Marilyn   Steve would you give me ten seconds?

Steve   Shoot.

Marilyn   I'm trying to tell you something!

Steve   Don't 'try' and tell me; just tell me.

Marilyn   God!

Steve   Was that in vain?

Marilyn   What?

Steve   The Lord's name is *always* taken in vain.

Marilyn   (*bemused*) Are you like this?

Steve   (*sees desktop calendar*) Oh no . . . (*reflexively checks bare wrist for watch.*)

Marilyn   What?

Steve   Fifteen . . . fifteenth?

Marilyn   What is it?

Steve   The Japs . . .

Marilyn   Japs?

Steve   Japs!

Marilyn   A meeting?

Steve   Oh no . . .

Marilyn   What time is it?

Steve   What am I gonna do?

Marilyn   What time is your meeting?

Steve   7.00 am.

Marilyn   That's OK.

Steve   (*pulls on tuxedo*) I have to bomb.

Marilyn   You've got five hours.

Steve   I have to shave, I have to get some proper clothes, I . . .

Marilyn   You look great.

Steve   No jive.

Marilyn   You look wonderful.

Steve   Marilyn, I'm about to sell 50,000 dollars of equity to a Japanese consortium. I mean I'm not going to Liz Taylor's wedding.

Marilyn   Then we'll get you a suit, we'll have you shaved. I'll order a limo – where's your meeting?

Steve   San Francisco.

Marilyn   Half an hour.

Steve   Oh man . . .

Marilyn   We'll get you there.

Steve   I'm shot.

Marilyn   Uncoil, honey.

Steve   Would you have like any OJ?

Marilyn   I'm afraid we only have freshly squeezed.

Steve   I can live with that.

Marilyn   (*goes to fridge*) Tell me about your business.

Steve   My business?

Marilyn   What line are you in?

Steve   Solid state human hypothermia.

Marilyn   Uh huh? – How did you get involved in that?

Steve   Because I love life.

Marilyn   You do?

Steve   I relish every nanosecond. In fact, the emotion I can think of stronger 'n my love of life is my total and absolute hatred and loathing of death and the universal deathwish. Which, as I guess you know's been running kinda wild lately. (*Gulps juice; points at watch.*) Could I borrow that?

Marilyn   (*removes watch*) You can have it.

Steve   (*takes watch*) Lifepact.

Marilyn   So what do you actually do?

Steve   Do? We operationalize! Freeze, wait, reanimate. Hey, you think that would make a good rap single?

Marilyn   Rap single!

Steve   (*rap*) 'Freeze, wait, reanimate'. Hey, that's the kind of synergy I should be throwing at the Japs. (*Checks watch.*) Shit. I have to bomb.

Marilyn   Steve . . .

Steve   Will you do me one last favour? Bruce Blase: 525 2525: tell him we go with the chopsticks – I don't care what he says . . . and tell Briest I have to cancel – I *may* have to cancel tonight . . .

Marilyn   I have to tell you something.

Steve   (*ties laces*) Uh huh.

Marilyn   This meeting. Was scheduled for 7.00 am, June 15th, 1983?

Steve   Correctamente.

Marilyn hands **Steve** desktop calendar.

Steve   So?

Marilyn   Look at the date.

Steve   Yes.

Marilyn   . . . Well?

Steve   15th . . . July!

Marilyn   Yes.

Steve   (*faint*) You . . . you're trying to tell me I've been here over an entire month?

Marilyn   I am.

Steve   (*laughs*) No. (*Pause.*) Why?

Marilyn   Because you have not been well.

Pause.

Steve   (*panicking*) What've I schitzed out?

Marilyn   No.

Steve   Oh, my God . . .

Marilyn   You are not mad.

Steve   (*reeling*) What've . . . what are you people?

Marilyn   You're blanking out, Steve.

Steve   Fuckin' kidnappers.

Marilyn   What day did you come in on?

Steve   Where've I . . . ?

Marilyn   What day did you come into hospital?

Steve   What've you done to me?

Marilyn   June 10th 1983. What did you come in for?

Steve   (*near tears*) I came in for a bloodtest!

Marilyn   Why?

Steve   The fuck difference is it now!

Marilyn   Why did you need a bloodtest? Steve, I know this is very cathartic for you, you can remember! Why did you come in for a bloodtest?

Steve   (*pause*) Because . . . because my insurance company reques . . . oh, my God no (*He remembers.*) . . . leukemia?

Marilyn   I'm afraid so.

Steve   No.

Marilyn   Honey, it's OK . . .

Steve   No. No. No way. Oh no . . .

Marilyn   That was on June 10th, 1983.

Steve   I can't . . .

Marilyn   On Saturday, the twelft of January, 1984, 3.44 pm, after taking a massive overdose of Vitamin A, you were certified clinically dead.

Steve   (*redeathing*) Ah . . .

Marilyn   At exactly 3.45 pm, a 'New Hope' suspension team, under the supervision of Morty Kronenborg and Susan Plaski put you on a heart–lung bypass and began perfusion with CPA, slowly reducing your bodyheat to −196 degrees centigrade, at which temperature it was maintained (*Near tears.*) until your full bodily, mental and spiritual resurrection in the early hours of this morning . . .

Steve *opens his eyes.*

Marilyn   (*drying her eyes*) Sorry . . . I'm sorry, I'm really out of my depth here. You see I'm a closure therapist; you really need a resurrection counsellor.

Pause.

Steve   The white blood corpuscles are dead?

Marilyn   Retroviruses are wiping them out as we speak.

Steve   This baked alaska sensation is just . . .

Marilyn   Frostbite.

Pause.

Steve   Bullshit.

Marilyn   No.

Steve   It's all bullshit.

Marilyn   No!

Steve   Perfectly formed bullshit! (*He starts to go.*)

Marilyn   Wait . . . Wait! (*She switches on recording.*)

Steve v/o   No I do not believe; I know. (**Steve** *has stopped.*) To say 'I believe' is to confess 'I doubt'; to say 'I know' is to say 'I know'; and either you know or you don't.

Steve *takes a beat, exits through French windows.*

Mike *enters from cryotorium, just as* **Steve** *goes out; he rushes back through swing doors.*

Mike   (*in corridor*) Doc . . . Doc . . . I found him . . .

Makoto *enters from cryotorium wheeling gurney, followed by* **Mike**.

Mike   Outside.

Makoto   (*wheels gurney through French windows*) Call Security.

Marilyn   (*radiant*) It's OK . . .

Mike   (*over intercom*) Security.

Marilyn   Mike . . .

Mike   Get someone to the Departure Lounge.

Marilyn   He's absolutely fine!

Mike   You stupid idiot! (*Exits via French windows.*)

Marilyn   (*exits after him*) He's just a little disoriented.

Jay *enters left, crosses to drinks cabinet, pours himself a drink.* **Don** *enters behind him.*

Don   (*undoing tie*) Supercilious blimps! You see me dancing the Governor's wife? So Strauss was a Kraut – he did not write goosestep! I mean, break a little wind. (*He slides couch, revealing waxwork.*) Jay? You give me a hand?

Jay   (*gazing out of windows*) Come here.

Don   (*crosses to windows*) What's doing?

Jay   (*numb*) The President.

Don   Pardon?

Jay   He's alive.

Don   Alive.

Jay   I just saw him.

Don   Are you shitting me?

Jay   Over there.

Don   Where?

Jay   On the lawn.

Don   The croquet lawn?

Jay   Yes.

Don   What would he be doing on the croquet lawn?

Jay   Playing croquet.

Don   (*turns away*) You disappoint me, Jay.

Jay Don, I . . .

Steve *enters via French windows holding croquet mallet. He crosses to fridge, fixes himself another glass of OJ. He seems greatly clarified and rejuvenated.*

Jay (*whispers*) You see?

Don (*mouthing, speechless, about to faint*)

Jay Don?

Steve Is he OK?

Jay (*holding* **Don** *up*) Don?

Steve (*crossing over*) He swallow something?

Jay I . . . I don't know.

Steve (*to* **Don**) Is something caught?

Don (*retches*)

Steve He needs the Heimlich.

Jay I don't . . .

Steve Hold it right there.

Steve *goes behind* **Don** *and gives him the Heimlich.*

Don No . . .

Jay No?

Don No!

Jay He didn't swallow anything.

Steve His heart?

Jay Could we . . . ?

Steve We gotta give him some CPR.

Steve *gets* **Don** *on his back on the floor. Flailing around in panic,* **Jay** *takes the opportunity to kick the waxwork back under the couch.*

Jay Could we wait . . . ?

Steve (*sitting astride* **Don**) It's OK, pal, it's OK . . .

Jay Could we wait for a doctor?

Steve I know what I'm doing, OK? (*Jabs hard into* **Don***'s chest.*)

Don Ahhhh . . .

Jay Oh shit.

Makoto *rushes in wheeling gurney, followed by* **Mike**.

Mike   Thank God . . .

Don   (*moans*).

Steve   Just in time.

Makoto   (*wheeling gurney up to* **Steve**) Mr President . . .

Steve   I think it's his heart.

Makoto   Please lie down.

Jay   (*to* **Don**) It's OK . . .

Makoto   (*takes* **Steve**'*s arm*) Please – lie down.

Steve   (*still sitting astride* **Don**) Hey, wait a minute.

Makoto   Lie down on the gurney.

Steve   What do you . . . ?

Makoto   You are not well.

Steve   Pal, you've got the wrong guy.

Don   Pills . . .

Jay *slaps* **Don**'*s face*.

Makoto   Please do as I say.

Mike   You're not well, Steve . . .

Steve   It's him needs helpin' out!

Mike   (*holding syringe*) Just lie down nice 'n easy and we'll . . .

Steve   (*getting up off* **Don**) Hey, hey back-up, OK?

Makoto   You're not . . .

Steve   Back up and back off!

Don   My pills . . .

During this, **Jay** *goes to drawer, searches for* **Don**'*s pills, runs out for glass of water.*

Marilyn *re-enters*.

Makoto   (*continuing*) You don't understand.

Steve   Will someone . . . ?

Marilyn   Wait.

Mike   You're not well, Steve.

Steve   I feel absolutely great.

Marilyn   Leave this to me.

Steve   Let go of my arm.

Makoto   Please relax . . .

Steve   You're fuckin' hands off me!

Marilyn   It's OK, Steve. (*Whispers to* **Makoto**.) He has this thing about Doctors.

Makoto   What?

Steve   I have this thing about doctors.

Makoto   What thing?

Steve   Everything.

Makoto   Would you like me to sugarcoat this?

Marilyn   It's OK, Steve.

Makoto   (*with difficulty*) I'm afraid there have been some slight complications.

Steve   Such as?

Mike   We just got the results on your first blood test . . .

Steve   . . . Go on?

Pause. **Makoto** *looks to* **Marilyn**.

Makoto   I'm afraid this may come as a slight shock to you.

Marilyn   What is it?

Steve   Quite fucking me around!

Makoto   I'm afraid our tests appear to indicate you're on the brink of multiple systems failure.

Marilyn   No.

Steve   What?

Mike   Heart, lung, liver and kidneys.

Marilyn   Oh no . . .

Steve   I feel great.

Makoto   I'm really sorry.

Steve   I mean, I feel absolutely fine!

Marilyn   This is impossible . . .

Steve   Doesn't that mean anything to you?

Makoto   But I'm afraid we don't seem to have fully eliminated the leukemia from your blood cells.

Mike   This is real, Steve.

Marilyn   Oh, my God . . .

Pause.

Steve   So what do you want me to do?

Makoto   I'm afraid we're going to have to put you back on ice.

Steve   You want me to get back in the fridge?

Makoto   I'm really sorry. I realise how this must feel.

Steve   . . . You fucking assholes!

Mike   Just for a couple more years.

Marilyn   This is impossible.

Makoto   A couple of decades at most.

Steve   Bullshit.

Mike   Steve, you may feel cool, you're standing on the edge of an abyss.

Steve   Just bullshit!

Makoto   You don't . . . he doesn't understand.

Steve   Neither do you, pal.

Marilyn   Can't you just put him in intensive care?

Makoto   We can't let him take that risk.

Mike   This is heavy, Steve.

Steve   Can't let me?

Makoto   Can't you see he's in an acute confusional state?

Steve   Hey, screw you!

Makoto   Dr Shriver, please section this patient.

Marilyn   (*conflicted*) We can't do this.

Mike   Doc, you . . .

Makoto   He's delirious.

Steve   Marilyn!

Marilyn   We can't . . .

Makoto   He could be on the brink of irreversible death.

The **Security Guard** *enters.*

Steve   (*to* **Marilyn**) Please . . .

Marilyn   You have to go back to bed.

Makoto   (*to* **Guard**) We've just sectioned this patient.

The **Guard** *takes* **Steve** *by the arms.* **Jay** *comes back in, gives* **Don** *pills and water.*

Marilyn   Stop it!

Steve   Your hands off . . .

Mike   Doc, you can't . . .

Makoto   Nembutal. (*Grabs* **Steve**'s *legs.*)

Steve   Let go!

Marilyn   Let him go . . .

Mike   You can't do this!

The scuffle.

Marilyn   Stop . . . Stop it!

Don   (*now completely recovered*) Whoa, whoa, whoa, whoa, whoa . . .

Steve   Let go of me . . .

Don   (*to* **Guard**) Can't you see who this is?

Makoto   Hypodermic.

Jay   It's The President!

The **Guard** *lets go.*

Makoto   (*still struggling with* **Steve**) Hypodermic . . . Hypodermic!

Don   Take him away.

The **Guard** *takes* **Makoto**'s *arm;* **Jay** *takes his other arm.*

Makoto   What are you doing?

Mike   Wait!

Don   Throw him the fuck out.

Steve *and* **Marilyn** *each take one of* **Makoto**'s *legs, flip him up onto the gurney, heave gurney towards cryotorium.*

Steve   Here's lookin' at you, Doc . . .

Makoto   This is murder!

Mike   Stop!

Jay *and* **Guard** *and* **Marilyn** *wheel him through swing doors, followed by* **Mike**.

Steve   Way to go.

Makoto   Murder . . .

Don   (*he has hastily re-tied his bow-tie*) Steve, I am so sorry.

Steve   Sorry?

Don   That was unforgive . . .

Steve   You just saved my life, pal!

Don   (*shakes his hand finding it hard to conceal his physical repulsion*) Don C Strohmeyer, President of Offshore Operations . . .

Steve   (*presses* **Don***'s flesh*) Lifepact. (*Pause;* **Don** *is holding his breath.*) You OK, now? (**Don** *nods.*) Hey, sorry if I was a little rough back then. I've been waitin' to try out the Heimlich for absolutely years.

Don   (*clipped*) That's fine.

Steve   (*still holding* **Don***'s hand*) Do you have asthma? (**Don** *shakes his head.*) I just made a bad smell or something? (**Don** *shakes his head.*) You sure? (*Smells his armpit.*) Oh man . . .

Jay *and* **Marilyn** *re-enter.*

Don   Could I introduce . . . ?

Steve   Excuse me.

Marilyn   Fresh as a daisy, Steve.

Don   This is Jay Snyder . . .

Steve   Hi Jay.

Jay   So pleased.

Steve   Feel free to vomit.

Don   Jay'll be acting as your personal resurrection counsellor.

Marilyn   May I suggest . . . ?

Steve   So this is it?

Jay   What?

Steve   This is the party?

Marilyn   Party!

Steve   I don't get a party?

Don   You'd like a party?

Steve   I just kicked death in the ass, guys.

Don   Champagne.

Steve   Guess you folks are pretty blasé about that now.

Don   As a matter of fact, no.

Jay   Absolutely not.

Marilyn   You know, he really should go back to bed.

Steve   It's partytime!

Marilyn   (*anxious*) . . . Don?

Jay *goes for champagne.*

Don   Steve: for a guy who's just . . .

Marilyn   Honey, could we . . . ?

Don   Been through . . .

Steve   What I've just been through – yeah?

Don   You're in . . .

Steve   Absolutely shit-hot shape.

Don   Absolutely.

Steve   'That which does not kill you will make you strong.'

Don   Take that down.

Marilyn   Thank you for being so strong.

Steve   Hey, thank you for being such a pretty woman.

Don   That's right.

Steve   For real. You're really in touch with your feminine side.

Marilyn   But I still think you should be in intensive care.

Steve   No way.

Marilyn   At least let me call another doctor!

Steve   Marilyn, you want to help? You seriously wanna help?

Marilyn   You know I do.

Steve   Like how about getting me something to eat!

Don   Food.

Marilyn   . . . OK.

Steve   OK?

Marilyn   OK, what would you like?

Steve   What would I like?

Don   Choose anything.

Steve   Oh boy . . . (*Closes eyes.*) Would you have like any . . .

Marilyn   Grated carrot?

Steve   Yeah, that would be nice.

Don   Check it out.

Marilyn   No problem. (*She goes out.*)

Steve   Hey, – there are no 'problems' . . .

Don   Just problems of perception.

Steve   Which is actually just a problem of 'reception'.

Don   Take that down.

Steve   Stay tuned.

Jay   (*holding tray with champagne flutes*) May I propose a toast? To your second lifecycle.

They toast.

Steve   So how's business?

Jay   Business?

Steve   This is 'New Hope' 'm I wrong?

Don   Absolutely not.

Steve   So cut to the chase. Clue me in. (*beat.*) How's business?

Don   Jay? The President would like . . .

Steve   Steve, *Steve*, OK . . .

Don   I'm sorry . . .

Steve   Skip the corporate shit.

Don   Would like an appraisal.

Jay   Where would you like me to begin?

Steve   Freeze, wait, reanimate – it take off?

Don   (*smug*) Did it take off?

Jay   Steve, on this island alone, we've got over a quarter of a million suspension holders, right here, under your very nose.

Steve   Blow me away.

Jay   In the next five years, over three million suspensioners will take the big sleep.

Steve   This is global?

Jay   Well, principally American, but we are breaking into the global market.

Steve   (*softly*) Blow me away. (*Shakes his head.*) Blow me away. (*Pause.*) We won. (*Laughs.*) I was right. We won out. We kicked ass. We kicked ass with the universal deathwish! (*Smacks fist.*) Wo! Yeah. Fuckin' ay! We won out! 'Hey death; where is thy sting?' (*Exultant laughter.*) Oh man . . . I guess this is all pretty nine to five to you guys?

Don   It's a job.

Steve   Yeah, well let me remind you where I just came from the whole of humanity was like poised over this toss up between eros and thanatos and believe me, the smart money was not on life.

Jay   Except it was.

Steve   Except it was! And I scooped it, I scooped out – hey, what about the competition?

Don   (*smug*) Competition?

Steve   Alcor?

Jay   Who?

Steve   Transtime? The Bay Area Cryonics Society?

Don   A handful of dust.

Steve   (*smacks fist*) Motherfucker! Fuckin' ay. Make my day. I knew neuro-suspension was a dead apple. (*Pause.*) Did they . . . ? Did they all . . . ? Mike Darwin? Durk Pearson . . . ? Jerry Leaf . . . ? they're all . . . ?

Don   Pushing up pod, Steve.

Steve   Hey, fuck you man, they were my friends! (*With pity.*) All gone? All of 'em? (*He wipes away a tear.*) Fuckin' freaks. Why they have to go neuro? The stupid fuckers went neuro.

Jay   Neuro?

Steve   One way trip, man. OK, who's king? Who's king?

Jay   (*tight*) I am.

Steve   Hail to the chief, Don. So what are we waiting for? I want a board meeting now.

Don   Board meeting?

Steve   Put me onto my trustees.

Jay   You want us to convene an extraordinary meeting?

Steve   Right now.

Don   May I ask why?

Steve   Why? This is my company, pal! (**Don** *and* **Jay** *exchange glances.*) Hey, chill, guys. Just 'cause I'm back on the bridge don't mean I'm gonna napalm my entire management.

Don   You mean you're planning to resume an executive role?

Steve   Am I planning . . . ? Hey, come on! The hell d'you expect? Sure, I'm gonna be on a real steep learning curve, it's gonna be like a paradigm shift for me: I can handle it, I'm functioning fine, I feel great – alpha state – now put me onto my trustees!

Jay *picks up phone, glances at* **Don**.

Jay   Steve . . . there's something we . . . something you don't . . .

Steve   You think I can't cut it?

Don   No, no . . .

Steve   What am I deadweight?

Don   Absolutely not . . .

Steve   You better believe it, pal.

Jay   It's just the situation isn't as straightforward as it might seem.

Pause.

Steve   You know what? You guys are a real downer. A real bad blue to wake up to.

Don   Steve, it's time we . . .

Steve   It's time for you to kiss ass, counsellor. 'Cause first thing I do I'm back on top I'm gonna have you both an appointment with outplacement.

Jay   We're just trying to . . .

Steve   I don't have to take this from you! You're not even players. What am I doing here? (*Gets up.*)

Jay   Where are you going?

Steve   I'm going to give a press conference.

Don   Press conference!

Steve   You got it.

Jay You don't want to do that.

Steve Sure I want to do it . . .

Jay Listen, wait . . .

Steve I wanna make the cover of *Time* magazine.

Don Steve, if you do that, I give you my word that by the end of the week New Hope'll've filed for receivership.

Steve (*amused*) Oh yeah?

Jay Without a shade of doubt.

Steve And how's that?

Don Tell him, Jay.

Jay You see, what you don't realise, Steve, is that you have resurrected very premature.

Steve Is that a fact?

Jay Your reanimation was not expected for at least half a century.

Don If ever.

Steve So what? You want me to climb into an incubator for fifty years?

Don We want you realise Steve, that you're the first body ever to have been reanimated.

Steve I am?

Jay That's right.

Steve First ever?

Don Ever.

Steve (*pause*) Shit me. I . . . I just made history? (*Shakes head.*) Man. This is . . . this is awesome. (*Pause.*) I'm like walkin' on water here.

Don Go ahead and try.

Steve Hey, wait a minute. This is gonna blow our stock price through the roof!

Don *shakes his head.*

Steve Sure it will.

Don Only in the short term.

Steve What are you talkin' about?

Jay Time to pay, Steve.

Steve   (*pause*) Pay?

Don   That's right.

Steve   How do you mean?

Don   We mean people figure you're back, we gotta bring all the others back.

Jay   Over 350,000 suspension-holders.

Don   Pay up their money.

Jay   Hundreds of millions of dollars.

Steve   (*pause*) I don't see the problem.

Don   The 'problem', Steve, is we don't have that money.

Steve   Don't have it?

Jay   That's correct.

Steve   Nothing?

Jay   Niente.

Don   Not a bean.

Steve   (*beat*) What happened?

Don   (*shrugs*) Human error.

Steve   Human error?

Jay   We made some bad deals . . . bad loans . . .

Pause. **Steve** *sits down.*

Steve   So you want me to keep a low profile, huh?

Don   Steve . . . we regard you as an invaluable resource.

Steve   You want me to go Trappist?

Don   And we want you back on board. We want you adding all the value you can.

Pause.

Steve   Go on.

Don   OK, OK, let me suggest, for the first twelve months – just as an hors d'oeuvre – let me suggest a consultancy contract worth 5 million dollars with a signing bonus of 3 million dollars. Cold, hard cash.

Steve   Canapes.

Don   Jay:

Jay   We'll augment your portfolio with options on five thousand 'New Hope' shares . . . we'll fund your pension, suspension, life and afterlife assurance with a two million escrow account . . .

Steve   Keep talking.

Don   As non-executive director, you'll have your own limosine, your own jet . . .

Steve   Gulfstream 4?

Don   (*to* **Jay**) Make a note of that – plus exclusive use of a suite in any city you care to name . . .

Pause.

Steve   Sounds . . . interesting.

Jay   Money is time, Steve.

Don   Prime Time.

Jay   And you've certainly earned every second of it.

Don   You like oysters, Steve?

Steve   I love oysters.

Jay   Ever feel like checking out the Eight Wonders?

Don   . . . Or maybe you just wanna kickback . . .

Steve   Relax . . .

Jay   Toke away.

Steve   Tend my garden.

Don   Grow things.

Jay   Take a load off.

Steve   No, it sounds very, very interesting.

Don   Oyster time, Steve.

Steve   In fact, I only have one tiny wrinkle with the whole proposition.

Jay   Yes?

Steve   My conscience.

Jay   Your what?

Steve   My conscience.

Don   (*pause*) What do you mean by that, Steve?

Steve   I mean pal, that you'd be keepin' people froze in order to pay me off.

Don   So?

Steve   It's called fraud, Don.

Jay   Only if you choose to call it that.

Steve   They placed their trust in you.

Don   That's true. But so did our stockholders.

Steve   Your stockholders?

Don   That's right.

Steve   You're not serious.

Don   I'm deadly serious.

Steve   You'd keep these people froze to protect your fucking stockholders!

Don   I certainly would.

Steve   No.

Don   (*implacable*) I would not resurrect one body even if I knew they were gonna be on Prime Time . . .

Steve   (*almost laughing*) No.

Don   And I have the company, the board, our investors – in fact I have the entire Northern Hemisphere with me on this.

Steve   You're not serious. You can't be . . . (*Pause; he covers his face with his hands; he is beginning to look and feel increasingly unwell.*) They're . . . these people are your patients! Doesn't that mean anything to you?

Jay   (*gently*) Where would we put them, Steve?

Steve   Put them!

Jay   Start resurrecting hundreds of thousands of people we gotta put them somewhere, don't we?

Steve   Hey, come on!

Don   Or was the population explosion before your time?

Steve   You can't be . . . !

Don   Whereabouts?

Steve   We put a man on the moon. Bring him back from the dead. And you can't get your tiny minds around that!

Don   You still haven't said.

Steve   What do you want – acres per person? Yeah, we're gonna have to rethink a few structures – few fiefdoms gonna come tumbling down – do us good. I mean it's an engineering problem, it's a marketing problem – we got enough oxygen to go round don't we? Got enough seafood. We . . . we can use condoms can't we?

Jay Condoms?

Steve Trash cans of America's enough to feed the world five times over! I mean, these are not problems – they're just political problems. Yeah, so maybe we gotta ease up on the carbon dioxide, eat a little less prime beef – I mean just how greedy do we have to be?

Don I'm sorry, Steve . . .

Steve We can find room!

Don You're out of your depth.

Steve Don't patronise me!

Don No, maybe you should learn a little humility yourself! You waltz in here . . .

Jay (*cautionary*) Don . . .

Steve I created this company, pal. This. All this. Your job!

Don Humbug.

Steve I created it!

Don (*sudden vehemence*) And who built the salesforce, huh? Who collared the business?

Jay Guys, please . . .

Steve It was *my* vision.

Don Whose idea was it to move 'New Hope' offshore? Due respect, Steve . . .

Steve You call that creative?

Don Creative!

Jay It was the secret of our success.

Steve I knew it.

Don So maybe you should quit bitching and salute that!

Steve (*bitter laugh*) I knew it . . .

Don 'Cause you just lucked into the high double digits, asshole!

Steve Just like Karl Marx and . . . and Christianity and all the other guys . . .

Don My heart creams for you.

Jay (*restraining*) Don . . .

Steve   Eaten up by the assholes . . .

Jay   If you please!

Steve   The accountants . . .

Jay   Guys, please . . .

Steve   The carpthinkers . . .

Don   So what are you gonna do about it, huh?

Steve   (*almost philosophical*) Bottom line, profit line assholes!

Don   What are you gonna do?

Jay   This is precipitate . . .

Steve   What am I gonna do?

Jay   Please!

Steve   I'm gonna turn you over to the District Attorney and go set up on my own. (*He starts to go.*)

Don   Oh, get off it.

Jay   At least think about it.

Steve   Cause life wins, pal.

Don   I mean who are you kidding!

Steve   And that's where you fucked up.

Jay   Stop . . .

He storms out, thrusting **Jay** *aside.*

Don   I'll tell you what you put into this company, pal: a well hung stiff!

Jay   Save it, Don.

Don   (*after him*) Think they'd let you boss a Fortune 500?! 'Freeze wait reanimate'. The fucken jerk! You couldn't get your head round a Christmas cracker!

Long pause.

Don   Shit.

Jay   We have a problem.

Pause.

Don   (*over intercom*) Security, would you see that Mr Arbeit does not leave the premises.

Jay (*beat*) What are we . . . ? what are you doing?

Don He needs to cool off, Jay.

Jay What do you mean?

Don What d'you think I mean?

Jay You mean . . . ?

Don I mean he needs to chill out.

Jay We're gonna . . . you're gonna . . . we're gonna use force!

Don Of course not.

Jay Then what do you mean?

Don Exactly what I said.

Pause.

Jay You gonna . . . (*laughs.*) No . . . !

Don That's right.

Jay We're gonna put him back on ice!

Don You said it.

Jay Don, we can't do that.

Don Do what?

Jay (*weak*) Just . . . (*Mimes killing.*) him?

Don Kill him?

Jay No.

Don Who said anything about 'kill'?

Jay Don, we can't . . .

Don No, we're gonna *chill* him.

Jay You can't . . . !

Don We're gonna *ice* him.

Jay (*giggles*) This is . . .

Don Yes we can. And we are gonna get Dr Makoto and he is gonna put him back on ice!

Jay How?

Don I don't know how. It doesn't matter.

Jay Doesn't matter!

Don   No.

Jay   That we'll be accessory to . . . !

Don   To what?

Jay   To . . . to . . .

Don   No-one's gonna die, Jay.

Jay   Come on!

Don   Yes, a certain individual is gonna be *incapax* again. That's all.

Jay   (*shrugs, hopeless*).

Don   This is no time to go quichey on me, Jay.

Jay   I can't do this.

Don   Goddamnit! We have a job to do. I pay you to do that job! What are you gonna just let him turn us in? You wanna disappear? Spend the rest of your life island hopping?

Jay   No.

Don   Then wise the fuck up.

Jay   . . . I can't . . .

There is a cry offstage. **Marilyn** *appears at door, gasping for help, goes back out.*

Beat. **Don** *and* **Jay** *go out after her. They re-enter, plus* **Security Guard**, *carrying* **Steve**, *lower him onto couch.*

Guard   I never hurt him mon, I swear – he just collapse!

Jay   Steve?

Marilyn   Get help.

Don   Where's Doc?

Guard   We threw him out.

Don   You what!

Jay   (*slapping* **Steve***'s face*) Steve?

Guard   We 'threw him the fuck out'.

Marilyn   (*slaps* **Jay** *full in the face*) Get help!

Don   Which way?

Jay   Shit . . .

Marilyn   Get a doctor!

Don   (*to* **Jay**) Let's get him.

They rush off, left.

Marilyn *gets* **Steve** *into recovery position. She rushes to fridge, gets Coke.* **Steve** *comes to, sits up; he is deathly pale.* **Marilyn** *gives him the Coke, feels his forehead, checks his pulse.*

Steve   Oh man . . .

Marilyn   Steve . . . ?

Steve   What've they . . . what've they done to me?

Marilyn   It's OK.

Steve   Feel so weak, I can hardly . . .

Marilyn   Honey, it's OK, just drink up now; drink up.

Steve   (*drinks*) What happened?

Marilyn   Help is coming.

Steve   Help!

Marilyn   It's alright. You're going to be OK.

Steve   (*clarifying*) Hey . . . hey, wait a minute, I am OK, I'm fine, I'm just a little dizzy is all.

Marilyn   Just relax.

Steve   Just gotta get my blood-sugar up . . . I . . .

Marilyn   You just need a little rest.

Steve   Man, I could crash . . . I haven't slept in ages . . . what are you looking at me like that!

Marilyn   (*miserable*) Like what?

Steve   I look that bad?

Marilyn   You look beautiful, Steve.

Steve   Bullshit.

Marilyn   It's true!

Steve   I know what you're thinking.

Marilyn   Steve, please . . .

Steve   You think I gotta get back in the fridge, don't you?

Marilyn   (*helpless*) I don't know.

Steve   Don't lie to me.

Marilyn   Maybe a little while.

Steve   (*numb*) Little while . . .

Marilyn   Just a couple more years . . .

Steve   No way. Never . . . (*Starts to get up.*)

Marilyn   What are you doing . . . ?

Steve   I'm going for a swim.

Marilyn   You can't . . . !

Steve   I'll never get back in there! Never.

The blood drains from his head; he collapses back onto the couch.

Marilyn   (*giving him the Coke*) Drink. Drink it.

He drinks the Coke; he is sweating profusely.

Marilyn   Why did you have to do this to me? Why couldn't you have just stayed in intensive care?

A faint glow of dawn light is beginning to appear through the French windows.

Steve   Could we go sit on the beach a while? I mean, maybe if I could just cool out and listen to the waves I'll feel better?

Marilyn   (*with great sorrow*) You're not well, Steve. You have to accept that.

Pause.

Steve   (*near tears*) Those fucking assholes! Can you believe it? Bring me back before there's a cure! Blow my only chance . . .

Marilyn   That's not true!

Steve   I'll sue them off the face of the earth!

Marilyn   Just a five minute nap.

Steve   I'll fucking kill 'em!

Marilyn   Honey, please try and uncoil.

Steve   I'm dying, Marilyn.

Marilyn   (*imploring*) Don't say that.

Steve   I can feel it.

Marilyn   Steve, they will cure you, they'll find a cure . . .

Steve   Do you realise how ageing this is?

Marilyn   Then they'll rejuvenate your cells.

Steve   (*shakes his head*).

Marilyn   Steve, they will – you don't realise the incredible advances they have made – they have a fruit fly can live a hundred and fifty years . . .

Steve   Oh yeah?

Marilyn   Yes – and they will heal your body and kill the leukemia once and for all. So maybe it'll take a little time, maybe ten years, even twenty, I don't know, it doesn't matter.

Steve   Doesn't matter.

Marilyn   It's the twinkling of an eye.

Steve   You really think these assholes would bring me back again?

Marilyn   Don't think that way.

Steve   Not in a million years.

Marilyn   (*small*) I'll still be here for you.

Steve   Come on.

Marilyn   Honey, I will. And I will make it happen!

Steve   In 10 years time?

Marilyn   Yes.

Steve   In fifty years time!

Marilyn   (*solemn*) Every single day.

Steve   Bullshit.

Marilyn   Look – (*she grabs remote, illuminates empty tomb.*) you'll be there for me – right there and I'll be here – I'll be praying for you every minute of the day . . .

Steve   (*Gazing at tomb, aghast*) Praying . . . ?

Marilyn   Steve, you don't realise – I know you so much better than you think – we have an intense spiritual communion . . .

Steve   What!

Marilyn   And I will be here for you as long as it takes, I'll be here for you while you're asleep and I'll be here for you when you come back!

Steve   An old woman?

Marilyn   If it takes that long.

Steve   Come on, Marilyn – I step out that fridge thirty-eight years old I'm gonna shack up with an old crone!

Marilyn   (*miserable*) Don't say that.

Steve   Then wise up – you're an attractive woman – you have a life.

Marilyn   You called me, Steve.

Steve   Called you?

Marilyn   You called for me to come here.

Steve   I did not call you to come here!

Marilyn   Oh, yes you did.

Steve   Look, I'm not a spiritual person, I don't even know what the word means . . .

Marilyn   But you knew, Steve . . .

Steve   I'm just blood flesh 'n bone, OK?

Marilyn   You *knew*.

Steve   Now will you give me a break?

Marilyn   That interview you gave! Your tapes . . .

Steve   Burn them.

Marilyn   Steve, this isn't you . . .

Steve   So who is it?

Marilyn   You're blanking out.

Steve   I'm not blanking out!

Marilyn   You're just a little tired . . .

Steve   Look lady, I don't know who you are, I don't know where you're coming from, this is a one way trip, OK?

Marilyn   It's not.

Steve   You need help.

Marilyn   (*slaps him in the face*) How dare you . . . ?

Steve   You're fucking nuts!

Marilyn   Can't you understand!

Steve   Hit a sick guy.

Marilyn   I am trying to save your life! (*Pause.*) You're dying, Steve. Dying in front of my eyes. And I have held a candle for you and you are stabbing it out in my face!

Steve   Why can't you just let me go?

Marilyn   Let you what!

Steve   Oh God . . .

Marilyn   How dare you! You goddamn wimp you! You loser! Just lay down and die?

Steve   Forgive me . . .

Marilyn   You . . . you asshole! This is *you* Steve. This sick sack of flesh is your *life*! (*She picks up bodybag.*) You want to go out in this? (*Pulls zip.*) Just zip out your life? Zip out the sun and the wind and the sky and . . . and everything you love? Just throw you in a ditch – throw dirt in your face – and let the worms win-out? Is that what you want? To let the bugs and the worms and the lice just pig-out on your life?

Steve *is weeping silently.*

Marilyn   (*increasingly desperate*) Then get back in the fridge! Yes, it's going to fuck you up real bad, you'll be gone a hundred years, even longer, at least you'll still have a chance . . . And you should get back in that fridge and rejoice – yes, rejoice! that you can still have your vitality . . . (*Near tears.*) and you can still have your beautiful body . . . and all this will be just a dream . . .

Long pause. Distant sound of surf.

Steve   (*without conviction*) I guess so.

Marilyn   Just a five minute nap.

Steve   One short sleep past.

Marilyn   Even less than that . . .

Steve   . . . I guess.

Marilyn   (*weeping openly now*) And you'll be back.

Pause. **Steve** *suddenly gets up, starts towards cryotorium. He pauses briefly at swing doors, pushes on through.*

A few seconds later **Makoto**, **Guard**, **Jay** *and* **Don** *burst in S.L.; see doors still swinging; they rush through to cryotorium.*

Marilyn *exits via French windows.*

Long pause. The sound of surf. Daybreak. The tomb fades to black.

A fax feeds out.

Eventually, **Mike** *enters holding liquid nitrogen canisters, empties them into base of tomb.*

Don *re-enters, goes to drinks cabinet, pours himself a shot. He sees fax, rips it from machine, reads it.*

Makoto *enters shaking down thermometer, hands it to* **Mike**, *who exits back to corridor.* **Makoto** *empties another canister of liquid nitrogen.*

Don *illuminates tomb;* **Steve**'s *discoloured body is now back in place.*

Don   Nice work.

He passes **Makoto** *a shot.* **Makoto** *downs it, starts towards cryotorium.*

Don   So what's the prognosis?

Makoto   Prognosis?

Don   You saved him?

Makoto   I think his chances should be pretty good.

Don   How soon?

Makoto   As soon as we have a cure for leukemia.

Don   When's that?

Makoto   (*shrugs*) Five to ten years.

Don   Five years!

Makoto   I'm afraid so. But look on the flip side. He was just a test pilot. He knew there was a risk of termination. Think of the others! We'll have them up and about in no time!

Don   Uh huh.

Makoto   Believe me.

Don   No, I do, Doc. I do.

Makoto   This is a . . . giant step forward! (*Starts towards cryotorium.*)

Don   There's just one little factor you left out the equation.

Makoto   What?

Don   You're under arrest.

Makoto   What!

Don   You heard.

Makoto   What are you talking about?

Don   I'm talking about the fact you cremated one of our patients, Ken.

Makoto   . . . You're not . . . you can't be . . . !

Don   And you are going down for murder one.

The **Security Guard** *re-enters from cryotorium.*

Makoto   This is insane!

Don   Kindly place Dr Makoto under citizen's arrest.

The **Guard** *comes forward, takes out handcuffs.* **Makoto** *pauses, puts his hands out, suddenly grabs the* **Guard** *by the balls; he collapses.* **Makoto** *darts for cryotorium, just* *as* **Jay** *is coming through: for a split second they face each other, frozen;* **Jay** *punches him hard in the diaphragm;* **Makoto** *collapses.*

Jay   Luck's out, geek.

The **Guard** *picks him up.*

Don   You have the right to potassium chloride, 50,000 volts or the firing squad. Take him away.

The **Guard** *takes him off.*

Don   (*passes scotch and fax*) Nice work.

Jay   (*drinks shot*) Shit.

Don   That was shave-ass, huh?

Jay   You gonna have him charged?

Don   Culpable homicide, Jay.

Jay   He'll fry for that!

Don   So he'll fry.

Jay   Shit.

Don   You want him at large?

Jay   (*weak*) I guess not.

Don   (*of fax*) Read that. Come on, lighten up.

Jay   What is it?

Don   A raise.

Jay   A what?

Don   Read it.

Jay   (*examines fax*) Planning permission! 55,000 acres?!

Don   Tutankamen kiss my ass.

Jay   His lips ascend.

Don   Lady luck go down on me.

Jay   Her lips descend.

Don   (*slaps fist*) Ye-ah!

Jay   Croesus, Don!

Don   Croesus who?

Jay   We're going to . . . we're going to be so rich – we'll sink the whole freakin' island!

Don   It can happen.

Jay   (*toasts* **Steve**) Hail to the chief.

Don   Long live the king!

They toast.

Jay   Hey death: where *is* thy sting?

They giggle.

Jay   Shit. He doesn't look too great.

Don   He looks terrible, Jay.

Jay   I mean – he looks like shit! We can't let the old folks check out on that!

Don   No. (*Beat.*) We can't.

Jay   What's the prognosis?

Don   Where's Marilyn?

Jay   I don't know. Don?

Don   (*gazing out French windows*) Throwing stones in the sea.

Jay   What's the prog?

Don   Lock up. (*He removes panel at base of tomb.*)

Jay   What are you doing?

Don   Our job. (*He inserts end of croquet mallet into nozzle.*)

Jay   Oh, my God.

Don   It's OK.

Jay   No!

Don   I switched off the alarm.

Don *presses hard. Dry ice gushes out, slowly becomes a trickle, finally stops.* **Jay** *looks on, horrified. All the colour drains out of* **Steve**'s *body.*

Don   You just gonna stand there, or what? (*Dislluminates the tomb.*)

Jay *stands, speechless.* **Don** *exits through swing doors; a couple of seconds later, he re-enters struggling with* **Steve**'s *cadaver, drops it on floor.*

Don   (*he is panicked now*) Get me that. (*Pointing at bodybag.*) Get me the bag!

Jay   (*frozen*) I can't . . .

Don   Can't what?

Jay   You can't make me do this.

Don   You fucking wimp, you gonna pull out now? (*Grabs him.*) Goddamnit, we have a job to do! And we are gonna do that job. (*Kicks couch revealing waxwork.*) Who commissioned that, huh? Whose idea was that? Now do your job!

Jay *suddenly scuttles into action, grabs bodybag, frantically tries to get* **Steve** *inside it, retches, struggles to do up zip.*

Don *picks up waxwork, rushes out through swing doors.*

Jay *yanks the bodybag over to the couch, slides it over it, stands gasping and ashen-faced.*

Don *re-enters, also breathless, replaces panel, goes to drinks cabinet, pours two stiff shots.*

Jay   (*almost inaudible*) We killed him, Don. We killed him!

Don   Don't say.

Jay   You think . . . you think it's too late to get a doctor?

Don   Sure, let's go get Doctor Makoto back.

Jay   Shall . . . ?

Don   Any more suggestions?

Jay   (*shakes his head, ashamed*)

Don   Congratulations. You got the job done. (*Downs shot.*)

Jay   I feel terrible.

Don   So you feel terrible. Deal with it.

Jay   I'm an . . . I'm an accessory to homicide!

Don   Only if you choose to call it that.

Jay   It was murder, Don.

Don   Don't sound so surprised.

Jay   I'm not a murderer, Don! I'm an accountant.

Don   (*shrugs*) Same difference.

Jay   What've . . . what've I . . . ?

Don   What the hell did you expect?

Jay   Expect!

Don   The wages of sin are death, pal. Plus a shit load of dough to be getting on with.

Jay   Oh, my God . . .

Intercom   Dr Shriver, I have Yorrick and Donna Blumenthal in reception. (*Discreet.*) They have two pugs with them.

Don   (*presses button*) Could you ask them to hold on a dime? (*to* **Jay**.) Better get that in the back of your Estate.

Jay   My Estate!

Don   You wanna wait till Marilyn gets back?

Don *unlocks and opens door down left. Beat.* **Jay** *slides couch, starts yanking bodybag over towards* **Don**.

Jay   What am I going to do with this?

Don   Hell, I don't mind. Dig a hole; cremate it; lighten up a little for God's sake!

Jay   Dig a hole!

Don   He's biodegradable, Jay.

Jay   (*retches*).

Don   It's feeding time!

Jay *retches again. He pulls bodybag out.* **Don** *closes the door, pours himself another shot, picks up the remote.*

Marilyn *enters via French windows. She looks totally washed out. She starts gathering up her things. She ignores* **Don**.

Don   (*pause*) We saved him, honey. We saved him. Marilyn? What are you doing?

Marilyn   It's over, Don.

Don   What!

Marilyn   I was there with him.

Don   What do you . . . ?

Marilyn   His heart was no longer in it.

Don   How can you say that!

Marilyn   (*near tears*) He let go, Don. He let go of the body. He just wanted out. (*Continues packing.*)

Pause.

Don   (*pressing the remote into her hand*) 'Labour not for the meat which perisheth but for that meat which endureth unto everlasting life . . .' Amen.

He downs shot and exits. Beat. **Marilyn** *puts down the remote, finishes packing her things. She starts to go.*

Intercom   Dr Shriver? (*Confidential.*) The Blumenthals are waiting to come through.

She pauses, evidently conflicted.

Intercom   Dr Shriver?

Beat. She picks up the remote, closes her eyes, presses it.

The waxwork gradually illuminates. It glows with health and vitality, even more so than the original.

Marilyn *opens her eyes, looks on in disbelief. She sinks to her knees, stifles a sob.*

Intercom   Dr Shriver . . . ?

Marilyn   Forgive me. God forgive me . . .

Intercom   Dr Shriver!

Marilyn   (*tears of joy*) Send them through. (*Presses the button.*) Send them through!

The door opens. She turns towards it with outstretched arms. An elderly, richly-dressed couple, each holding pugs, their faces nipped and tucked to a waxen perfection, enter the room . . .

Blackout.

The Life of the World to Come

The Life Of The World To Come struck me as one of the most ambitious plays to be written about contemporary America since *Glengarry Glen Ross*. I was immediately excited by it and wanted to direct it. The play's comedy is dark, often grotesque, but Williams tightens his satiric grip so firmly that our laughter cools into disquiet, then horror.

Half laughing and half horrified, Williams plays with the deep absurdities of a culture coming into existence in America, where Cryogenic Suspension, Afterlife Insurance, Closure Therapy and Resurrection Counselling have been embraced by the ruthlessly self-interested world of the Corporation. New Hope Life Extension has found an ingenious way of dealing with ethical objections to euthanasia by marketing a new-age, pseudo-religious form of afterlife. To the reassuring sound of surf in the Departure Lounge, under the sleeping eye of the flawlessly preserved body of Steve Arbeit, the company has created new rituals of prayer and faith, of consummation and illumination. Steve, the life-affirming Californian guru, not only 'believes' but 'knows' that cryogenic suspension is a passport to a 'life in this world to come.'

The play mixes black comedy and farce, but there are deeper roots to its preoccupations: phenomenal advances in medical science mean that human lives are longer in this century than in any century before. But by extending life, we are also extending the years of disease, so New Hope's unspoken promise of 'consecrated euthanasia' seems both plausible and seductive.

Williams' vision is rooted in an America where founders of corporations are revered with an almost religious awe, an America which has perfunctorily proposed therapy and personal growth as panaceas, an America still contaminated by the greed and ruthlessness of the Reagan era. Behind this play lie the Wall Street takeover battles of the 1980's (particularly the stories of Ross Johnson, Henry Kravis and R. J. R. Nabisco, and the brutal ousting of the entrepreneur Steve Jobs by his own board at Apple), the breaking of established company loyalties in an era when longterm employees were cursorily dismissed and became 'trespassers' overnight.

Arbeit may echo Jobs – in more than just his name – but his origins are more complex: he possesses the ideals of that generation which despised the futility and destruction of the Vietnam War, and the paranoid profligacy of the nuclear arms race, what Steve calls 'the universal death wish' where 'the smart money was not on life'.

Like the Californian 'immortalists', Steve believes in the cult of youth and health, and that death is literally optional, a final insult we should have the courage to defy. Envied and resented by Don for his idealism and his beautiful body, Steve is also mocked by his cynical successor as a 'fucking jerk' who 'couldn't get his head round a Christmas cracker'. For Steve is an entrepreneur who has tried but failed to cash in on his beliefs. A richly contradictory character, partly comic, partly tragic, Steve is finally obliged to confront death as an inescapable reality; the defeated life affirmer embraces euthanasia.

As the play opens Jay explains that under the new jurisdiction of this island 'cryogenic suspension does not constitute clinical death, but "a temporary cessation of vital processes".' Indeed the play looks to a time when the legal status of clinical death becomes increasingly obscure. It hints ominously at recent developments in cryobiology, anticipating a time when scientists can extend the life-span of a fruit-fly to one hundred and fifty years, and touches intriguingly on the emerging science of nanotechnology. It satirizes scientists who 'guinea-pig' with their patients, but remain morally oblivious to the human costs of their research in an already over-populated world.

Seamlessly plotted, *The Life of the World to Come* projects us into a recognizable future. As a play it's far from reassuring. It's not fashionably 'feelgood' and its satire of each character is essentially cold. Williams allows us no emphathy with these characters, but under the surface we can sense his anger at their phoniness, gullibility, mendacity and ruthlessness. *The Life of the World to Come*, as has been observed, possesses the authentic voice of America, infused with a richly enjoyable seam of English black comedy. Alarming and funny, I think it will prove to be a deeply prophetic play about the world just around the corner from our own.

My warm thanks to the original cast of *The Life of the World to Come*, and to the numerous people who made its premiere at the Almeida Theatre possible, particularly Cole Kitchenn, Paul O'Leary, Sue Plummer, Jon Linstrum, John Leonard, Simon Bernstein, Rod Hall, Jo Jenkinson, Kevin Fitzmaurice, McCabes, Stephen Wrentmore, Mike Wade and John Moysen.

Derek Wax
September 1994

Rod Williams is thirty years old and lives in London. His first play, *No Remission*, won second prize in the 1988 Mobil Playwriting Competition and was first performed by the Lucky Porcupine Theatre Company at the Edinburgh Festival in 1990. The English première was at the Lyric Studio, Hammersmith in 1992 with Midnight Theatre Company, directed by Derek Wax, and was followed by an Arts Council-funded national tour. The play has since been translated into German and Flemish. His second play, *Creative People*, set in a telesales office, has yet to be produced. A television adaptation was commissioned by BBC Screenplay. *The Life of the World to Come* was started in 1990. Its completion was made possible by a grant from the Polonsky Foundation.